QUILTS OF ILLUSION

FRONTISPIECE: Tumbling Blocks (Cross variation) pattern pieced quilt, c. 1850, Warren County, Kentucky. Made by Margaret Calvert. 77" x 72". Silk, cotton, wool, and mohair. (*Collection The Kentucky Museum, Western Kentucky University; photo courtesy The Kentucky Quilt Project.*)

QUILTS OF ILLUSION

Tumbling Blocks, Delectable Mountains,

Stairway to Heaven, Log Cabin,

Windmill Blades, and

Other Optical

Designs

LAURA FISHER

THE MAIN STREET PRESS • PITTSTOWN, NEW JERSEY

Dedicated to Gary with thanks for his constancy and positive thinking, to Frances and Herman Fisher for their hope and support, and to the road not taken.

Published by
The Main Street Press, Inc.
William Case House
Pittstown, New Jersey 08867

Pubished simultaneously in Canada by
McGraw-Hill Ryerson Ltd.
330 Progress Avenue
Scarborough, Ontario M1P 2Z5

Cover and text design by Frank Mahood

Printed in Japan

Library of Congress Cataloging-in-Publication Data

Fisher, Laura, 1945-
   Quilts of Illusion.

   Bibliography: p.
   Includes index.
   1. Quilts, American. 2. Quilts—United States—History—19th century. 3. Quilts—United States—History—20th century. 4. Optical illusion in art. I. Title.
NK9112.F57 1987   746.9′7′0973   87-5653
ISBN 1-55562-010-8
ISBN 1-55562-009-4 (pbk.)

88 89 90 91 92 10 9 8 7 6 5 4 3 2 1

CONTENTS

PREFACE

Our eyes look, but our minds see. . . .

An optical illusion fools the eye. Scientifically, it is a visual experience in which a discrepancy exists between what we perceive and the real physical characteristics before us. Quilts, forms that are essentially planar, or two-dimensional, become illusionary when their design appears three-dimensional. Through touch, we acknowledge the quilt's flat surface, but in our mind's eye, we sense differing psychic effects—a kinetic pattern, multiple layers, or several designs seeming to occupy the same space simultaneously. Here is more than initially meets the eye.

The literature of quilting has taught us to appreciate antique American quilts first as historical and social artifacts, and more recently as fine art, remarkable and pleasing for their graphic images, the relationship between and manipulation of form, color, and line, and the presentation of repeated or sequential images. Antique illusionary quilts invite a fresh analysis, for they present what is by now familiar in unfamiliar, often enigmatic, ways. They challenge us to try to interpret ambiguity: are the patterns reaching out toward us or away from us? Are the lines straight or curved, connected or separate? Are we looking at designs from above or below? Are we seeing openwork layers? Is the surface raised or depressed? Such bedcovers affect our perception by dispelling familiar notions of such fundamental concepts as near and far, right and left, above and below. In many examples included in this book, these concepts are interchangeable, presenting an altered vision that can be read in more than one way. For example, familiar series of squares, triangles, or rectangles often exhibit a shift in direction, a suggestion of volume or space, or the illusion that several designs are at play simultaneously—all through the manipulation of shape and color.

Many types of illusions exist, generated mostly through the use of angular shapes and strong tonal contrasts. In some illusionary quilts, a sense of space is conveyed by varying the size, color, and shape of some pieces; by interrupting a logical or expected pattern of alignment; or by placing shapes in unexpected and unconventional relationships. Other quilts include sections (called pattern blocks) which read individually as flat planes, but, when combined and multiplied, generate design elements that seem to exist on several levels. In still others, forms that can stand alone as distinct images—a star, a tree, a flower—produce kinetic, complex optical designs when combined. Often, the juxtaposition of light and dark alone conveys a sense of movement as lines appear to waver and elements seem to advance or recede. Different areas demand recognition all at the same time. Layers build, lines shift, forms pop out and disappear.

Optical illusion quilts are compelling because they vary from the norm and they vary within themselves. Their designs involve the viewer intellectually, not just aesthetically, by disturbing the accustomed confined space of a simple bedcover, making it active, mysterious, and unpredictable. In many cases, the viewer cannot control what he or she is seeing. Many of these quilts gain optical impact from their negative, as well as their positive, spaces. The negative is the field between the pieced (the positive or designed) segments, typically of solid color or configuration. Although quiltmakers probably treated this aspect as a suitable background for the piecework, from the viewer's perspective it gains dominance, disturbing our understanding of the quilt, but in a stimulating, intriguing way.

For the needleworker of old, quiltmaking was all about *imagination*. The challenge was always to organize a group of scraps or small pieces into a whole cloth of pleasing appearance as well as utility. To me, antique illusionary quilts represent perhaps the most captivating exercise of the quiltmaker's need for self expression. Undoubtedly, many were constructed without a knowledge of perspective, of mechanical drawing, or the use of specialized tools to facilitate the task of design. In them is expressed a freedom of spirit and lack of restraint. Yet at the same time they required considerable thought, precise handling, and enviable concentration. Such quilts could not have been made in a hurry. Highly personal and individualized, even in the simplest patterns, their execution offered quiltmakers the opportunity to explore ideas and test designs. What commitment, perhaps even obsession, enabled quilters to plan, count, coordinate materials, then cut, count, and stitch to ensure that the whole would come out right? The attention to detail in these examples must have been intensely different from that of quilts made of just enough pretty blocks to yield a beautiful bedcovering. Many optical illusion quilts cannot be called beautiful in the conventional sense. To quilt lovers accustomed to visual presentations of tiny stitches and serene images, these quilts may appear chaotic or confused. Such confusion exists only in the viewer's perception, not in the construction of the design.

When I solicited collectors, dealers, and curators for quilts to include here, they first located examples of illusions among the classic Tumbling Blocks and Log Cabin variations. Often, bold graphics alone were considered to be optical illusions. Asked how quiltmakers managed to create such complex designs in a time of limited technical knowledge and design training, these experts replied, "serendipity," "luck," "chance," or "accident," coupled, of course, with innate artistic skill. Some felt that the existence of such designs must reflect a mathematical or geometrical education or inclination, while others insisted that most designs were simply the result of tinkering with small pieces of cloth with no awareness that a masterpiece would emerge. Happily for us, those artists had imagination, which allowed them to explore in fabric what today a painter or sculptor might create. And they had courage, which allowed them to defy conventional standards of taste and beauty to pursue the abstract fantasies of their mind's eyes.

As in other visual arts, the creator had to confront the issue of organization, or how to make sense of the patches. Some quilts illustrated here include thousands of pieces so intensely composed that viewers may be unable to decipher what they are seeing. The density of piecing greatly affects our ultimate perception, as do the relationships among colors employed. But even in simple two-color compositions that repeat a single form, provocative illusionary results are possible.

All of these examples have an order, but it may not be apparent at first glance. After the initial stunning impact, the elements can be dissected and the composition analyzed and understood. In none of the chosen quilts is there a pattern element that is unique to illusionary quilts. Their familiar forms—a square, a hexagon, a strip—appear countless times in everyday quilts. Their distinction as intriguing designs stems from the creative interaction of form, color, and pattern, and their consequent transformation into large, abstract surfaces.

This exploration of quilts of illusion encompasses several chapters. First is an explanation of the dynamics of these quilts: the quiltmaking traditions; principles of design and composition in art and needlework; perceptions and perspectives that color our appreciation of the designs; the types of visual illusions, and the forms with which they have been created. The second chapter reviews historical inspirations that might have influenced the appearance of optical illusions in American quilts, such as motifs in ancient textiles, woodwork, tile work, and architectural ornamentation. The third chapter is a portfolio of optical illusion quilts, organized by the basic geometric shape used to construct the design. A final chapter presents four examples of optical illusion quilts—a Tree of Life, a Tumbling Blocks, Three-Dimensional Fans, and an Eccentric Star—for readers to reproduce or modify to create their own illusions.

Each viewer has options for examining the quilts illustrated in this book, for everyone brings along a host of past experiences—an ability to judge size and distance; habits of seeing; knowledge of art and design; processes of perception; and even the unique physical properties of your own eyes. The illusions presented here may be more apparent, therefore, to some people than to others.

Take your time examining the quilts, at least enough for the natural process of vision fatigue to cause a shift in image. Most examples increase in complexity and kinetic illusion with concentrated attention. Turn the book sideways and up-side down. Explore the effects of a difference in perspective or light source upon the patterns. Look first at the dominant form or forms from which each design is constructed, using them as a visual point of reference as the motifs begin to shift and as elements emerge and recede. Then concentrate on a different aspect—for example, the light or dark field, the center block, or the ellipse—and let yourself be mystified, and I hope delighted, by all you see. Look for repeating elements, or the common denominator, such as the star, the triangle, or a strip of a certain color or tone. When you mentally dissect the quilt surfaces, greater appreciation for their remarkable qualities will follow.

I consider this study a beginning, for it is only recently that quilts have been acknowledged as the visual precursors of many of the design "innovations" and color systems that were later employed by practitioners of Op Art and other con-temporary painting. Although many of our examples are of the nineteenth cen-tury in materials, patterning, construction, and cultural sensibility, their designs are compatible with the most contemporary home or corporate environment. As collectors hang their antique patchwork "Eschers" and "Vasarelys" alongside modern paintings, the optical illusion quilt is bound to achieve its rightful place in art history.

As sensory beings, we delight in visual trickery, often seeking optical stimula-tion from such relatively modern innovations as 3-D movies, strobe lights, and holograms. These illusionary quilts, far older, are as remarkable and enticing a visual experience.

1.
THE DYNAMICS OF ILLUSION

ANTIQUE AMERICAN QUILTS, long revered as our most colorful naïve folk art, have a familiar form and construction. Quilts of illusion employ that form, but present it with an unfamiliar face. They are mysterious and intriguing, offering multiple images, a rich unity of opposites, visually dynamic spatial forces, a sense of movement, and constant visual stimulation—all within the familiar confines of a bed-sized expanse of fabric. The three-dimensional visual appearance of these flat, two-dimensional forms led to the development of *Quilts of Illusion*.

In its early years, quiltmaking was considered a craft. Young ladies and even young men were taught basic sewing skills in order to make bed-covers for colonial families. Over the years, the artistic possibilities of the craft became increasingly refined and a native folk art was developed as quilters invented more and more patterns to utilize their precious scraps of fabric. In so doing, needleworkers tested combinations of color, shape, and design, spurred by an innate sense of creativity.

The fascinating, inherently graphic content of antique quilts was brought to the attention of a wide contemporary audience at a landmark 1971 exhibition at New York's Whitney Museum, "Abstract Design in American Quilts." The exhibition's organizers, Jonathan Holstein and Gail van der Hoof, helped to alter our perspective on these textile treasures by presenting them as significant works of art.

Quilts of illusion have more in common with the art of the twentieth century than they do with other historic American textiles. Few of the quilts illustrated in this book have the charm or quaint sentimentality of friendship or album quilts, the historic content of presentation or commemorative quilts, or the beautiful needlework of appliqué quilts, acknowledged quilt heirlooms that have been cherished from one generation to the next and often exhibited in prestigious museums.

Illusion quilts are generally patchwork mosaics, incorporating many pieces organized by shape and color into a harmonious whole. That so many have survived to this day is remarkable when one considers that the humble patchwork quilt (in contrast to the special occasion appliqué) was created for everyday household use, and rarely intended to be treasured for posterity. The intricacy with which many were composed suggests, however, that their makers took special pride in the skillful execution of the fabric bits and never actually used the finished quilts.

While many of these bedcovers have the appearance and construction of utilitarian quilts, their designs are anything but ordinary. In many examples, little stars "pop", octagons "float", lines zigzag, blocks tumble and twist, and designs seem to move in and out of the quilts' flat surfaces. As early Kentucky quiltmaker Aunt Jane best expressed it: "How much piecin' a quilt is like livin' a life. You can give the same kind o' pieces to two persons, and one will make a Nine Patch and one will make a Wild Goose Chase, and they will be two quilts made out of the same kind of pieces and jes' as different as they can be. And that is jes' the way with livin'. The Lord sends us the pieces, and we can cut them out and put them together pretty much to suit ourselves, and there is a

FIG. 1.1. Right Angles Patchwork pattern pieced quilt top detail, c. 1875, Midwest. Maker unknown. 90" x 72". Cotton. An extraordinary sense of solidity, volume, and depth is conveyed in this rarely seen pattern. The "Y" shape seen so clearly in this detail is repeated hundreds of times across the quilt surface. It has been created by joining three identical L-shaped or chevron pieces. To understand the construction of this design, think of cubes whose diamond-shaped sides have been clipped at the centers to allow the insertion of a neighboring element, making a composition that is perhaps more akin to Tumbling Blocks than quilt patterns which bear that title. The optical effect is like an aerial view, looking down into the space of a densely packed cityscape of calico high-rises. (*Author's collection*.)

heap more in the cuttin' out and the sewin' than there is in the caliker" (Hall and Kretsinger, *The Romance of the Patchwork Quilt in America*, 83).

Pieced quilts were always planned to some extent, as the seamstress determined what shape the elements would take and how many were needed to complete the bedcover. Occasionally, designs were sketched in advance and the fabric pieces laid out according to a plan. But other designs may have resulted as the quiltmaker played with colors, shapes, and patterns until a pleasing solution emerged. Organizing the pieces and blocks by color and line was one of the few creative outlets available to women in the heyday of quiltmaking, yet there is a consensus among quilt experts that any design planning was limited to the preparation of the individual pattern blocks and that no quiltmaker could have planned the extraordinary optical illusions which enliven the surfaces of the most kinetic examples.

Many quilters worked from patterns, either directly copying design and color, or applying a personal creative touch to prepare an unusual example. Quilt patterns, both classic and novelty designs, were available commercially and could be swapped with neighbors, copied, or purchased directly from newspapers, periodicals, batting manufacturers, and even professional quilt designers. The quest for new designs was an integral part of the pleasure of quiltmaking and frequently led to the creation of beautiful quilts. It is unlikely, however, that instructions on how to compose some of the masterful illusions illustrated in this book were ever communicated through a pattern book or commercial source. In the earliest published books that discuss quilt patterns, there is little mention of the eye-dazzling potential of the designs, even for those patterns called "puzzle", the likeliest to generate "trick" results. Ruth Finley addresses the visual qualities of only a few of the hundreds of patterns described in *Old Patchwork Quilts and the Women Who Made Them*.

Until Jonathan Holstein's book, *The Pieced Quilt: An American Design Tradition*, very little had been written about the optical impact of quilts. But much had been reported about women's joy and excitement in exploring the art of patchwork. As Alice Morse Earle wrote in 1898, "Women revelled in intricate and difficult patchwork; they eagerly exchanged patterns with one another; they talked over the designs, and admired pretty bits of calico, and pondered what combinations to make, with far more zest than women ever discuss art or examine high art specimens today" (*Home Life in Colonial Days*, 271). She noted that, through quilting, "women were able to express their longing for decoration, their pride in needlework, and their love for color" (ibid., 26). Through social interchange, women learned how to improve their compositions' interest and appeal and were challenged to try out new patterns, all within the proper framework of making a useful household article.

Among the tens of thousands of quilts that have been stitched in America in the last two centuries, why do some display designs of illusion while others, using similar patterns and pieces, do not? For the illusionary quilts pictured here, their makers must have derived an intellectual and artistic pleasure in creating designs that exceeded the traditional goal of making a functional, attractive object.

As with other art forms like painting and sculpture, the quilt artist must have relied on standard principles of design composition, such as:

establishing a point of emphasis (figs. 1.12, 3.9 and 3.66);

creating an appearance of either perfect or imperfect balance; that is, countering a small area of full intensity with a large area of half intensity, or little with big, or solid with void (fig. 3.18);

establishing unity through a repetition of different elements (figs. 1.24, 1.25);

creating a rhythm that may be curvilinear, echoing, or repetitive (figs. 1.4, 1.6, 1.21);

establishing proportions of the parts to the whole by pre-determining the size and relative scale of the pattern elements (figs. 3.1, 3.10, and 3.24).

The quilter had to have been intuitively aware of those elements of organization which any artist employs to create a composition, including:

Line, the basic device to create form or define pattern. Even without including actual physical lines to indicate design, a quiltmaker can suggest lines through the edges of the pattern pieces, as in figures 1.12 and 4.1. Diagonal lines imply activity, movement, and direction, while verticals and horizontals generally are inactive. Countless examples here convey agitated linear effects because they include, or imply, diagonal lines.

Plane, or the location in visual space of any aspect of the design. The quilt artists inventing illusions have manipulated planes by including elements that appear parallel to the quilt surface, along with others that suggest depth or a third dimension because they are diagonal or curved, as in figures 1.11, 3.63, and 3.81.

Solids and voids, or *masses and space,* which suggest visual variety because they play something against nothing. Optical illusion quilts often suggest solids floating above a flat surface, convey a sense of occupied emptiness, or transform the ground into an imaginary occupied space, as in figures 3.15, 3.27, and 3.40.

Perspective, in which the relative size of the elements of the design seems increased or decreased. This can be either one-point, or linear, which gives the impression that all lines in a composition are parallel, receding, or will meet at a vanishing point (fig. 3.4); two-point, where the lines need not be parallel to the surface, but the foreground appears foreshortened to convey an illusion of depth (fig. 3.46); or aerial, in which imaginary lines in the distance are made smaller or lighter to sharpen the foreground (fig. 3.2).

Color, which has hue (the wavelength of reflected light); value (the amount of white or black present in or modifying the hue); and intensity (the saturation or transparency, depth, or lightness of the hue). The attributes or sensations of color are threefold: hue (color or shade); brightness (lightness or darkness, luminescence); and saturation (extent to which the color departs from a neutral gray).

To create an illusion, the quiltmaker would manipulate all those elements and create a somewhat formal composition which had a symmetrical, almost mathematical, structure that organized the size, position, and direction of the pattern elements. Because they were not structured, informal compositions like crazy quilts generally could not produce an illusion. When joining the patchwork pieces according to a pre-planned scheme, one quiltmaker might repeat the same block over and over to build a quilt surface (fig. 3.1), while another might vary the blocks, achieving an overall pattern from the interaction of various aspects of the blocks when they merge (fig. 1.6).

The quiltmaker had several choices when planning her composition: she might build up a repeat design in the "English" patchwork or "allover" method, joining identical geometric shapes continuously without first grouping them (fig. 3.93). Or, she could build a pattern in blocks or in strips, first combining a number of patches in a design and then joining these to create a larger surface (fig. 3.95).

The most extraordinary examples of optical illusion quilts began to develop from the mid-nineteenth century onward, as block-work quilts became the preferred American system for construction, supplanting the

FIG. 1.2. Album Patch pattern pieced quilt, Amish, c. 1930, Mifflin County (Nebraskan Community), Pennsylvania. Maker unknown. 92" x 84". Cotton. The eye gets no rest in studying this illuminated composition of four-patch corner blocks, nine-patch center blocks, and fence-rail framework. A coral cotton grid seems to cross tessellated squares which read as octagonal green forms. Verticals and horizontals direct the eye to coral X's, which compete for attention with the nervous dark green outlines beneath (or are they above?) the delicate crisscross grid that links together all this energy. Where should one look first? (*Author's collection.*)

FIG. 1.3. Roman Stripe pattern pieced quilt, Amish, c. 1930, Holmes County, Ohio. Maker unknown. 80" x 63½". Cotton. In its vertical position, as shown, this vibrant quilt appears to contain black triangular tabs emerging from its surface, ready to be pulled to reveal an imaginary surprise. When viewed horizontally, black mountain peaks seem to progress up into a distant landscape amid a field of strips in desert sunset colors. The blacks vie for dominance with identically sized triangles pieced of narrow strips of pastels; together, these triangles read as shadowy diamonds that weave a mysterious diagonal pattern across the quilt surface. (*Photo courtesy Esprit Quilt Collection.*)

1.2

FIG. 1.4. Indiana Puzzle pattern pieced quilt, Amish, c. 1920, Indiana. Maker unknown. 82″ x 70″. Cotton. Here is the most direct form of illusion: a figure/ground, or positive/negative counterpoint in which the eye cannot decide if the light or dark forms are dominant. Although the pattern appears to be composed of gracefully interlocking curvilinear forms, in fact it is created with large center squares from which four triangles extend. The tiny four patches at the intersections read as sinuous extensions of the form because of the careful tonal coordination. (*Photo courtesy Esprit Quilt Collection.*)

FIG. 1.5. One Thousand Pyramids pattern pieced quilt, c. 1890, Pennsylvania. Maker unknown. 75″ x 72″. Cotton. An unseen force at the pinwheel center seems to be sucking the quilt surface into a vortex. Although triangles are typically straight sided, these give the illusion of having curvilinear sides receding inward. This effect is called a logarithmic spiral, wherein the distance between circles appears smaller toward the center. Conceivably, the quiltmaker could have prepared the design by drawing overlapping circles, adding lines to divide them, and creating patchwork pieces from the resulting diagram this way. Or the optical effect could have been the result of imprecisely cut pieces, which in most cases would distort the finished quilt, but in this case would only accentuate the optical illusion. This striking quilt is a later innovation of the colonial tradition which dictated that a young girl collect a thousand triangles of calico, after which she would meet the man who would become her husband. Here, the maker probably combined her patches first into eight larger triangles which were then united with their points facing inward. (*Collection of George Kiberd; photo courtesy Sandra Mitchell.*)

whole cloth quilt, the framed center medallion, and other early quilt formats. Quiltmakers found that the repetition of one block, or the combination of two or more different pieced blocks, could produce wonderful and often dramatic designs. (The block is traditionally a 10″ to 14″ square incorporating small patches of fabric cut to predetermined shape and varied in color and/or size.)

Blocks could be composed either symmetrically, that is, of uniformly shaped and arranged pieces; asymmetrically, incorporating diverse pieces; or split, that is, comprised of two equal parts (usually triangles) where half is a solid piece, and the other half combines smaller geometric pieces. According to Jonathan Holstein, "in the case of either symmetrical or asymmetrical blocks, it is extremely difficult to envision what the overall results will be from the contemplation of a single block" (*The Pieced Quilt*, 53). The quilter would find that making square symmetrical blocks meant to be linked would "always form the same pattern no matter how she would turn the blocks," but asymmetrical or split blocks could be combined to produce many different graphic designs "by varying their orientation within the format" (ibid.). It is likely that very striking and unanticipated designs resulted from the latter process.

In quilts that are illusionary, blocks are frequently joined together without the physical or visual separation of a sashing strip or a solid intervening ground block. This allows internal elements within the patterned

FIG. 1.6. LeMoyne Star and Four Patch pattern pieced quilt, c. 1890, Shawnee, Oklahoma. Shoshone Indian maker. 81″ x 68″. Cotton. Serial ranks of three-dimensional pattern seem to step up, and back, and up again in a unique combination of classic geometric shapes. This four-color scheme of diamond and square shapes unites patterns of stars, cubes, and four patches. Could the maker have anticipated this dramatic, constantly shifting optical illusion? Different motifs vie for attention when the quilt is viewed horizontally or vertically. Stars incorporating two diamond arms of each of the four colors become more or less visible; plateaus appear; cubes advance or recede; and hexagonal forms emerge as the quilt is studied. (*Author's collection.*)

Fig. 1.7. Tumbling Blocks (Cross variation) pattern pieced quilt, c. 1850, Warren County, Kentucky. Made by Margaret Calvert. 77″ x 72″. Silk, cotton, wool, and mohair. Perhaps the most extraordinarily dimensional of all the Tumbling Blocks patterns ever executed, the Cross variation achieves a remarkable, almost surreal illusion of cubes floating free above a cross which itself appears superimposed above an hourglass figure. All of the forms appear to be suspended above a separate field. This startling abstract creation was a hundred years before its time in artistic freedom, eliciting great curiosity about the motivation and artistic background of its creator and the meaning of its imagery. The three-dimensional sense which all Tumbling Blocks patterns convey is heightened here by underlying images which differ from the cubes. (*Collection The Kentucky Museum, Western Kentucky University; photo courtesy The Kentucky Quilt Project.*)

Fig. 1.8. Delectable Mountains pattern pieced quilt, c. 1890, locale unknown. Maker unknown. 80″ x 79″. Cotton. Contrasting triangles are arranged in a composition that reverberates to the outer edges of the dramatic design. It appears as if six squares of decreasing size have been layered atop sawtooth grounds. In addition, a large crisscross form pulsates outward diagonally like an artist's rendition of radio waves. In reality, there are no layers. The quilt design has been organized by adding a sawtooth element to each row, implying a line that links the bases of those forms and tricks the viewer into thinking that separate planes of pattern exist. The design suggests activity radiating beyond the perimeter of the quilt. (*Photo courtesy Darwin D. Bearley.*)

FIG. 1.9. Touching Stars (String Star variation) pattern pieced quilt, c. 1900, Berks County, Pennsylvania. Maker unknown. 81″ square. Wool. Bold diamonds set in contrasting squares appear to be the predominant pattern around which this quilt was composed. Closer study reveals a busily pieced version of a figure/ground dichotomy in which the background vies for attention with the actual pattern of touching stars. These stars, pieced like a crazy quilt, are also called String Stars or Log Cabin Stars because they are made up of narrow, irregular segments of scrap fabric. Because the star points "touch," the solid areas of fabric which form the field come forward instead as a distinct geometric element. (*Collection of Kelter-Malce.*)

1.9

FIG. 1.10. Hummingbird Star pattern pieced quilt, c. 1900, locale unknown. Maker unknown. 79″ x 72″. Cotton. A variety of visually competitive forms energizes this graphic composition. The major element appears to be pale diamonds with dark centers, but it is a challenge to decide what design dominates: is it the concave white forms caught at their four corners with dots? Or four-armed stars of dark elongated diamonds centered with matching dots? Or the octagonal forms surrounding white concave diamonds? It is endlessly intriguing to see how combinations of unusually pieced blocks are capable of generating different visual illusions. (*Photo courtesy Darwin D. Bearley.*)

1.10

FIG. 1.11. Baby Blocks pattern pieced quilt, c. 1870, Queensboro, Kentucky. Made by Julia Wickliffe Beckham. 86″ x 82″. Silk and velvet. In this classically executed example of the Baby Blocks pattern, made by a woman who was the daughter, sister, and mother of governors of Kentucky and Louisiana, a solid velvet diamond shape constitutes what reads as both the top and bottom of cubes with patterned sides. Our perception shifts. We see cubes from above and below, as well as rows of patterned or solid fabric diamonds undulating like ribbons across the quilt surface. The placement of light, medium, and dark tones here has been carefully orchestrated to produce a flowing, elegant, three-dimensional surface design. (*Collection of the Owensboro, Kentucky Area Museum; photo courtesy The Kentucky Quilt Project.*)

FIG. 1.12 Thirty-nine Borders Enigma pattern pieced quilt, c. 1875, Pennsylvania. Maker unknown. 90″ x 88″. Cotton. Technically, this powerful graphic is a variation of the Single Log Cabin and "framed center" pattern formats. The main body of the quilt features concentric squares pieced of narrow strips which have been coordinated by color and print. The wider pieced borders were probably intended to hold the vibratory effect of the center in check, just as a Victorian frame would border a print. Instead, those borders emit their own dynamism because of their rich prints and contrasting lights and darks. The quilt's flat surface gives the illusion of receding inward toward a vanishing point, an illusion heightened by the imaginary line that appears at the mitered corners of the squares. The quilt's current owner, when asked her opinion of the maker's motivation, replied that "she probably felt trapped!" Viewers familiar with contemporary art may find the quilt startlingly like a Frank Stella painting. (*Collection of Susan Parrish.*)

blocks to "touch" or visually link and create additional lines of pattern across the quilt surface. In some examples, however, sashing adds visual strength to combined blocks, becoming a grid, at times dominant, at times subordinate, but always occupying a different visual plane than other aspects of the overall design. Some blocks can stand alone as images (fig. 3.55), but when combined may appear subordinate to new design elements (fig. 1.9). Other blocks form no clear design independently and must unite in order to create a geometric pattern (fig. 1.14).

Quiltmakers of old found they could create completely different surface designs using the same basic structure but shifting its position (fig. 3.6). While they may have been aware of the potential for creating the various patterns inherent in using asymmetrical blocks, most optical illusion designs were likely produced as happy accidents rather than as careful orchestrations. The interaction of color, contrast, and form might have been planned to some extent, but the kinetic impact of the final design was probably more fortuitous than anticipated.

1.12

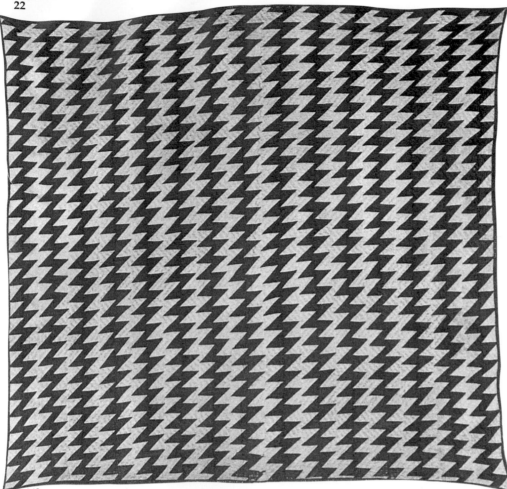

1.13

FIG. 1.13. Zigzag pattern pieced quilt, c. 1910, Pennsylvania. Maker unknown. Dimensions unavailable. Cotton. This classic figure/ground illusion in red and white is totally reversible. The viewer cannot decide if the dark or light (positive or negative) zigzag streak is dominant. A contemporary seamstress might think the quilt was composed of lengths of rickrack skillfully positioned to interlock. In reality, hundreds of identical rhomboids have been artfully combined to produce a crisp, dramatic abstraction whose stepped effect conveys a sense of motion and instability. (*Collection of Guernsey's.*)

FIG. 1.14. Log Cabin (Light and Dark variation) pattern pieced quilt detail, c. 1880, locale unknown. Maker unknown. Dimensions unavailable. Silk satin. This quilt detail illustrates how four small Log Cabin squares have been arranged so that the light triangular halves join at the intersection of four identical squares to create a larger diamond. Innumerable varieties of large-scale design are possible with the Log Cabin pattern, depending upon the juxtaposition or turning of the light and dark elements. (*Photo courtesy The Main Street Press.*)

1.14

FIG. 1.15. Log Cabin (multiple variations) pattern pieced quilt detail, c. 1880, locale unknown. Maker unknown. Dimensions unavailable. Cotton. Three Log Cabin pattern variations—Barn Raising, Light and Dark, and Streak of Lightning—have been successfully combined on one surface using thousands of strips of fabric. Extraordinary attention to the organization of the light and dark pieces of the small Log Cabin blocks and to the rotation of those blocks resulted in a flawless geometric composition. (*Collection of Buckboard Antiques.*)

In many of these examples, the structural blocks disappear within the visual activity of the overall composition uniting them (fig. 3.71). In others, the block is readily identifiable but appears in the company of other complex design elements (fig. 1.2). A number of the illusions presented here are of form and shape, rather than color. In some, two pattern elements are perceived simultaneously (fig. 1.6) or merge into a new pattern (fig. 1.23). Some are spatial illusions, where one pattern is seen as existing above or below another (fig. 1.7).

Quilts of illusion appear vibrant, changeable, and intriguing because *the eye* may receive impressions, but *the mind* interprets them. Through various processes of perception, the viewer makes conclusions about the various optical clues of size, shape, position, direction, color, texture, and the forces transmitted by the patterns. Perception occurs, and differs, among people, always in the context of prior experiences, present circumstances, and visual abilities.

The Gestalt theory of psychology deals with the concept of perception and refers to the "whole," the "configuration," or the "form." It concludes that there are laws or principles of organization at work which show that how an object is perceived cannot be predicted just by adding up our knowledge of its parts, and that those parts may become unobservable when they are combined with other parts. This theory is the essence of illusionary quilts. Quilts of illusion are ambiguous: when the eye is stimulated by shape and line, more than one pattern can easily be seen. The different elements cannot be observed simultaneously; only one shape will predominate at any given moment, varying as our observation is prolonged. The immediately visible shape is called the figure; between it and the viewer is the ground, of indeterminate distance.

FIG. 1.16. Log Cabin (Light and Dark variation) pattern pieced quilt, c. 1880, locale unknown. Maker unknown. Dimensions unavailable. Wool. Through the consistent combination of the light and dark elements of the basic Log Cabin block, this classic pattern produces a totally reversible image—a positive/negative configuration—on the quilt surface. Four blocks are grouped with their dark triangular halves abutting so that the light halves also unite to form a similar large diamond element. Typically, the Log Cabin pattern allows the quilter to incorporate thousands of different scraps of fabric; the power of this simple graphic is accentuated by the limited selection of fabrics used to create the design. (*Collection of Avis, Flora, and Alex Skinner Medawar.*)

1.15

1.16

FIG. 1.17. Log Cabin (Barn Raising variation) pattern pieced quilt, c. 1860, locale unknown. Maker unknown. 68" x 62". Wool. The simple act of setting the Barn Raising configuration on an angle is in itself uncommon, but the more unusual achievements of this dazzling example lie in its illusions of visual texture, interwoven composition, and illuminated palette. Thousands of strips of gray, blue, and golden brown have been precisely coordinated to give the impression of bargello needlework, as if yarns had been sewn through a backing to build up the beveled-edge diamond latticework. Placing the lightest (gray) strips at the edges of the Log Cabin blocks has made these areas appear raised in contrast to the black diamonds at the center of each segment. The gray strips also link visually as a network of light thread claiming our attention at the same time as the golden concentric squares pulsate to the sawtooth borders of the quilt. (*Courtesy Dr. Robert Bishop; photo © Schecter Lee.*)

To enhance our enjoyment of illusionary quilts, it is helpful to know what factors might influence our perceptions of shape. As Julian Hochberg outlines them, the principal Gestalt laws are (1) "the smaller a closed region, the more it tends to be seen as figure;" (2) "objects that are close together tend to be grouped together;" (3) "areas with closed contours tend to be seen as figure more than do those with open contours;" (4) "the more symmetrical a closed region, the more it tends to be seen as figure;" and (5) the eye tends to see "that arrangement of figure and ground. . . which will make the fewest changes or interruptions in straight or smoothly curving lines or contours" (*Perception*, 87).

What does all this mean to the viewer of a quilt of illusion? As one tries to focus on a particular area to gain visual stability and to determine the pattern, the visual system will become fatigued, and there may seem to be: a sensation of shifting or overlapping images (fig. 1.21); a sensation of ambiguity in the figure/ground relationship (fig. 1.9); a visual tension which makes it hard to separate figure from ground (fig. 1.10); or a change in the orientation of the pattern which causes the viewer to read different spatial effects (figs. 3.46 and 3.85).

The delightful, often unanticipated, and almost unexplainable tricks of perception create several types of illusions:

Figure/ground illusions, where the mind cannot separate an object (figure) from its environment. The figure element has the principal shape and should exist visually some distance from the ground.

FIG. 1.18. Log Cabin (Sampler variation) pattern pieced quilt, c. 1880, Ohio. Maker unknown. 88" x 76". Wool challis. This richly hued quilt contains an eye-filling sampling of potential designs which the basic Log Cabin pattern block can generate. By differing the arrangement of the colored strips that are pieced around a tiny central square to form the basic block, the quiltmaker created the illusion of solid diamonds, diamonds in squares, crosses, triangles, and medallions. Signed in ink, "To George," this may have been a creative gift from a maker who loved the Log Cabin's visual variety and did not want to restrict the quilt surface to only one possible design. (*Author's collection.*)

1.18

1.19

FIG. 1.19. Double Wedding Ring pattern pieced quilt, c. 1935, Atlanta, Georgia. Maker unknown. 83½″ x 71″. Cotton. This quilt's maker has produced a very different graphic from the classic Double Wedding Ring by using a bright (red) cotton fabric as the "ground" for her rings. As a result, the background looks as if it is the foreground, with its concave diamonds surmounting a field pieced of contrasting arched strips. The quilter fortified this visual trickery by placing a fabric of related, but not equal, tone within the elliptical areas between the ring curves. In traditional examples of this pattern, the ground and ellipses are usually white and thus typically read as subordinate to the pastel rings. (*Photo courtesy The Museum of American Folk Art; gift of Dr. Robert Bishop.*)

FIG. 1.20. Mosaic (Stars variation) pattern pieced quilt detail, c. 1860, Midwest. Maker unknown. 70″ square. Wool challis. Hexagonal "cells" or "rosettes" are linked like a honeycomb with hexagonally pieced triangular areas which together read as large-scale six-pointed stars. Using hexagons only, the quiltmaker manipulated two geometric forms to create a design of multiple images rather than of space or movement. The hexagon, although difficult to piece because some of its sides are cut on the bias, is nevertheless one of the most enduringly popular patches. (*Author's collection.*)

1.20

FIG. 1.21. Robbing Peter to Pay Paul pattern pieced quilt, Amish, c. 1904, probably Midwest. Maker unknown. 77" x 65". Cotton. An intense blue/green network of concave squares aligns diagonally across the quilt surface, while, simultaneously, glowing red circles form a similar network. Each set of forms competes for visual dominance in this figure/ground illusion. The pattern here is perceived as reversible; the eye focuses on neither element exclusively. To construct this complex pattern, the blocks are fashioned by carving off elliptical forms from each side and using those slivers as an element in the construction of the neighboring contrasting-colored block. This borrowing or sharing of design elements enhances the kinetic visual sensation of the design, as do the complementary colors used in this example. (*Photo courtesy Barbara S. Janos and Barbara Ross.*).

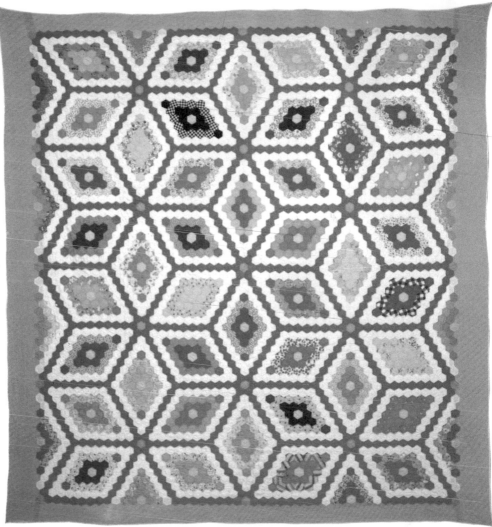

1.22

These illusions are perceived as reversible or equivocal relationships, in which the mind cannot choose between the positive or negative shapes and shifts attention repeatedly from one area to the other (figs. 1.3 and 1.21);

Closure illusions, where the viewer tends to perceive closed gaps or filled spaces where there are incomplete visual patterns (figs. 3.57 and 3.90);

Size and direction illusions, where there is a discrepancy between what we see and what is measurable fact. These can range from simple linear suggestions to complex superimposed images. Strong directional forces within a given pattern may alter our perception of the geometric shape at the core of that pattern (figs. 3.21 and 3.109);

Interrupted systems illusions, where space and depth are conveyed because the repeat or periodicity of certain pattern systems has been altered, or the logical flow has shifted in direction, thus introducing planes on a flat surface (figs. 3.24, 3.73, and 3.81);

FIG. 1.22. Rainbow Tile (Hexagons variation) pattern pieced quilt, c. 1920, probably Ohio. Maker unknown. 78" x 74". Cotton. Thousands of tiny hexagons have been grouped into diamond-shaped segments rather than the "Granny's Garden" rosette format with which quilt lovers are more familiar. These diamonds are then employed as in a Tumbling Blocks composition, creating large-scale cubes and stars that vie for visual dominance. This optical effect is called an illusion of pattern and periodic structure, in which geometric figures pop out or turn in with equal regularity as the quilt is observed. Lines of lavender hexagons direct the viewer's attention in all directions in this rollicking graphic illusion. (*Author's collection.*)

FIG. 1.23. Foundation Rose and Pine Tree pattern appliqué quilt, c. 1850, Carlisle, Pennsylvania. Maker unknown. 85" square. Cotton. Mid-nineteenth-century floral appliqué quilts are rarely illusionary. They are prized instead for their needlework and representational qualities. Until the nation began to appreciate geometric design as "worthy" art (see chapter 2) this form of red and green appliqué was regarded traditionally as a "best" quilt. But in this dramatic creation, the floral imagery has become subordinate to the geometric illusions formed by the convergence of the appliqué blocks. Sharply pointed, propeller-like stars emerge from the luxurious appliqué work, as do four-pointed stars formed by the touching clusters of rounded shapes, while scalloped dots appear within octagonal forms. This multiplicity of design elements in visual competition, unusual in an appliqué quilt, rivals the best illusionary effect of geometric compositions. (*Photo courtesy Darwin D. Bearley.*)

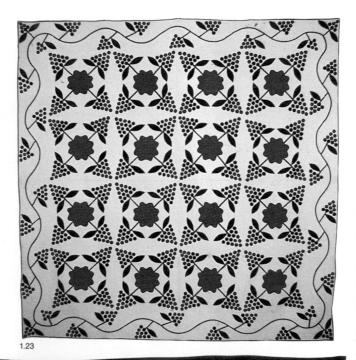

1.23

FIG. 1.24. Flying Geese and Tudor Rose patterns pieced quilt, c. 1930, locale unknown. Maker unknown. Dimensions unavailable. Cotton. Two distinct pattern blocks have been alternated to produce a composition in which each pattern advances and recedes simultaneously. Using contrasting triangles, the quiltmaker arranged the Flying Geese elements to link across blocks set on point so that they read as a delicate horizontal and vertical grid above a patterned ground. Where triangles from the Geese blocks intersect matching corners of the Tudor Rose blocks, the viewer perceives a grid linking those blocks as well. (*Photo courtesy Frank Ames.*)

1.24

FIGS. 1.25, 1.26. Flo's Fan (New York Beauty variation) pattern pieced quilt details, c. 1925, Greene County, Tennessee. Made by Minnie Swatzel. 76½ x 61½. Cotton. This densely patterned quilt surface is a study in contrasts. Dramatic sawtooth circles appear to be whole, and also to rotate, as if anchored beneath a dark grid by a series of square bolts. The mechanical looking sawteeth seem to squeeze in toward the white squares, but the squares are strong enough visually to compete for the viewer's attention as they shift and pop up from their "curtained" frames. As the enlarged detail shows, the quilter's use of intricate patches—with pointed edges, curves, and diagonals, all expressing movement—gives the design great illusionary potential. (*Collection of Marjorie Armstrong; photos courtesy Quilts of Tennessee.*)

1.25

1.26

Pattern and periodic structure illusions, where a consistent geometric pattern may be small enough or viewed at such a distance as to be perceived as having a single color value, producing a variety of perceptual effects (figs. 3.20 and 3.26);

Distortion, where the viewer tries to focus to correct what is perceived as a visual aberration (figs. 3.5 and 3.42);

Brightness contrast illusions, where how light or dark a certain area seems depends upon comparison with surrounding areas of lighter or darker value (figs. 1.29 and 3.3);

Irradiation, where light and dark areas of equal size may be perceived as unequal because a white area is thought to produce a retinal image that affects the eye's receptors less selectively than a dark image (fig. 1.3).

In layman's terms, here is some of what you are likely to see as you study quilts of illusion. The quilt surfaces will appear activated; pattern elements will seem to shift or reverse themselves as you watch (fig. 3.115). Pattern blocks that were constructed of certain shapes will seem to

FIG. 1.28. Center Diamond pattern pieced quilt, Amish, c. 1910, Lancaster County, Pennsylvania. Maker unknown. 80" square. Wool. In this spectacularly colored diamond, the similarity in value and intensity between the two shades of pink wool blurs the distinction between the edge of the diamond and its surrounding field. The quilt surface appears to throb and radiate, the hallmark of the best Pennsylvania Amish quilts. This effect is intensified because the colors are complementary on the color wheel, a situation which can generate stunning optical tricks. (*Private collection, photo courtesy Barbara S. Janos and Barbara Ross.*)

FIG. 1.27. Double Four-Patch pattern pieced quilt, Amish, dated 1901, Holmes County, Ohio. Maker unknown. Dimensions unavailable. Cotton. The entire quilt surface seems to implode and explode simultaneously. The viewer's focus shifts from the suggestion of a deep, dark "background" to a lighter "foreground" grid conveyed by the linkage of the pieced double four-patch pattern blocks. A constant visual tension has been expressed through the decision to place the pattern blocks on point, creating a shadowy zigzag inner border that appears to throb at the edges of the body of the quilt, where the similarity in tone of some of the squares in the smaller four patches to the larger black squares has caused the red and camel elements to "float" above the darker ground. (*Collection of Barbara S. Janos and Barbara Ross.*)

1.28

FIG. 1.29. Crown of Thorns pattern pieced quilt, Amish, c. 1915, Indiana. Maker unknown. 80" x 76". Cotton. The same pattern pieces of strips and triangles comprise each of the twenty blocks in this quilt, yet the blocks read as very different designs because of the juxtaposition of contrasting or complementary fabric pieces within each block. Some look like curved squares with pointed extensions; others, like crosses within diamonds, as "T" formations, or as combinations of these variations within each block. The changing images result from either the contrast between light and dark pieces or from the similarity in value of the pieces to their surrounding field or to contiguous patches. (*Photo courtesy Darwin D. Bearley.*)

disappear or to be transformed into other shapes (fig. 1.10). And, most remarkably, space will loom out at or back from the viewer, even though we all know we are looking at flat surfaces. Elements within the quilts will seem to advance or recede, to switch from left to right, or to be visible from above or below. That is what most illusion quilts portray; they express space on flat planes which do not overlap.

Only appliqué quilts have physically overlapping elements (layered flower petals, for example), yet very few of them exhibit surface designs which qualify as illusionary. The several examples in chapter 3 (figs. 3.88, 3.101, and 3.102) convey illusions through the manipulation of their negative spaces.

Quilts of illusion are not collages, nor are they three-dimensional in reality, yet they communicate a sense of volume or space through the skillful manipulation of color and shape. In some, a change in a logically anticipated sequence of pieces, such as a reversal or a tilt in angle, is enough to create a perception of imbalance or volume (fig. 3.62).

Diagonal lines, whether actual or implied, draw the eye along their length and imply depth or height. They are more difficult to handle in quiltmaking because they are usually cut on a bias to the grain of the fabric, giving them the potential to stretch out of shape and distort the alignment of the quilt surface. They convey depth by implying outward or inward motion or variation in plane. Planes may become apparent because some aspects of a sequential design merge in our perception as inclined lines (fig. 1.12).

Contrasting elements, whether of color or scale, may appear to float off the surface in an illusionary quilt (fig. 3.15). Lights and darks, whether black and white or contrasting colors, constitute positive and negative spaces which are primary generators of illusions. Many of these quilts depend on their inner spaces—the field or ground—to evoke the illusion. This use of reverse or contrasting value also conveys an illusion of movement or space (fig. 3.117). Even where the light and dark tonal contrasts may not be "pure," as in the case of patterns incorporating many different scraps of fabric in related tones, the eye manages to compensate for irregularities in sequence so that the optical effect is carried through.

Contrast also helps to create illusions where heavy grids appear to dominate patterns which are actually the pieced blocks constituting the primary design elements (fig. 3.3). Several examples here show a grid, either through the unification of sashing elements—the strips bordering the blocks (fig. 1.2)—or through our perception of a linkage of design elements within neighboring pieced blocks (fig. 3.8).

All grids appear to exist on different planes from the patterned quilt surfaces; some are dominant (fig. 3.111), while some are mysteriously subordinate (fig. 3.26). Designs based on grids actually emphasize the patterned motifs because of their clear geometrical structure.

Other quilt patterns gain a sense of illusion from repetition, either of forms scaled to fit within themselves (fig. 3.93), or of hundreds and even thousands of patches (figs. 3.34 and 3.39). Repetition creates a rhythmic patterning which exaggerates the geometric order and clarifies the visual field. The continuity of shape or color in rows causes the eye to follow a network of pattern (figs. 3.4, 3.39, and 3.41).

Finally, some of the most mysterious illusions are those in which the apparent visual pattern looks as if it is sharing pieces with the neighboring blocks. Yet in terms of the actual construction of the quilt, this could never occur (fig. 3.85). Certain elements, such as an elliptical leaf, a pine tree, or an elongated diamond, read as if they occupy two places at once. This results from the skillful piecing of blocks with many geometric shapes, and from the direct annexation of each block to its neighbor. As the size of such antique quilt surfaces increased, it is a wonder that their makers could actually have completed some of these extraordinarily eye-dazzling compositions.

2.

A HISTORY OF ILLUSION- ARY FORMS

THE OPTICAL ILLUSIONS present in these vibrant, extraordinary American quilts may have had as their inspiration styles that originated in other cultures and other eras. The growth of the United States in the eighteenth and nineteenth centuries brought immigrants who carried with them the crafts, concepts of design, and artistic traditions of their native lands to enliven and transform their new domestic environments.

The earliest American quilts reflected the fashions and tastes of Europe. Standards of beauty and design were narrowly proscribed. Two quilt formats prevailed: the center medallion, or framed center, which featured an appliqué motif often cut from naturalistic printed cottons and centered within multiple borders; and the simple block-work or one-patch variations incorporating squares of different fabrics. As the nineteenth century progressed, divisions and subdivisions of the pieced format ensued, leading to the extensive vocabulary of quilt patterns now regarded as an American design legacy. Few of these classic quilts are illusionary, however.

The distinctly American style of quiltmaking produced a broad range of recognizable, reproducible patterns that Sandi Fox considers "the common denominator of American culture in a constantly evolving environment." The representative quilt produced, she writes, was one "of challenge as well as circumstance, and it was stitched by rich and poor alike. The challenge was to take the lines of a pattern that had been worked by a thousand other hands and through dimension, color, and craftsmanship, make it uniquely one's own. It was a challenge well met, and in the doing, perhaps America's greatest glory" (*19th Century American Patchwork Quilt*, n.p.).

Quilt historians regard the explosion of patterns and styles in the nineteenth century as reflecting the genesis of an American identity from the multitude of ideas, cultures, and inventions brought by newcomers to our vast land. The strong visual statement that quilts made was national in scope and perhaps reinforced the patriotic cohesiveness that was binding an ever larger Union. Trends in the collection of patterns occurred in America's early days, just as fads ignite the design-conscious imagination today. Any interesting pattern or material would have been shared, while a natural spirit of competition probably stimulated many attempts to improve upon any new idea.

The combination of a single color with a white ground, for example, was a stylistic convention that developed as quilters expanded their repertoires beyond appliquéing fancy fabrics or piecing dark utility quilts. As Edward Binney and Gail Binney-Winslow note, "by working in one color on white, a quiltmaker was better able to refine, manipulate, and create designs, the distraction inherent in a multitude of printed fabrics or colors thus obliterated" (*Homage to Amanda*, 51). This led to advancements in the development of geometric patterns, from which optical illusions could naturally emerge.

Little formal training in the creation of patterns existed in the early years of the nation. Young women's education in handicrafts focused on

FIG. 2.1. Star of the East pattern pieced quilt, Old Order Amish, c. 1930, Holmes County, Ohio. Maker unknown. 75" x 66". Cotton sateen. Using the sparest of forms and materials, the maker of this simple yet eloquent quilt has communicated a variety of optical illusions that suggest a lesson in plane geometry. Each of the star's six points appears as a solid three-dimensional form whose peaked edge advances towards the viewer. The effect is like looking down upon pyramidal volumes composed of light and electric blue tetrahedrons. The alternation of color in each point conveys the impression of a light source originating simultaneously from the upper right and lower left—each arm appears half in light and half in shadow. This strict alternation makes the star appear to rotate towards the light. Perhaps the drama of the finished quilt was anticipated; the quiltmaker could have experimented by folding a piece of paper, as in Japanese origami, and placing it on a dark ground. (*Collection of Morgan Anderson; photo courtesy Toli Pappas Photography.*)

needlework for the preparation of household articles and garments. Instruction covered music, literature, and etiquette, as well, but concentrated on the practical housekeeping skills. In the early academies or female schools to which girls of the upper classes were sent, art training was restricted to needlework or painting on paper or velvet. Students learned representational drawing of naturalistic forms—flowers, fruit, foliage, animals, people, and landscapes. Drawing manuals, prints, and engravings were their sources of design. The stenciling and découpage skills which might have inspired a creative quiltmaker to attempt transparent, layered effects did not occur until the second half of the nineteenth century.

Few women were able to obtain training in the arts or even to gain appreciation of the fine arts in colonial days; their education increased only as the nation expanded westward. According to Carrie Hall, "There were no schools of design open to our pioneer mothers; for the most part, the patterns were of quite simple geometric shapes, many of them having been used for generations" (*The Romance of the Patchwork Quilt in America*, 260). Moreover, there was little access for women to the basics of construction, mathematics, and geometry which young men would have needed to acquire as practical skills for their livelihood. But, "who shall say that woman's mind is inferior to man's, when, with little knowledge of mathematics, these women worked at geometric designs so intricate, and correlated each patch to all others in the block?" (ibid., 4).

A review of the indexes of books dealing with quilts and quiltmaking reveals, surprisingly, that few authors have established a category for optical effect, optical design, or illusion as a subject. Only Jonathan Holstein has analyzed the concept to any degree. He reviewed popular women's publications of the period 1830-1898, such as *Godey's Lady's Book*, and found only seventy-five published piecework patterns (among a multitude for crazy quilts and appliqué work). Of those patterns, only a handful were designed in the block style which had the greatest potential for variation. Other journals of the period were addressed mostly to rural audiences, barely mentioned quilts, and contained no patterns, Holstein concluded, since their audience was not the "middle class aspirant, but rather rural folks who made cotton and wool quilts strictly for warmth. The women who made functional quilts—and made up the patterns— were largely unschooled and certainly not trained in geometry. Yet they, and perhaps their husbands, had a practical knowledge of design which they used in their daily work" (*The Pieced Quilt*, 56).

Early authors researching old quilts were apt to be sentimental about them and were often unable to identify origins for the designs. Pioneer women may have written letters and kept diaries, but rarely described their creative processes in detail, reporting instead on the social interaction of quilting bees or their personal feelings about familial experiences. Books of the 1920s and '30s, with diagrammatic explanations of pattern construction, characterized earlier graphic quilts as "dramatic," "interesting," or "complicated to make," but gave few clues to the manipulation of pattern that led to some of the livelier examples featured here.

What, then, might have inspired quiltmakers to create designs of illu-

Fig. 2.2. Roman Square (Basketweave variation) pattern pieced quilt, c. 1925, Ohio. Maker unknown. 78″ x 69″. Cotton. Square blocks made of light and dark strips pieced in careful sequence to afford the greatest contrast have been alternated in direction across the quilt surface. The result of this arrangement is an illusion of three-dimensionality that resembles woven material as it might appear under a magnifying glass, or a network of woven ribbons. Because of the illusion of closure, the viewer mentally completes the linkage of the strong diagonals, even though these lines are interrupted by blocks facing in the opposite direction. (*Photo courtesy Darwin D. Bearley.*)

sion? There is a wealth of probable sources, ranging from elements in the natural environment to everyday household objects like textiles and woodwork, architectural ornamentation, tile work, and motifs in stone, metal, and wood from other cultures and ages. During the Victorian and Edwardian eras (1837-1910), cultural changes in England and the United States encouraged education in, and the application of, design, and revolutionary ideas in the fine arts fostered an environment that liberated creative expression.

Of course, a quilter needed to look no farther than her window, where light casting shadows, filtered by lace curtains or architectural ornaments, left a geometric image that could be translated into cloth. Natural objects like the growth rings of trees, the planes of a crystal geode, or the tracery of a snowflake could be equally suggestive. Patterns abounded in the landscape, modulated by light and ready for interpretation in fabric by a creative person.

Woven fabrics used for domestic textiles were also a ready source of

40

FIG. 2.3. Double cloth (double weave) geometric coverlet, c. 1840, probably Northeast. Maker unknown. 74″ x 64″. Wool and cotton. Durable bed-coverings of this type were composed of two separate layers of cloth which were connected in the weaving process to form the geometric motifs. Commonly, only two colors were used: an indigo blue for the dark (wool) component and a natural (cotton) for the light component which, woven together, provide the contrast. This particular coverlet is an unusual combination of three colors—red, black, and yellow. Professional weavers using multiple-shaft looms generally manufactured these more complex bedcovers: the simpler overshot coverlets and blankets were most commonly made at home. It was possible to achieve a considerable variety of weaving designs on even the simplest home looms. Household bedding and linens appear in weaving patterns called twill, tabby, diaper, blanket, and damask variations, among others. Because most coverlets were set up schematically in blocks, and all incorporate an over-and-under formula to compose a design, their patterns were easy to emulate in quilt piecework. (*Author's collection; photo by Peter W. Glasser.*)

geometric designs. For example, gingham checks have a warp of one color and a weft of another which cross over and under in sequence to create a third color. Madras plaids, originating in India and exported the world over for centuries, are composed of woven cotton threads in vertical and horizontal schemes that create mixed-color blocks. Tartan plaids and argyle checks, with their colorful backgrounds and strong geometric shapes, make easily translatable designs (fig. 3.56).

Weaving and basketry, both ancient arts, produced interlaced designs sugggesting depth. American coverlets, woven in two or more colors, developed intricate geometric designs that were precursors of some quilts

FIG. 2.4. Carpenter's Wheel (Broken Star variation) pattern pieced quilt, Mennonite, c. 1880, Lancaster County, Pennsylvania. Maker unknown. 76″ square. Cotton. A great ribbon of pink and green undulates around a group of eight-pointed stars which seem to pop forward from this rich background because of the contrast of their scale to the overall graphic design. The single large-scale Carpenter's Wheel pattern is always associated with Lancaster County, Pennsylvania. Typically, it reads as flat and boldly colored, despite its angled edges. Here, the inclusion of tiny stars in the blocks between the central star and outlying pointed border adds spatial dimension that makes this pattern strikingly contemporary in its artistic impression. Ancient floor-tile patterns achieve a similar sense of undulating depth by incorporating various shades of marble or stone. (*Author's collection.*)

FIG. 2.5. Parquetry work, English and American, nineteenth century. Wood, shell, and/or papier maché. For several centuries, the surfaces of many household articles, small storage boxes, and furniture have been decorated with tiny pieces of wood, paper, or shell of various colors and geometric shapes. The most frequently encountered graphic design is some variation of the Tumbling Blocks pattern, but many three-dimensional geometric motifs associated with quiltmaking were executed in wood, stone, marble, and other materials long before they were translated to fabric. (*Author's collection; photo by Peter W. Glasser.*)

FIG. 2.6. Strip Star Maze pattern pieced quilt, c. 1875, probably Pennsylvania. Maker unknown. Dimensions unavailable. Cotton. This visual whirlwind actually has an orderly construction of fine narrow strips pieced first in diamond forms and then joined in an arrangement much like mosaic tile. The varying angles of the strips and the edges of the pattern elements draw the eye in, out, and around the composition, simultaneously veiling and revealing the star-like plan of the design. Such a turbulent effect most likely reflects the quiltmaker's need to use up precious scraps of fabric and her artistry in conquering the challenge of organizing the pieces. (*Photo courtesy Darwin D. Bearley.*)

of illusion (see figs. 2.3 and 3.77). The manufactured printed textiles which replaced handwoven goods by the nineteenth century were also inspirations for quilt patterns; simulated patchwork designs of great complexity and intricate scale could have been models for quiltmakers.

Probably the greatest sources for illusions, however, were found in architectural ornamentation and woodcraft. Ancient motifs from many cultures—Greek, Roman, Etruscan, early Christian, Middle Eastern, Islamic, Moorish, and Oriental—are echoed in quilt patterns. As early as the fifth century, B.C., glass mosaics and architectural ornaments in wood, stone, and metal evinced elements of design that were optical illusions. Some quilt patterns that appear multi-layered echo architectural support systems of webbed and balanced construction, stained-glass joinery techniques, or cloisonné or damascene metalwork, in their tracery designs.

In ancient Greece, Mesopotamia, Egypt, and the Orient, mathematical systems influenced the development of ornamental decoration. According to Stuart Durant, "Roman craftsmen were expert in setting out geometrical designs and were in possession of almost all the drawing instruments known to us, including compasses, proportional dividers, and set squares" (*Ornament*, 63). Some early mosaic designs were based on a grid of equilateral triangles combined to make an overall pattern of hexagons (figs. 3.81 and 3.114). Many of these designs were brought to Great Britain, where they reappeared in mosaic floors, in Celtic crosses, and in knot work.

The highest development of ornamental art based on geometry stems from the Islamic culture, where animal forms could not be represented in any artistic medium. As early as the thirteenth century, Islamic designs were emulated in European paving stones. Helen Fairfield has noticed the similarity of some quilt patterns to ancient Italian stone floors in Florence and Venice: "Some 400 years of effort, whose geometric designs stem from the eleventh through the fifteenth centuries, could have been designed for working in patchwork. With clever use of shape and shade, the paviors of Venice created intricate designs, many of which possess remarkable illusions of a third dimension" (*Patchwork from Mosaics*, 7).

Dozens of familiar quilt designs, including such patterns as the Le-Moyne Star (fig. 1.6), Carpenter's Wheel (fig. 1.14), Star of the East (fig. 2.1), and Baby's Blocks (fig. 3.54) can be traced to ancient tile work. Italian masters of mosaic migrated throughout Europe, introducing their designs to many other countries. Some quilts are assembled from a group of pre-formed parts set within sashing, much as ancient stained glass, cloisonné, or mosaic tesserrae are set in a matrix of plaster or joined with a network of metal solder, iron bars, or stone tracery. This style of piecing visually links a grid which in many quilts appears to overlay other pattern elements. As in stained glass, a quilt image may seem to "continue" beneath the grid which separates the colored pieces from each other (figs. 3.10, 3.57, and 3.73).

The venerable art of woodcrafting may have inspired quilt designs. Elaborate parquetry inlays embellished fashionable tea caddies, writing boxes, case furniture, and decorative accessories which were brought to the United States from Europe. These pieced designs, showing depth through the use of different shades or types of wood inlay, frequently resemble Tumbling Blocks patterns (fig. 2.5).

Decorative furniture was carved, veneered, inlaid, or painted. Some painted furniture was made to convey the illusion of carving with *faux* modelled forms and incised lines to suggest depth. Those who could not afford inlay or marble could re-create the look through *trompe l'oeil* graining or marbleizing. Many early colonial polychrome chests show geometric elements akin to illusionary quilt designs, such as segmented circles representing the Tudor Rose that transposed realistic forms on a flat surface.

Increased consciousness about design that would have encouraged experimentation with quilt patterns flourished in the nineteenth century, as revolutions in the industrial and applied arts began to affect the creation of everyday objects. Scientists and laymen alike began to investigate the notion of what makes form. A scientific movement begun in the 1830s to study the "persistence of vision" led to the invention of devices to "capture" motion. This merging of magic and science captivated a widening lay audience. Experiments filtered down to many households in the form of paper ephemera and post cards that included images layered to produce depth. Optical toys of many varieties created movement from inertia and revealed hidden images. There was great interest in investigating the magical properties of the eye. The kaleidoscope, invented in 1817, transformed shapes through the use of lenses which distorted angles of

FIGS. 2.7, 2.8. Mosaic toys, United States, England, and Germany, commercially manufactured. Late nineteenth and early twentieth centuries. Wood, paper, and clay. Many middle-class households from the beginning of the Victorian era onward were likely to include playthings for children which taught design while they promoted dexterity. These examples of boxed mosaic games contain small pieces in various geometric shapes and colors which could be arranged in endless patterns. Such toys may well have been used as the inspiration for quilt designs. (*Author's collection; photos by Peter W. Glasser.*)

vision rather than changing the shape of the actual object. Other toys focused on the idea of anamorphic images, where a hidden form emerges from a relatively straightforward combination of designs.

Pattern books on optics, folding toys and cards that transformed images, and some highly sophisticated motion toys were popular and undoubtedly inspired creative people to explore optical phenomena in other media. Among the devices invented were magic lanterns; thaumatropes (where two images when spun merge as one); zoetropes, which convey an illusion of motion through a spinning drum mounted with different pictures; polyrama pyroptiques (home version dioramas); as well as the more familiar stereopticon and, later, the camera. Through all of these inventions, an awareness was undoubtedly fostered that two dimensions could be made to appear three-dimensional using perspective, distortion, and lenses or manipulated sources of light. As with these optical toys, quilts of illusion merge old images into new ones, create a suggestion of movement, and reveal that *what we get is not always what we see.*

Needleworkers began to imbue their quilts' flat surfaces with suggestions of a third dimension during the Victorian era, a time when concepts of design, works of art, and materials from other cultures were brought in great quantity and variety to a growing America. Because most antique quilts reflect the social climate in which they were made, an increasingly complex society was likely to have stimulated increasing intricacy in quilt design. The expansion of trade and travel educated

Americans to the art and culture of other places; people traveled more widely, and artists exchanged design ideas freely.

The concurrent Industrial Revolution transformed society, mechanizing handwork and spawning a variety of new designs. The corresponding emergence of a middle class, with newfound time and money which could be used to experiment with home furnishings, led to an increased awareness and acquisition of decorative objects. From the 1870s onward, books and journals on decoration of the household, including Charles Eastlake's *Hints on Household Taste* and Clarence Cook's *The House Beautiful*, proliferated. The everyday domestic environment of the emerging middle class contained endless sources of inspiration for the quilter. Wallpaper patterns, textiles, carpets, ceramics, metalwork, glass and china, advertising trade cards, painting and sculpture, and even book design contributed significantly to the design aesthetic of American quilts. Motifs from Middle Eastern, early European, and Oriental sources were commonplace. Patterning abounded; objects with strong graphic designs might be created of multiple layers of material. Japanese art, with its surface designs mostly flattened and stylized, exerted considerable influence.

During the design explorations of the aesthetic movement of the 1870's and '80s and the arts and crafts movement of the early 1900s, quiltmakers may have been exposed to the newly popular philosophies that anyone could create art and that everything could be made beautiful through the application of design. The concept of layering or juxtaposing different patterns was the hallmark of the aesthetic movement, whose principles of art filtered into all aspects of domestic life. The strong linear motifs of the movement inspired a stylized, geometrized flattening of forms which dominated ideas and design and could be found in goods manufactured at the end of the nineteenth century. In addition, women were beginning to gain increased acceptance as professional artists, applying these philosophies of design to needlework, ceramics, and textiles. Art, and formal education in art, became important; consciousness about design was rampant. As interior design became a recognized profession, American homes were illustrated in journals that exposed their lavish detailing for all to copy. National schools of design were opened; art clubs and art schools that taught more than needleworking skills were established.

Stuart Durant reports that, from the 1880s onward, the making of pattern was actually taught in manuals which showed how repeat patterns could be constructed using grids (*Ornament*, 73). Instructive toys were invented, among them the Froebel architectural stone blocks said to have inspired Frank Lloyd Wright, and other mosaic amusements featuring small bits of wood or tile which allowed children to experiment with geometric form (fig. 2.7).

In 1880, Frederick Ad. Richter and Company, the foremost manufacturer of pattern-making toys, construction blocks, and puzzles, produced a mosaic set with plans to create patterned floors and walls. Such toys actively involved children in design. Even machines for drawing patterns, such as the "epicycloidal geometric chuck" (1910), which might have been used to design quilt patterns as well as home interiors, were developed (ibid., 75). During the Victorian era, an age in which the family unit was inviolable, children were included in many household projects, including that of quiltmaking. They began early in life, had ample free time, and reaped the benefit of new educational methods of training which encouraged experimentation.

From the mid-nineteenth century onward, radical innovations in the art of painting seem to parallel the increasing experimentation in quilt design. The impressionists, whose work was first exhibited in the United

FIG. 2.9. Workbook of interwoven and folded designs, dated September 21, 1888, locale unknown. Made by Edith L. Aldrich. Paper. This fascinating workbook/scrapbook contains handmade plates that are exercises in geometric design. Some have been folded, as in Japanese origami, others are composed of interwoven shiny paper cut into strips. Different graphic effects have been created by varying the sequence of strips in the interlacing. (*Author's collection; photo by Peter W. Glasser.*)

States in 1886, investigated the representation of light on canvas. Seurat and other post-impressionists were interested in the science of optics: through their technique of pointillism, dots of separate color, when seen from a distance, merge into solid objects. In subsequent art movements like cubism, surrealism, and abstract expressionism, painters began to treat their subjects in new ways. Surfaces became flattened and images broken into stylized planes. Artists like Bracque, Picabia, Duchamp, and Picasso created geometric abstractions. Experimentation flourished on both sides of the Atlantic, reaching a zenith in the creations of the Wiener Werkstätte, whose principal designer, Koloman Moser, produced textiles of reversible imagery that resemble some of the quilt patterns featured here (figs. 3.105 and 3.115). At the same time, American quilters were achieving parallel innovations in design, for a spirit of experimentation was in the air.

During the 1920s and '30s, modernistic designs were found stamped on every kind of domestic product from pressed-glass dinnerware and icebox doors to the packaging of laundry soap. Such motifs were omnipresent, and quilters were likely to have been influenced by the streamlined environment around them, whether or not they were aware of the radical changes taking place in the art world.

M.C. Escher (1898-1972) is perhaps the principal artist whose name evokes images of optical illusion in design. This Dutch painter created illusionary volumes of shifting perspectives on flat surfaces in such designs as metamorphoses, cycles, and approaches to infinity, designs which are also seen in some of the quilts featured here (figs. 1.22 and 3.2). There are strong similarities between Escher's work and that of quilt designers working in the same period (the 1920s and '30s), as there are between mid-twentieth-century movements such as op art and pop art and much earlier quilts. As Jean Lipman suggests, op art painters, who created large-scale geometric abstractions by juxtaposing bold colors for dramatic effect, may have been inspired by quilts conceived as much as a century earlier (*Provocative Parallels*, 117). For example, while contemporary artist Ellsworth Kelly may carefully plan the color harmony and contrast inherent in his paintings, nineteenth- and early twentieth-century quilters are felt to have had an intuitive sense of color that produced much the same result long before Kelly was born.

Perhaps some makers of quilts of illusion did not look at all to the outside world for inspiration, but came to their remarkable graphic designs motivated solely by some inner vision and personal creative genius that needed no external confirmation. After all, it was an indomitable group of pioneers and adventurers who conquered the American West. The hardships they faced and the ingenuity needed to overcome them might have found expression in complex quilt patterns that transform a seeming chaos into order. The truly creative quiltmaker always tried something different, rather than going along with the crowd. Someone without that creative inspiration would make a serviceable but unremarkable quilt, while the same patches organized by special hands and minds achieved artistic brilliance.

3.
QUILTS
OF
ILLUSION:
A
PORT-
FOLIO

TO A MODERN ART LOVER, the following portfolio may suggest the works of such artists as Frank Stella, Victor Vasarely, Richard Anuszkiewicz, Georges Bracque, Francis Picabia, Kolomon Moser, and other twentieth-century painters, rather than an album of quilts of illusion. And at first glance, quilt admirers accustomed to seeing elaborate flowers or eagles as representative of their favorite art form may not be able to appreciate these intricate, shifting patterns. But on further examination, the complex, mysterious, and dramatic qualities of these stunning quilts will emerge.

Ask a group of quilt aficionados to name an optical illusion pattern and almost unanimously the answer will be "Tumbling Blocks." Yet there are many other patterns that create optical illusions, including great series of Log Cabin variations, Stars, Bow Ties, Roman Stripes, and even Double Wedding Rings and floral appliqués. Probably any traditional geometric design, and the familiarly shaped elements within it, can be grouped and modified to generate striking graphic, illusionary results. Readers who think they "know" the Tumbling or Baby Blocks pattern may be surprised to see the optical tricks those cubes can play.

The pieced (and infrequently, appliqué) quilts that follow generally have an overall geometric design which is based on the repetition of a single element or pattern block. The colors chosen and the juxtaposition of pieces within the total framework of the design have led to some remarkable optical effects. Although their first role was to serve as ordinary and useful household objects, these patchworks have become visually engaging works of art in the hands of imaginative quilters. While hard-pressed pioneer women had little time to consider decorating their rustic log cabins with works of art, their subconscious needs for self expression were met in some measure in their quilting. The more talent a seamstress possessed, the more complicated her designs were likely to be.

The quiltmaker of illusions may have had an innate facility for, or understanding of, mathematical or geometric concepts to guide her design, but more than likely the most disarming of the optical effects occurred spontaneously because of the unpredictable interactions of cloth and color and line. Many of the examples of the quilter's art included here are akin to geometric forms such as the tetrahedron, the hexahedron, and so on, but few quiltmakers are likely to have had training in geometry to the degree that would have directed the creation of patterns. Although most blocks comprising the overall quilt surface are assumed to have been planned beforehand, some of the powerful results shown here undoubtedly astonished their makers with unanticipated dimensions of movement and depth.

In all of the examples which follow, the visual "whole" is greater than the sum of its actual parts—seemingly impossible in reality, but a magical by-product of the quiltmaker's artistry.

Any quiltmaker, anywhere, could create an optical illusion quilt. Examples have surfaced in all parts of the United States and cannot be attributed to any particular region or group (unlike antique Broderie Perse quilts, for example, which stem from the original Thirteen Colo-

FIG. 3.1. Kaleidoscope pattern pieced quilt, fabrics c. 1930, made in 1974, Chattanooga, Tennessee. Made by Bets Ramsey. 84" x 70". Cotton. This is one of the few instances in pattern nomenclature where the name conveys the image. An eye-dazzling composition of circles and triangles seems to spin and twist in constant motion. Simultaneously, the viewer perceives concave four-pointed stars, small dark circles composed of wedge-shaped triangular segments, and illuminated disks that seem to overlay the surface's kinetic underpinnings. Because each pattern piece is shared by neighboring designs, an illusion of interrupted systems conveys the impression of transparency as some areas veil other aspects of the overall design. (Collection of Bets Ramsey. Photo courtesy Quilts of Tennessee.)

nies, or Baltimore Album quilts, which originated at a certain period of time in a particular place). Interestingly, many of the best examples come from Amish communities, where a tradition of sensitivity to color in its purest form, without the distraction of pattern, led to an eloquent expression of design. Certainly twentieth-century color-field artists and theorists like Josef Albers could look to these Amish illusions to study the interaction of color. It is ironic that the Amish produced so many examples of illusionary quilts, because in the earliest, most orthodox settlements, some sect leaders forbade the piecing of quilts. Interaction with their non-Amish neighbors introduced these simple people to American quilting traditions which, coupled with their indigenous color sensibility, led to the creation of truly radiant graphic masterpieces.

Any seamstress, whether Amish or not, probably began a new quilt with a basic form in mind and let her creative instincts motivate the preparation and assembly of her pieces. By experimenting, she could explore possible patterns from scraps without having to compose an entire design. Or she might have created a pattern using graph paper or paper templates folded in equal parts upon which different colors or design elements could be drawn to explore combinations for their effects. After deciding on her overall design, the quiltmaker might have created her own patterns from paper, pressboard, or other stiff template; marked the patches; figured out the amount of material required for the different components; and begun to sew.

This portfolio of quilts is organized according to the predominant geometric forms that comprise the blocks or pattern segments, just as the quiltmaker would have approached her project. The *basis* for the illusion is our starting point, as the geometric forms employed are the piecing elements most familiar to quilt lovers and quiltmakers alike: the square and the triangle; the diamond and the cube; the rectangle and the strip; curvilinear forms, including circles and hexagons; and, finally, combinations of representational, eccentric, miscellaneous, and unique patterns. The three basic geometric designs in earliest use in American patchwork quilting were the square, the rectangle, and the diamond. The circle and hexagon were considered secondary to these three basic forms. Together, these five geometric shapes, and the parts into which each can be easily subdivided, constitute the piecework vocabulary for the majority of quilts.

To demonstrate how the use of different tonal combinations and relative size can alter a traditional pattern, this chapter includes several examples of each of the more familiar quilt patterns, such as Baby Blocks, Stars, Log Cabins, and block work. In conjunction with the many illustrations depicting the full quilts, details are included to highlight interesting aspects of the designs. Some examples are one of a kind, taking off perhaps from a familiar concept, but modifying it in a highly original and sometimes explosive way.

Many of the examples included here have no recorded pattern names. The titles that accompany them either stem from the geometric format of the design closest to a traditional example, or are affectionate or picturesque descriptions which the owners have given them. Most pattern names were derived from historic, geographic, botanical, political, socio-cultural, religious, or familial sources. While the names are charming, they usually give no hint as to the formal composition of the block or the finished quilt. For example, quilts with the word "puzzle" in their name may have been so called because they contain a number of differently shaped geometric pieces. Or designs like Yankee Puzzle, Irish Puzzle, Chinese Puzzle, and others might have emerged at a time of mass emigration to the United States and have little to do with design complexity. The "puzzle" design closest to a real illusion is Tile Puzzle, whose frame of reference is the intricately webbed ancient Islamic patterning which seems to have influenced many of the quilts included here (see fig. 3.116).

Each illustration in this portfolio is accompanied by a legend which follows a basic format. First is noted the pattern name as recorded in a published source or submitted by the maker, family of the maker, or current owner. Next is the date, either preceded by "c." if estimated, or as recorded by the original source. Then the materials used to piece the top are cited, with the primary fabric listed first. Any regional or historical information, including the maker's name, has been included when known. When measurements are available, length precedes width. A description of the basic building blocks of the overall design follows, with some analysis of how the graphic effects are perceived.

Few legends contain information on family provenance, for most have been acquired through a network that dislocated them from their family of origin and any anecdotal material that might have shed light on how these designs came into being. After all, these quilts are prized for their artistic attributes, their graphic appeal, and their mastery of design. All too frequently, the social context which might have illuminated their creation has been obliterated by time.

Squares and Triangles

THE SQUARE, perhaps the most commonly used geometric shape in quiltmaking, is a rectangle with four equal sides. This basic unit of block design is the source for the term "block work," for the earliest known American pieced quilts incorporated some combination of square blocks. These could be employed to frame a central square with outer borders, as in the central medallion format, or be formed of scraps, creating a pleasing foundation from which to build a design. Patches could also be sewn into a square block which was treated as a single unit for purposes of larger composition.

This most basic unit of quilt-block composition can be easily cut and simply varied in scale or coloration to build a successful quilt design. Some variation of the square—the right-angle triangle, created by bisecting the square in half diagonally, or the rectangle, by bisecting it in half vertically—constitutes the basis for innumerable quilt patterns. The quiltmaker using triangles has the option of keeping some pairs in the same color and varying the colors of others to create a pattern using simple pieces. She does not need a template, other than the pattern for the square, to create triangles: they can be cut by folding the square on the diagonal and clipping it.

Compositions employing the repetition of one patch of identical size rely on variations of shading and color rather than form for their graphic effect. Other

Fig. 3.2. Diamond in a Square to Infinity (One-Patch variation) pattern pieced quilt, c. 1925, Muncie, Indiana. Maker unknown. 84" square. Cotton and rayon. Some 15,000 postage-stamp-sized pieces have been organized by color and shading to produce an extraordinary large-scale abstraction that conveys near and deep space simultaneously. At the center, subtly shaded pastels create small diamonds in squares, which appear to be laid on top of each other until they confront rust-colored perimeters. As the eye tries to decipher this microscopic activity, it is at the same time distracted by the quilt's corners, where deeply hued layers appear as if peeled back to reveal underlying layers. The pieces have been sewn edge to edge in the standard fashion, but the illusion is one of several planes of fabric. Around the time this quilt was executed, many national competitions were held with prizes given to quilts made using the greatest number of pieces; this one surely approaches a record and was generations ahead of its time in its sweeping, painterly treatment of its images. (*First published in* The Quilt Digest 5; *photo courtesy The Quilt Digest Press.*)

FIG. 3.3. Double Nine-Patch pattern pieced quilt, Amish, c. 1920, Ohio. Maker unknown. 79" x 70". Cotton. What at first glance appears to be a sampler quilt of twenty blocks separated by dark sashing is actually a group of identical nine-patch blocks which read differently depending on their color juxtaposition and relative intensity. In some blocks, a diagonal crisscross dominates; in others, the small solid squares "pop" to read as solid crosses, when actually they serve only to separate the smaller pieced patches; others look like solid checkerboards as their color differences merge; and in still others the small patches appear to float free. The blocks were probably made of scraps without any effort to coordinate the colors into a visual whole across the quilt surface. It's fun to examine each block to discover further variations that color produces. (*Photo courtesy Darwin D. Bearley.*)

multiple square patterns, using patches of different scale and color, tend to be grouped in larger squares, composed usually of four or nine patches, and set within a grid or framework to organize the design.

Examples given here range from illusions which include a few dozen squares of limited color variation where strategic placement of colors forms a pattern, such as Double Nine-Patch (fig. 3.3), to examples where thousands of pieces have been carefully coordinated to achieve the effect (fig. 3.2).

Squares are easy to multiply to form different designs. Probably at least half of all known pieced quilt patterns are formulated on some multiple of the square, with most assuming the four-patch or nine-patch configuration. In these, alternating the color in a regular fashion creates a visible, larger-scale, pattern.

The Bow Tie pattern and its variations are actually a version of a nine-patch pattern. In this grouping of nine squares, eight have their inner corners clipped diagonally to allow the inclusion of a small square at the center of the group. Bow Tie blocks are arranged most often with the center square and the upper and lower opposing patches cut from the same color fabric in order to display the bow tie configuration. Each pattern block of nine squares can be colored and rotated in relation to its neighboring blocks in ways that create a great variety of graphic quilt patterns. In some more dramatic examples included here, the viewer must search to locate the bow tie within the optical presentation. Among the Amish, with their particular color sensibility, the Bow Tie pattern achieved an intensity of exaggerated image—even though the use of bow ties by Amish men was eschewed as unnecessary adornment!

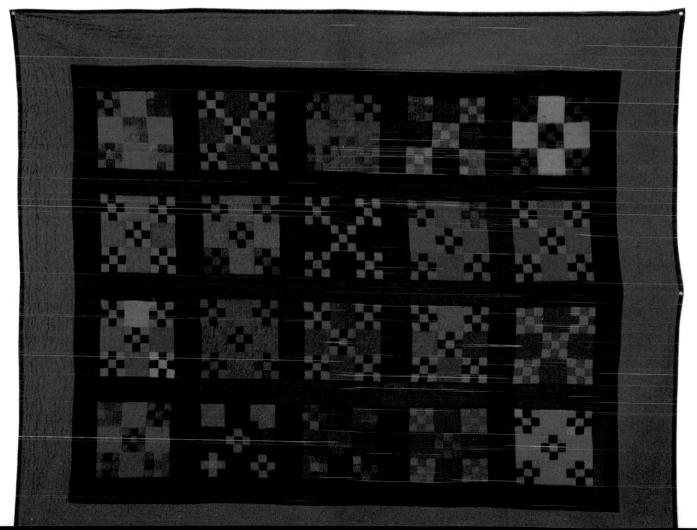

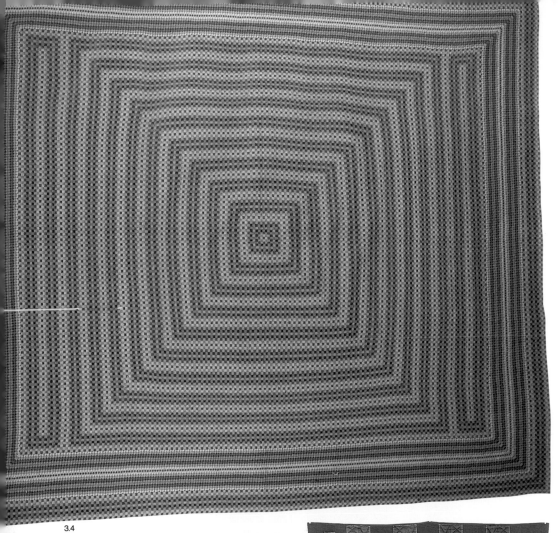

3.4

of a maze. This same sense of endless space conveyed by increasing or diminishing elements is expressed in figure 1.12. The illusion achieved masterpiece status in the hands of George Yarrall, a jewelry engraver reported to have taken up quilting to keep his hands limber. He began the quilt on July 2, 1933, and finished it on December 30, 1935, arranging ten colors of percale into a series of borders, panels, and a center to present an enigmatic vortex. (*Photo courtesy The Kentucky Museum, Western Kentucky University.*)

FIG. 3.5. Coarse Woven (One-Patch variation) pattern pieced quilt, c. 1910, locale unknown. Maker unknown. 79″ x 69″. Cotton. Gradient patterning creates an illusion of three dimensionality in this simply constructed One-Patch variation. Peaks and valleys outlined in dark shades appear as if in constant motion above a light ground. At the same time, the zigzags appear to bleed into the white areas and prevent the eye from focusing, thanks to the quilter's skillful shading of the zigzags in lighter tones. This pattern is also called Flamestitch or Fine Woven, inspired probably by needlework which is done in a continual up-and-down, in-and-out motion, rather than the contiguous piecing method by which a quilt is usually constructed. (*Photo courtesy Darwin D. Bearley.*)

FIG. 3.6. Hit-or-Miss pattern pieced quilt, c. 1920, locale unknown. Maker unknown. 79″ x 64″. Cotton. By imaginatively moving each rectangle of identical color one half length down, the quilter produces a dramatic graphic, which fools the viewer into thinking that the quilt has sagged in the middle, or that a thread has been pulled which distorts the quilt surface. A simple rectangular form in two primary colors is employed in a striking and unconventional manner with whimsical result. Where another maker might have aligned the ingots in rows like a Bars pattern, or in alternation like a checkerboard, this quilt's creator moves the image into the realm of the abstract through her employment of a novel geometric configuration. (*Photo courtesy Darwin D. Bearley.*)

3.5

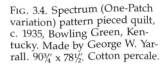

3.6

FIG. 3.4. Spectrum (One-Patch variation) pattern pieced quilt, c. 1935, Bowling Green, Kentucky. Made by George W. Yarrall. 90¾ x 78½. Cotton percale.

A composition which appears to be concentric squares made of strips is actually constructed of 66,153 pieces, each no longer than ¼″ or ⅜″. Their arrangement by shade within consecutive-length strips draws the viewer's attention into and out

FIG. 3.7. One-Patch Star pattern pieced quilt, Amish, c. 1930, possibly Midwest or Canada. Maker unknown. 80" x 72". Cotton. In this unusual Amish quilt, the elemental one patch has been organized by color to illuminate a brilliant star, atop a dark field, that seems to be pinned to the surface by a Diamond in the Square pattern. This unusual device gives the illusion of several layers of design. The dark and light contrasts also heighten the effect of pattern suspended above surface in the corners, where miniature Sunshine and Shadow graphics create additional visual trickery. (*Author's collection.*)

FIG. 3.8. Sunshine and Shadow (everted variation) pattern pieced quilt, Amish, c. 1915, Mifflin County, Pennsylvania. Maker unknown. 84" x 75". Wool and cotton. Look what can happen when a classic pattern is split down the middle and put together back to back. X marks the point of intersection with powerful optical effect. Because of the placement of related or contrasting shades, the X appears to be both chiseled into and beveled above the quilt surface. The use of a light outline underscores the three-dimensional effect. Through a trick of the eye, the four sides appear to be inching in toward the quilt's center, following imaginary lines that bisect the design vertically and horizontally. (*Photo courtesy Darwin D. Bearley.*)

FIG. 3.9. Double Nine-Patch pattern pieced quilt, Amish, c. 1930, Mifflin County, Pennsylvania. Maker unknown. Dimensions unavailable. Cotton sateen. The device of setting a pieced block on point adds variety to country quilts, and in the hands of a quilt artist can produce wonderful optical effects. Here, a multi-level, spatial illusion occurs from the linkages perceived both above and below the quilt's actual plane. A light horizontal and vertical grid has been created where the tiny nine-patch blocks join visually. This grid communicates a visual tension as it attempts to hold in check the wide, dark diagonal grid, which is actually the sashing separating the pieced blocks. (*Photo courtesy Judi Boisson Antique American Quilts.*)

3.7   3.8

3.9

3.10

3.11

Fig. 3.10. Four-in-Nine-Patch pattern pieced quilt, Amish, c. 1920, Mifflin County, Pennsylvania. Maker unknown. 80″ x 71″. Cotton sateen. Multiple planes of pattern appear simultaneously in a complex design built from the simplest of geometric elements—the square block or patch. Each larger block includes both the four-patch and nine-patch elements which the Amish traditionally incorporated in their quilts. Here, these groupings have been set on point so that when they touch neighboring blocks the smaller squares within link up like pastel light strings in a horizontal and vertical grid above the quilt surface. That grid seems to overlay a complex spatial illusion: the olive-green sashing that frames the four-in-nine-patch blocks looks instead like a subordinate lattice-work grid beneath the patterned layers. The solid squares that separate the four-patch segments in each large block seem to merge in yet a third layer of pattern—dark crisscrosses connected beneath the olive grid. (*Photo courtesy Judi Boisson Antique American Quilts.*)

Fig. 3.11. Bow Tie (Floating Octagons variation) pattern pieced quilt, Amish, c. 1930, Ohio. Maker unknown. 45″ x 30″. Cotton. This small-scale example captures the exciting illusory qualities which the Bow Tie pattern can generate in skillful hands. Here, each little square block contains a pastel bow tie all of one color with green segments at the remaining two corners. Groups of four such squares have been arranged with the bow ties facing diagonally at each corner. As a result, a larger scale, actively patterned surface has been created, appearing simultaneously as if holes have been punched out to reveal green beneath, or as if octagons are floating above the surface. (*Photo courtesy Darwin D. Bearley.*)

3.12

3.13

FIG. 3.12. Bow Tie pattern pieced quilt detail, c. 1880, Massachusetts. Maker unknown. 100″ square. Wool challis, silk, and cotton. This detail is included for comparison with other Bow Tie examples to show how the quilter's decision not to organize the light and dark tones of the patches has led to the absence of any clear Bow Tie design. If the Bow Tie pattern is to produce optical tricks, tonal contrasts, rather than the shapes of the pieces, must be carefully orchestrated. The entire composition contains nearly 4,000 clipped square patches of patterned Victorian fabrics, giving it an intricate, rich appearance. Yet the surface has little illusion of depth or movement except in the rare areas where some of the fabric tones have been accidentally aligned. (*Author's collection.*)

FIG. 3.13. Bow Tie pattern pieced quilt. Amish, c. 1930, Ohio. Maker unknown. 78″ x 70″. Cotton. Diagonal bands of the bow tie squares assume a variety of shapes because of the fanciful combination of intense lights and darks. The lightest shades seem to generate the most distinct bow ties. In areas where the bow ties are dark, and more closely related in hue to their neighbors, such images as octagons, butterfly hinges, and checkerboard blocks emerge. No one image dominates because there is so much movement conveyed by the consistency of shades on the diagonals that course up the quilt surface. (*Photo courtesy Darwin D. Bearley.*)

FIG. 3.14. One-Patch Diamond in a Square pattern pieced quilt, Amish, c. 1930, Midwest. Maker unknown. 80″ square. Rayon gabardine. By rotating the direction of a chief visual element and outlining it, the quiltmaker has visually suggested that there are two separate layers of pattern, which we know that technically there are not. Here is another example of how with a little imagination the most basic element of patchwork—the square block—can be transformed into a strikingly modern visual abstraction. (*Author's collection.*)

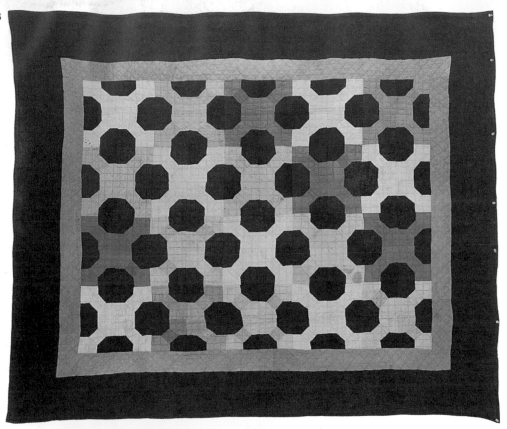

FIG. 3.15. Bow Tie (Octagonal variation) pattern pieced quilt, Amish, c. 1900, Iowa. Maker unknown. Dimensions unavailable. Cotton. In this infrequently attempted variation, two Bow Tie blocks are shifted in their diagonal direction so as to create bold black octagons at the central meeting point of each group of four bow tie squares. In such examples, the octagons appear to float above the quilt surface as if they have been applied on a backdrop. That background's visual interest is further enhanced by the consistent organization of light tones on the diagonal. (*Photo courtesy Judi Boisson Antique American Quilts.*)

FIG. 3.16. Checkerboard (Bow Tie variation) pattern pieced quilt, Amish, c. 1930, Ohio. Maker unknown. 74″ x 68″. Cotton. An entirely different visual effect from other examples of this pattern has been achieved by restricting the palette of the familiar bow-tie composition to just two contrasting shades. The bow-tie structural elements have become completely sublimated to the checkerboard. Its alternating squares shift in the viewer's perception from the appearance of light octagons afloat on a dark ground to a dark grid laid over a lighter ground. (*Author's collection.*)

FIG. 3.17. Diagonal Triangles pattern pieced quilt, Amish, c. 1920, Holmes County, Ohio. Maker unknown. Dimensions unavailable. Cotton. Which triangles point the direction in which to read this quilt design—the dark or the light ones? Each half of this quilt, which is bisected on the diagonal by a pale strip, incorporates hundreds of triangles in diminishing rows which seem constantly to switch direction. Their sawtooth edges communicate a dynamic quality that activates the quilt surface. (*Photo courtesy Judi Boisson Antique American Quilts.*)

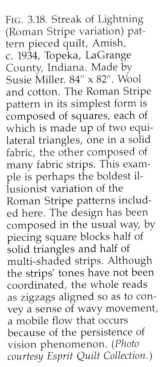

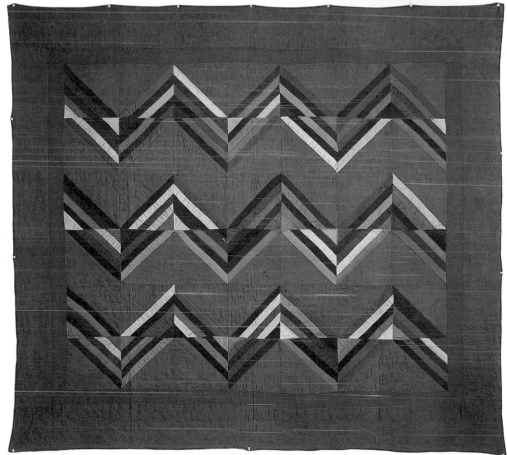

FIG. 3.18. Streak of Lightning (Roman Stripe variation) pattern pieced quilt, Amish, c. 1934, Topeka, LaGrange County, Indiana. Made by Susie Miller. 84″ x 82″. Wool and cotton. The Roman Stripe pattern in its simplest form is composed of squares, each of which is made up of two equilateral triangles, one in a solid fabric, the other composed of many fabric strips. This example is perhaps the boldest illusionist variation of the Roman Stripe patterns included here. The design has been composed in the usual way, by piecing square blocks half of solid triangles and half of multi-shaded strips. Although the strips' tones have not been coordinated, the whole reads as zigzags aligned so as to convey a sense of wavy movement, a mobile flow that occurs because of the persistence of vision phenomenon. (*Photo courtesy Esprit Quilt Collection.*)

FIG. 3.19. Ocean Waves pattern pieced quilt, Amish, c. 1915, Ohio. Maker unknown. 84″ x 79″. Cotton. Black diamonds appear to have fallen in a symmetrical pattern atop a turbulent background that looks like printed fabric, instead of the hundreds of richly hued pastel triangles of which it is pieced. The triangular piecework, which is characteristic of the pattern, is so dense here that it seems to merge visually as a solid field on which snippets of black float. The strongly optical effect of light and dark contrast is greater at the center than at the sides, where the gray, rather than black, diamonds are closer in value to their surroundings and thus exhibit less visual tension. (*Photo courtesy Darwin D. Bearley.*)

FIG. 3.20. Path Through the Woods pattern pieced quilt, c. 1890, Pennsylvania. Maker unknown. 83″ square. Cotton. Identically sized triangles of intricately patterned Victorian cottons have been coordinated by light and dark tones to produce concentric outlined squares that seem to expand from the quilt's center Broken Dishes square. While occasional deviations from this orchestrated harmony of tone occur, they fail to break the rhythm of the concentric pieced squares. In some areas, where the tone of contiguous triangles is related, shadowy diamonds appear to float up optically to capture the viewer's attention. (*Author's collection.*)

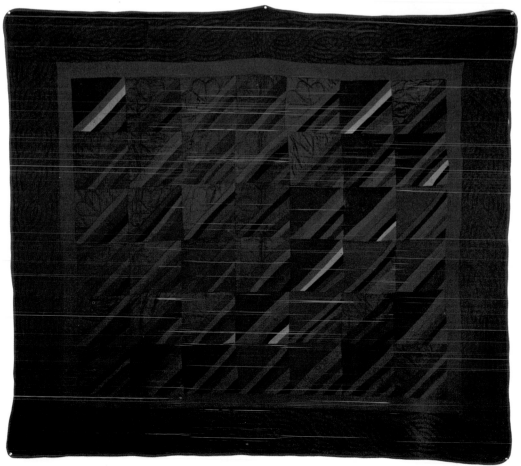

FIG. 3.21. Roman Stripe pattern pieced quilt, Amish, c. 1905, Holmes County, Ohio. Maker unknown. 78″ x 74″. Cotton and wool. This densely packed variation of a triangle-based pattern looks as if it was produced by three-dimensional computer wizardry. This modern, intergalactic landscape image is, surprisingly, a favorite pattern among the Amish, whose lifestyle and beliefs are very different from its contemporary style. The solid triangles, for which many different blacks were used, read as black or charcoal, matte or shiny, highly raised from the quilt surface or disappearing into the striped bands, because they react differently to the light source. Within this straightforward composition, there is much visual variety caused by light and color. The viewer cannot encompass the whole because a study of the parts reveals such differences. (*Photo courtesy Darwin D. Bearley.*)

3.22

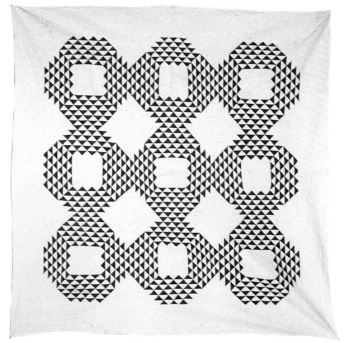

FIG. 3.22. Railroad Crossing pattern pieced quilt, Amish, c. 1935, Ohio. Maker unknown. Dimensions unavailable. Cotton. Patterns like this express an idea through abstraction rather than realism. The geometrics here direct the eye everywhere at once. Bold black solids appear as a grid placed over the subordinate beehive of activity conveyed by tiny solid-colored triangles, when in actuality these areas are one flat surface created by sewing patches together. The grid also recedes as the triangular areas merge as "town squares" in the viewer's perception through the phenomenon of closure, in which the eye perceives filled spaces that don't really exist. (*Photo courtesy Esprit Quilt Collection.*)

FIG. 3.23. Ocean Waves pattern pieced quilt, c. 1900, locale unknown. Maker unknown. 80″ square. Cotton. This crisp and dramatic graphic design seems to be two different things at once: light squares and diamonds laid on top of a patterned ground, and patterned fabric from which those geometric shapes have been cut out. By restricting the piecing to two fabrics (red and white), the powerful effect of the pattern has been heightened and emboldened. (*Photo courtesy Darwin D. Bearley.*)

3.23

FIG. 3. 24. Pinwheel pattern pieced quilt, c. 1920, locale unknown. Maker unknown. 75″ square. Cotton. A diagonal grid of miniature dark and white pinwheels seems to dance above and below a larger scale pinwheel ground. This illusion is caused in part by the effect of white pieces against white, which makes the grid seem at times like the absence of pattern. Its small scale in relation to other elements of the design also exaggerates the multi-level visual confusion and activity of the quilt surface. (*Photo courtesy Darwin D. Bearley.*)

3.24

FIG. 3.25. Kansas Dugout (Roman Stripe variation) pattern pieced quilt, Amish, c. 1925, Ohio. Maker unknown. 87″ x 66″. Cotton. The same basic block used for figure 3.18 here has been worked in groups of four, with the striped and solid areas abutting each other, rather than being aligned in rows. Although no effort was made to correlate the sequence of strips so that the matching fabrics align when the blocks are joined, the eye perceives concentric diamonds folding out from their centers. The striped diamonds appear to be reflected in a mirror; although their image is broken, we "know" the other half is there. In addition, the solid areas of fabric compete equally as a design element for the viewer's attention. (*Photo courtesy Esprit Quilt Collection.*)

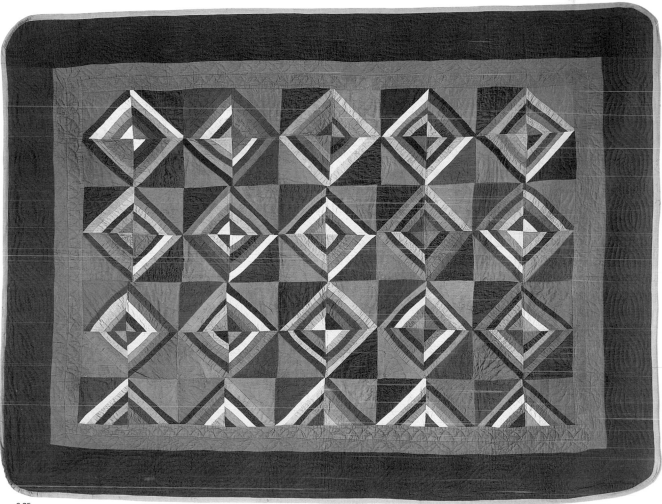

3.25

FIG. 3.26. Hayes' Corner pattern pieced quilt, Amish, c. 1930, Holmes County, Ohio. Maker unknown. 74" square. Cotton. The intense tonal contrasts of the diamond forms nearly dissolve the overlying stepped grid that is a hallmark of this infrequently executed pattern. In contrast to the other examples of the Hayes' Corner pattern included (figs. 3.45 and 3.120), here the concentric diamonds seem submerged beneath a light-toned veil, rather than floating on top. The closely related tonal values of the pattern pieces continually deceive as to which geometric form is dominant on the visual field. (*Author's collection.*)

FIG. 3.27. Ocean Waves pattern pieced quilt, Amish, c. 1930, Ohio. Maker unknown. Dimensions unavailable. Cotton. The solid centers of this intricate pattern seem to be surmounted by a highly sculpted, almost three-dimensional grid. It reminds the viewer of tramp art, where wood is chip carved and placed in increasingly smaller layers atop each other. Hundreds of tiny triangles suggest that wood effect and seem to raise the grid toward the viewer. In other Ocean Wave examples, the pieced triangles read more frequently as a printed fabric background. (*Photo courtesy Judi Boisson Antique American Quilts.*)

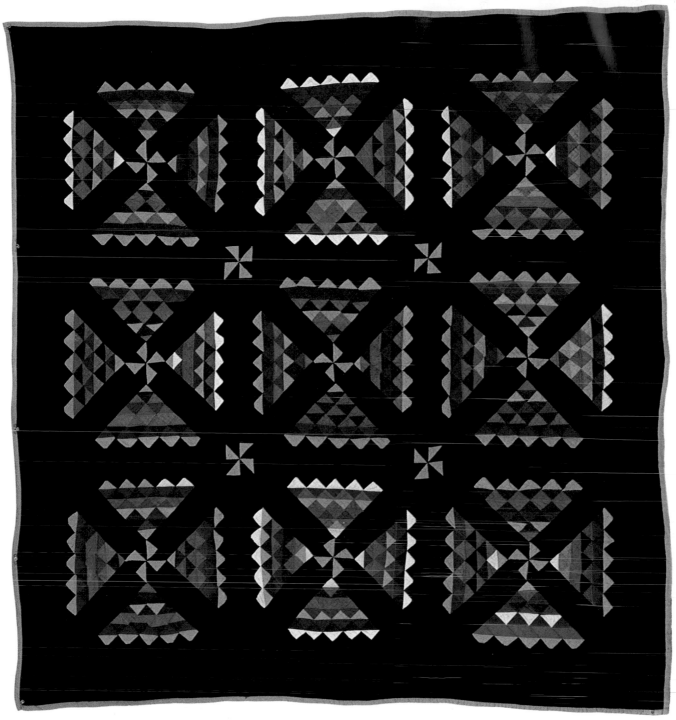

Fig. 3.28. Railroad Crossing pattern pieced quilt, Amish, c. 1915, Holmes County, Ohio. Maker unknown. Dimensions unavailable. Cotton. The black "tracks" converge in an iron-like diagonal and square grid visually raised above nine blocks of concentric sawtooth squares. The quiltmaker care-fully orchestrated her sawtooth strips of tiny mauve, pink, rose, and blue triangles so they would read in successive outline as a further illusion. The eye is led in many direc-tions at once from this design, traveling around the grids and pausing at the pink pinwheel intersections before taking off on another route. The black grid appears to have been laid down as a separate section, rather than joined contiguous-ly to the triangular pieces. Railroad Crossing is one of the rarest Amish patterns. (*Photo courtesy Judi Boisson Antique American Quilts.*)

FIG. 3.29. Kaleidoscope pattern pieced quilt detail, fabrics c. 1930, finished in 1974, Chattanooga, Tennessee. Made by Bets Ramsey. 84″ x 70″. Cotton. As this detail reveals, complex piecing and tonal coordination produce the illusion of transparent overlays and geometric designs of stars, octagons, and propellers in this richly textured country quilt. A variety of patterned fabrics have been strategically laid out with attention to lights and darks to create an intriguing surface which seems to roll over itself as the eye follows the diagonal and curved edges. (*Collection of Bets Ramsey; photo courtesy Quilts of Tennessee.*)

FIG. 3.30. Delectable Mountains pattern pieced quilt, c. 1925, Ohio. Maker unknown. 75″ square. Cotton. This uncommon variation of the Delectable Mountains pattern incorporates large triangles pieced of small pastel print squares to create the "mountains." Although the mountains are traditionally composed of triangles, the illusionary effect achieved here is the same. The quilt appears to be made of successive layers of squares laid on top of each other in decreasing size, but actually it is composed by the quilter adding one triangular element to each row as she moves outward from the center. The viewer imagines the mountain range expanding beyond the borders of the quilt. (*Photo courtesy Darwin D. Bearley.*)

FIGS. 3.31, 3.32. Pyramids (Triangles variation) pattern pieced quilt and detail, c. 1860, England. Maker unknown. 40″ x 34″. Silk. This luminescent crib quilt or parlor throw, composed of one-inch triangles, illustrates how the juxtaposition of light and dark tones, whether planned or accidental, can produce different geometric effects. Studying the quilt surface as a whole, the viewer may see hexagons, six-pointed stars, or pyramids, depending on the group of triangles observed. These illusionary effects are likely to have been accidental, since this seems to be a scrap bag quilt, albeit pieced of costly silk fabrics, prepared without an overall plan of tonal coordination that would have resulted in a more uniform design scheme. (*Author's collection.*)

Fig. 3.33. Footprints in the Sands of Time (Jacob's Ladder variation) pattern pieced quilt, Amish, c. 1890. Mifflin County, Pennsylvania. Made by Mrs. Samuel Sharp. 81″ x 68″. Cotton sateen. As its evocative name suggests, this quilt features lines coursing in every direction and different elements vying to dominate the visual field. Using the simplest shapes and tonal combinations, the quilter has produced an intricate network from blocks. Black provides a rich contrast to the lighter shades which form the four- and nine-patch blocks and the triangular fillers. A diagonal grid seems both to dominate the surface and to be subordinate to a square grid that weaves over and under the myriad pieces. (*Photo courtesy Barbara S. Janos and Barbara Ross.*)

3.31

3.32

3.33

Diamonds and Cubes

BOTH THE DIAMOND and the cube are variations of the square patch, but with angled sides that naturally add a dynamic quality to any design, since an angle automatically implies motion or depth.

A diamond is a four-sided figure, which can be equilateral—that is, with sides of equal length—or composed of elongated sides. Some diamonds are formed simply by turning squares on point.

In quiltmaking, the cube is a multiple patch formed of three diamonds, one of which is usually employed horizontally, and two of which are set at an angle. This grouping can be treated as one unit by using the same color for all three pieces, or by varying the shading, using two or three different colored or patterned fabrics within the unit to achieve a wide variety of optical effects. If the colors of the diamonds incorporated in a cube are varied, a sense of volume or depth results. If only one fabric is used for the piecing, the form will read like a hexagon.

The Tumbling Blocks cube design is the most familiar to quilt lovers. It is also called Stair Steps or Illusion and, most commonly in the South, Baby Blocks, and is the pattern most frequently acknowledged as capable of revealing an optical illusion, even in quilt studies compiled nearly a century ago.

If volume can be suggested in just one cube unit, imagine the sense of depth that can be communicated when cubes are repeated by the hundreds, and even thousands, as is quite common in quiltmaking. The architectural impression achieved in such repetition can be astonishing. By skillfully handling the colors of each cube, the quiltmaker can create tremendously powerful graphic designs, in many of which the top of one cube serves also as the bottom of the cube in the row above it. The entertaining visual confusion and constant shifts in perception that result are a hallmark of quilts of illusion.

Both the diamond and the cube are more difficult to piece than the straight-sided square because their angled sides require the quilter to cut the fabric on the bias. In so doing she could easily stretch the fabric, thus distorting the subsequent composition. Each angled side of a diamond or cube must be precisely measured to insure that contiguous pieces align properly and that the finished quilt top will lie flat.

FIG. 3.34. Leavenworth Star pattern pieced quilt, detail, c. 1920, Pennsylvania. Maker unknown. 88" x 86". Cotton. This captivating, intricate composition, full of pattern and depth, is simply constructed, repeating one pieced block several hundred times. That block has an eight-pointed star at its center, and a mitered border in which each side is pieced of three patches (two diamonds and a rhomboid). At each intersection of four such blocks, the diamonds link up to form another star pattern, which advances in the viewer's perception as four three-dimensional cubes. One's eye constantly shifts from the stars in the blocks to the stars at the intersections to the diagonal starry grid above a squared-off field. The sensation of depth is accentuated because all the elements look as if they have beveled edges. Patterned turn-of-the-century cottons comprise the more than 1,500 pieces in the quilt. It would be interesting to see the same design executed in solid fabrics. (*Author's collection.*)

FIG. 3.35. Trip Around the World (Sunshine and Shadow variation) pattern pieced quilt, Amish, c. 1900, Lancaster County, Pennsylvania. Maker unknown. 78″ x 76″. Cotton. A classic Pennsylvania-Amish design has been transformed through the use of shading to read like interwoven strips reaching back into a vortex, rather than as the concentrically pulsating diamonds with which this pattern is identified. Small diamonds in dusty tones merge in many areas and appear to undulate over and under each other. This unique visual effect probably occurred by accident as the quilter used up the scraps at hand; it is doubtful that the fabrics were carefully coordinated. (*Private collection; photo courtesy Judith & James Milne.*)

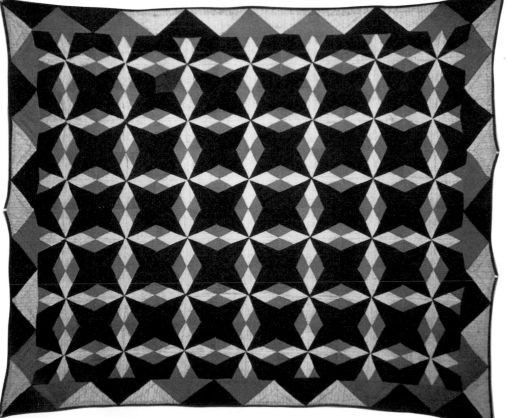

FIG. 3.36. Travel Star pattern pieced quilt, c. 1910. Texas. Maker unknown. 76″ x 64″. Wool. Each block of this dynamic quilt is centered with a four-pointed star made of dark wool suiting and is surrounded by lighter shades of diamonds. The strong, shifting images which activate the quilt surface emerge only when the blocks are joined. Together, these elements produce a pattern similar in effect to figures 1.6 and 4.1, in which several geometric designs vie for attention. The stars look as if set in octagonal rings, while elongated medium- and light-toned four-pointed stars emerge from a dark ground. Most wool quilts of this era were made for warmth from available clothing scraps, but this quilt's maker must have sensed the dramatic possibilities that lay in the contrasting wools she probably chose especially for this design. (*Author's collection.*)

FIGS. 3.37, 3.38. Touching Stars pattern pieced quilt and detail, c. 1883, Shelbyville, Tennessee. Made by Charlotte Waite Burditt. 95¼" x 78¼". Cotton. What looks at first glance like a series of Indian tepees or hexagons centered with stars is actually an imaginative large-scale composition of six-pointed stars. The variety of visual images stems from color juxtaposition and pattern repetition. The pale shades of the many diamonds in the arms of the stars cause them to merge with the background and exaggerates the darker aspects of the piecing. In addition, those areas converge perceptually like a diagonal grid framing hexagonal images. The stars disintegrate into other elements of the total composition until close inspection, when each intricately pieced six-pointed shape emerges. (*Collection of Charlotte N. Parrish; photo courtesy Quilts of Tennessee.*)

FIG. 3.39. Broken Star pattern pieced quilt, Amish, c. 1935, Holmes County, Ohio. Maker unknown. 89" x 79". Cotton. Three Amish quilts of the Broken Star pattern have been chosen to demonstrate the different visual possibilities inherent in the same design. In this first example, the choice of colors and their juxtaposition causes the design to appear less dense, even though all three versions probably contain the same number of diamond patches. The eye tends to focus here on the outside "star" ring, where bright patches link with the star arms to read like tufts or pompoms independent of the overall design. The lavender diamonds of the field between the star arms recede visually, as if these areas have been cut out of the quilt, rather than advancing as they do when black is used. (*Photo courtesy Darwin D. Bearley.*)

FIG. 3.40. Broken Star pattern pieced quilt, Amish, c. 1930, Holmes County, Ohio. Maker unknown. 79" square. Cotton sateen. This example of the Broken Star shows how the inner and outer points of the star form can be made to seemingly burst out toward the quilt's edges rather than to be contained within its borders. The outer ring, pieced of diamonds, appears to be a series of serrated star-tipped forms because the diamond patches relate in palette. The black fields between the inner and outer piecing seem to have acquired points themselves as they link up with the black diamonds in the surrounding pieced area. (*Photo courtesy Darwin D. Bearley.*)

FIG. 3.41. Broken Star pattern pieced quilt, Amish, c. 1935, Holmes County, Ohio. Maker unknown. 90" square. Cotton. Chromatic juxtapositions can produce a variety of optical effects. In this bold version of the Broken Star pattern, the eight-pointed star at the center nearly disappears amid the turbulence of the design. Two distinct elements advance. The large black diamonds (which are actually the ground or field between the star arms and the pieced surround) seem to float above the quilt surface; the pieced border reads like a scalloped ring or a network of intertwined links encircling the star, rather than as an extension of the central pattern. (*Photo courtesy Darwin D. Bearley.*)

FIG. 3.42. Zigzag (One-Patch variation) pattern pieced quilt, c. 1885, Berks County, Pennsylvania. Maker unknown. 80″ x 71″. Cotton. This unusual variation of a simple one-patch pattern is dazzling, its visible yet invisible lines and angles calling to mind heat waves rising from a hot summer pavement. Another Pennsylvania quilter might have taken these pieced diamond elements and turned them into a conventional Star of Bethlehem, but this anonymous artist gathered the diamond groups into bars and joined them with vertical strips pieced of two more diamonds, creating a chevron-like, kinetic composition. (*Collection of M. Finkel & Daughter.*)

FIG. 3.43. Triple Irish Chain pattern pieced quilt, Amish, c. 1905, Holmes County, Ohio. Maker unknown. 79″ x 65″. Cotton. Through the phenomenon of closure, the eye perceives big black dots in this sophisticated but disarmingly simple design. They appear to be either afloat on, or dropped out of, a checkered field which is the classic pieced design. Although the black areas have angular sides, they read as circular because the eye tries to compensate for the distortion and to justify the contrast between the vast expanse of black and the lighter surround. (*Photo courtesy Darwin D. Bearley.*)

FIG. 3.44. Arkansas Traveler pattern pieced quilt, c. 1880, Ohio. Maker unknown. 82″ square. Wool challis. The quilter's choice of just three contrasting fabrics results in design variations more clearly defined and dramatic than they would be if many fabrics had been employed. The viewer perceives four-pointed stars set within dotted octagons, but these motifs soon lose the competition for visual dominance to lighter diagonal bands which traverse the quilt surface. A somewhat shallow sense of depth is conveyed where pinwheels cover pointed stars. All this geometric effect has been accomplished using only two diamond-shaped pattern pieces—one elongated, the other, kite-like. (*Private collection; photo courtesy of the author.*)

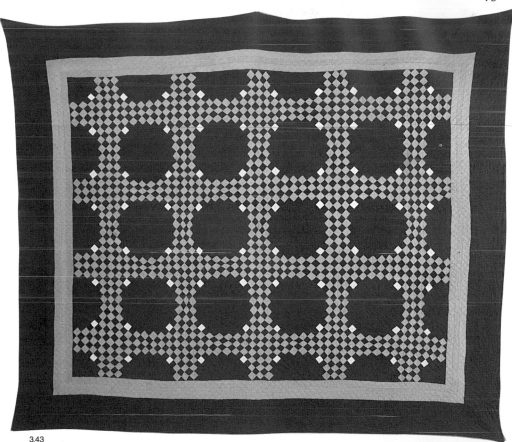

3.43

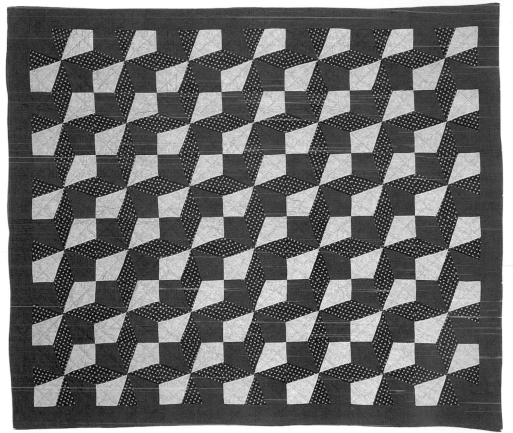

3.44

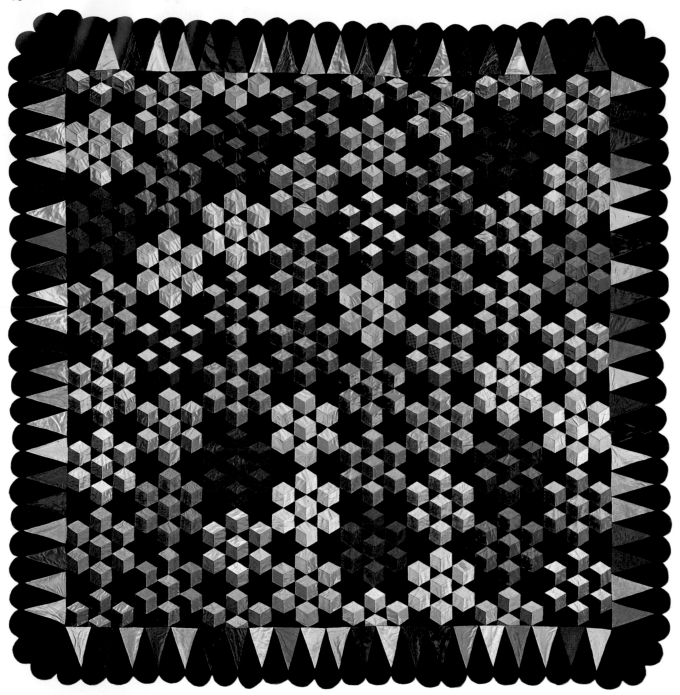

FIG. 3.45. Tumbling Blocks and Stars pattern pieced quilt, c. 1880, Portsmouth, Ohio. Made by Mrs. James Newman. 78″ x 74″. Silk and velvet. Seven cubes, arranged in a hexagonal grouping, touch to surround black velvet six-pointed stars. These geometric forms compete for visual dominance, and the quilt surface is in constant motion as these elements either advance or recede. In addition, the cubes' formations provoke differing spatial perceptions depending on the greater or lesser color contrasts within. Some appear as if seen from above; some, as if seen from the side; and others, as flattened hexagonal elements. This skillful and un-common treatment of Baby Blocks shows the extent to which a variety of effects can be achieved through the choice of colors and fabrics. (*Collection of Mr. & Mrs. M. Curtis; photo courtesy Stella Rubin.*)

Fig. 3.46. Tumbling Blocks pattern pieced quilt, Amish, c. 1930, Holmes County, Ohio. Maker unknown. Dimensions unavailable. Wool and cotton. The subdued palette of blues, violet, maroon, mustard, and green in this cubic composition emits a very different visual impression from the light-hearted, delicate example of figure 3.47. The pattern plays visual tricks at several levels of the quilt surface because of color similarity or contrast. Where closer in value, the rows read like horizontal strings of diamonds atop dark, undulating ribbons, as if viewed from above. Where more contrasting, the rows read as three-dimensional cubes seen from either the right, left, or above. The variation in shading transforms the basic cube from two dimensions to three as color contrast increases. Admirers of contemporary art may appreciate the architectural variations of shape and color, but the quilter probably had no such goal in mind—she used whatever shades were available. (*Photo courtesy Judi Boisson Antique American Quilts.*)

Fig. 3.47. Tumbling Blocks pattern pieced quilt, Amish, c. 1940, Michigan. Maker unknown. Dimensions unavailable. Cotton sateen. A pastel rainbow of cubes in striped rows reads simultaneously from above and below, from right and left, because of the color juxtapositions. Some of the bold, three-dimensional cubes have darkly shadowed left sides which suggest movement in that direction, while others march sprightly to the right; the direction constantly seems to switch. The overall illusion presented suggests a space-age weave of assorted high-tech colors, rather than the straightforward alignment of cubes that would have emerged if fewer colors had been employed. (*Photo courtesy Judi Boisson Antique American Quilts.*)

78

Fig. 3.48. Seven Sisters (Tumbling Blocks variation) pattern pieced quilt, c. 1875, Pennsylvania. Maker unknown. 82″ × 80″. Cotton. Six-pointed stars ringed by white hexagons are compressed into a multi-thousand piece composition that is actually a tiny Tumbling Blocks pattern. The blocks keep shifting into stars and back into blocks. The visual intrigue is compounded by the strong directional lines that have been generated by carefully coordinating the cubes' sides in the same fabrics so they link up across or diagonally upon the quilt surface. Even the stars vary as we study the design: some, in medium-tone Victorian calicoes, appear full bodied, while others seem to be composed of trilobed forms of white diamonds. (*Author's collection.*)

3.48

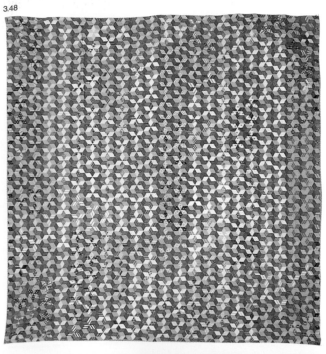

Fig. 3.49. Tumbling Blocks pattern pieced quilt, Mennonite, c. 1880, Pennsylvania. Maker unknown. 76″ × 66″. Wool. A variety of solid woolens has been incorporated in this unpatterned blocks variation. Both cubes and six-pointed stars become visible, but with no particular consistency. The diamond-shaped pieces are probably clothing remnants, making this quilt a true scrap composition. The cubes here were probably treated independently, rather than orchestrated by tone to further a grander design scheme. (*Photo courtesy Esprit Quilt Collection.*)

3.49

FIG. 3.50. Illusion (Tumbling Blocks variation) pattern pieced quilt. Amish, c. 1930, Holmes County, Ohio. Maker unknown. Dimensions unavailable. Cotton. Forceful diagonals, like streamers, are as dominant visually as the traditional cubes of this design. They read as ribbons, blocks, or rows, depending upon the variation in placement of the light, medium, and dark diamonds. The optical effect shifts particularly at the upper right and lower left corners in this dynamic and continually changing creation. (*Private collection; photo courtesy Esprit Quilt Collection.*)

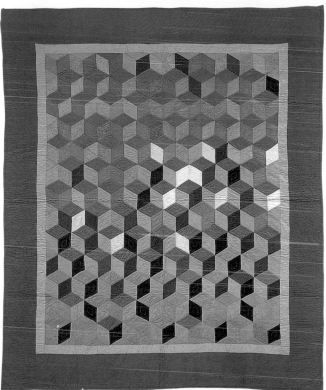

FIG. 3.51. Tumbling Blocks pattern pieced quilt, Amish, c. 1935, Holmes County, Ohio. Maker unknown. 80" x 76". Cotton. Because almost all of the cubes in this traditional pattern are topped with identical fabric diamonds, the quilt surface appears as if it were a three-dimensional composition observed from above. The absence of coordination of the medium and dark tones at the sides of the cubes restricts our perception to this more singular spatial illusion. The blocks seem to have been constructed as scraps became available, without adherence to a more formal scheme that might have organized the various intensities of shading. (*Photo courtesy Esprit Quilt Collection.*)

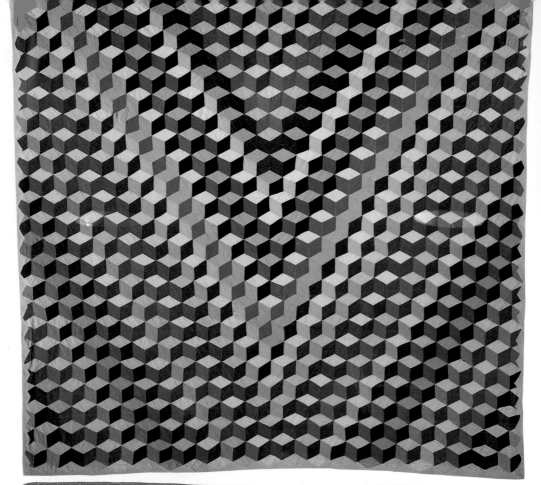

FIG. 3.52. Stairway to Heaven (Tumbling Blocks variation) pattern pieced quilt, Amish, c. 1940, Midwest. Maker unknown. Dimensions unavailable. Cotton. This masterpiece of color coordination and composition is aptly named. The eye is carried up and in and out of the quilt surface by the blocks which form the "stairs," as each diagonal row leads to a distant point seemingly beyond the quilt's borders. The design reads as steps whether right side up or upside down. Right side up, the stairs point in from both sides to create an inverted "V" peak; upside down, two sets of stairs diverge from a lower point beyond the quilt edges. In some blocks or cubes, the top diamonds are the lightest; in others, the two lower are identically colored; in still others, all three are the same color, but of different intensities. Yet all read as three-dimensional objects, conveying a feeling of depth and space. (*Photo courtesy Esprit Quilt Collection.*)

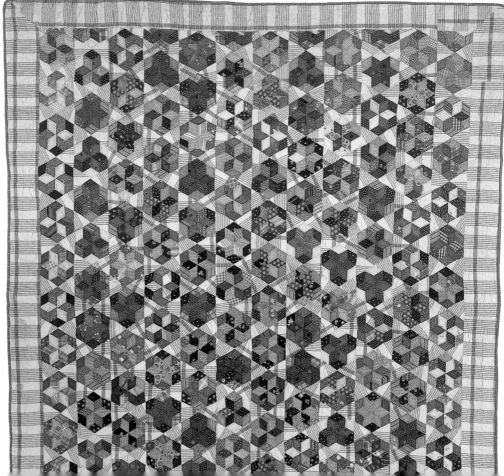

FIG. 3.53. Hexagonal Star pattern pieced quilt, c. 1880, Cumberland County, Kentucky. Made by Mary Alexander. 91″ x 76½″. Cotton. A close look at the little stars that seem to be set within hexagons reveals that each is composed of three cubes whose bases touch. Because of the varying color relationships of the Victorian prints used, some of these read clearly as stars, while others read as cubes in three dimension. By filling the spaces between the hexagonal segments with triangles of a lighter hue, the quiltmaker has created yet another geometric image—that of a larger six-pointed star in which each hexagon is centered. (*Photo courtesy of The Kentucky Quilt Project, Inc.*)

FIG. 3.54. Lone Star (Baby Blocks variation) pattern pieced quilt, c. 1885, Paducah, Kentucky. Made by Isabella Fleming and Doris Boucher. 81″ square. Cotton. Classic cubes in contrasting tones serve almost as background pattern to the powerful octagonal form and spidery star that try to dominate the surface. But even within this geometric complexity, the cubes still switch in perspective and convey a sense of depth and movement. (*Photo courtesy The Kentucky Quilt Project, Inc.*)

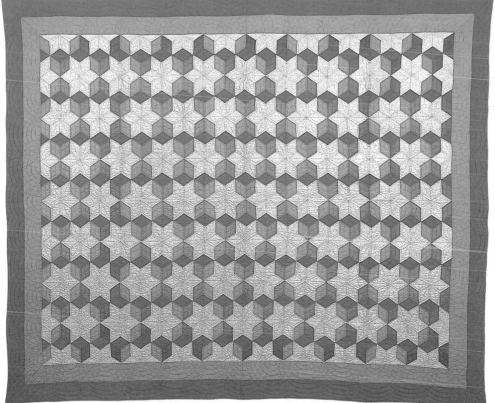

FIG. 3.55. Tumbling Blocks (Columbia Star variation) pattern pieced quilt, c. 1930, Ohio. Maker unknown. 90″ x 80″. Cotton. A restricted palette of complementary shades allows for sharp visualization of distinct tumbling blocks which seem to move around a series of white six-pointed stars. A similar construction is shown in figures 3.45 and 3.98. If the quilt is read vertically as originally designed, the blocks appear as a hexagonal surround for the stars; when read horizontally, the cubes appear to have been organized in zigzag rows with the deepest shade as their axis. (*Author's collection.*)

Rectangles and Strips

A RECTANGLE is a straight-sided figure in which the length exceeds the width, or vice versa. It is also defined as a four-sided figure with four right angles. In quiltmaking, strips are longer, narrower pieces of rectangular shape, such as those most familiarly seen in Log Cabin patterns. The rectangular shape can either be cut directly from cloth, or communicated visually by joining two or more squares of identical fabric to create the elongated element.

The boldest geometric quilt employing rectangles or strips is known as a Bars pattern. It is frequently made by needleworkers of the Amish and Mennonite sects, who arrange full length strips of fabric across the quilt surface. More common are abbreviated pieced bars, which enable a thrifty seamstress to incorporate small scraps of many printed or solid-color fabrics into a simple design. Using even a minimal two-color scheme, a quilter can combine rectangular patches and rotate them in direction according to a consistent plan to develop powerful graphic designs.

Log Cabin pattern variations are among the most versatile of quilt designs using rectangles or strips. They permit the quiltmaker to combine hundreds and sometimes thousands of strips to achieve limitless results just by coordinating the light and dark tonalities of the materials within the composition. The strips can be composed of scrap fabric in a multitude of prints or can be limited to a two- or three-color palette chosen to effect a particular visual goal. Such quilts' construction echoes the log shelter which became commonplace as colonists moved westward across the North American continent. Made in a fashion that emulates that building, the basic log cabin blocks contain strips surrounding a central square that symbolizes the hearth around which the home was built.

The Log Cabin pattern is a practical one, because it enables the completion of a quilt from small, otherwise useless scraps. It is also portable, since it can be composed of manageable blocks with no necessity to create complicated templates. Log Cabin quilts, though commonplace projects among mid- to late-nineteenth-century seamstresses, are remarkable for their variety, a variety made possible by the originality with which each quiltmaker orchestrated the placement of light- and dark-toned fabrics.

FIG. 3.56. Log Cabin (Courthouse Steps variation) pattern pieced quilt, c. 1850, New England. Maker unknown. Dimensions unavailable. Wool. Thousands of multi-patterned log strips compose small diamonds that have been combined without attention to a large-scale contrasting color scheme as is usual in more traditional Courthouse Steps variations. The result is an intricate, richly colored, almost textural composition that looks like ribbons of fabric woven over and under to create a whole cloth. In various areas of the quilt, crisscross images surface because of the harmony or contrast of neighboring strips. (*Photo courtesy Judi Boisson Antique American Quilts.*)

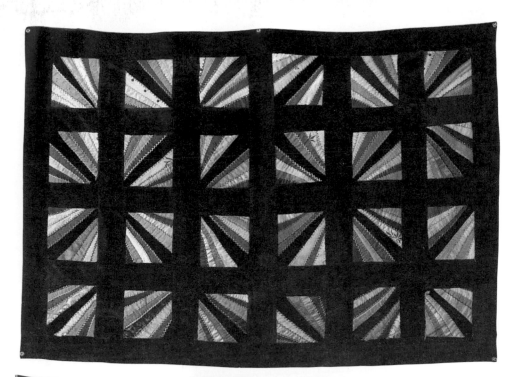

FIG. 3.57. Roman Wall pattern pieced quilt, c. 1895, locale unknown. Maker unknown. 45″ x 32″. Silk and velvet. This dramatic crib quilt looks as if an iron grid had compressed an array of fabrics so that they splashed out in all directions from its weight. In actuality, this sophisticated stained-glass-like creation, which the owner calls his "Franz Kline painting," has been made in blocks of wedge-like strips of fabric pieced as if they radiated from one corner. Their direction has been rotated almost symmetrically when joined, so that the narrow strips convey a subordinate illusion of concentric diamonds or four-pointed stars beneath the black grid which borders them. (*Photo courtesy Darwin D. Bearley.*)

FIG. 3.58. Carpenter's Square pattern pieced quilt, c. 1890, locale unknown. Maker unknown. 79″ square. Cotton. Resembling a classic meander or Greek key pattern in which a consistent geometric form interlocks, this maze-like design was created by the careful organization of narrow strips of just two fabrics. A sequence of layers is suggested in which a central square of interlacing appears to have been applied to a dark sawtooth area which tops a white ground, or vice versa. The lines and points communicate so much movement and interruption of image that the viewer cannot extract the figure from its field. Traditionally, this pattern employs dark strips on white; here the treatment has been reversed and the design so compacted that we are continually mystified as to what lies over or under, what is connected or separate, and what is moving in or out. (*Photo courtesy Darwin D. Bearley.*)

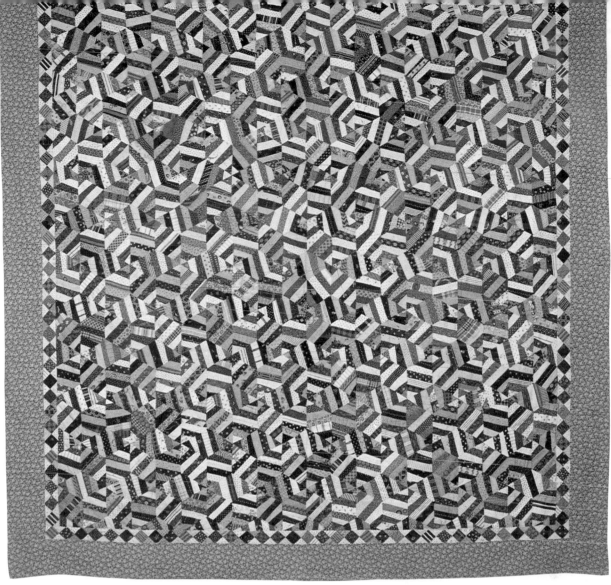

3.59

3.60

FIG. 3.59. Snail's Trails pattern pieced quilt, c. 1875, Pennsylvania. Maker unknown. 80″ x 79″. Cotton. Thousands of nineteenth-century, richly colored calico prints have been pieced in strips and organized to interlock visually, making it impossible for the viewer to judge which element predominates: the lines arching over and around, or under and up. The quiltmaker achieved a symmetry of composition that is remarkable in light of the blindingly small scale and dense patterning of the strips. In one of those rare designs whose pattern name truly reflects the image from which it has been drawn, the quilt surface is in constant motion, its squiggly lines leading the eye around an enigmatic, endless maze. (*Photo courtesy Darwin D. Bearley.*)

FIG. 3.60. Stars in a Diamond out of a Square pattern pieced quilt, c. 1920, probably Southern. Maker unknown. 72″ square. Silk and rayon. The whimsical title given by the current owner to her exuberant discovery conveys the quilt's three-dimensional trick imagery. The design has been pieced primarily of strips for the framework and large star, diamonds in the center star, and triangles to fill in. Nothing has been layered, yet the viewer perceives the major design elements as separate entities. It seems as if the quiltmaker created tiny glazier's points to hold down the black octagon that outlines the center stars, but nothing can visually contain the explosive eccentricity of the composition. (*Collection of Susan Parrish Antiques.*)

3.61

3.62

FIG. 3.61. Hayes' Corner pattern pieced quilt, Amish, c. 1930. Ohio. Maker unknown. 80″ x 72″. Cotton. The entire background, composed of narrow pastel strips, seems to be rotating like the sleeve-clad arms of a windmill, despite the imaginary efforts of the black "bars" to pin the composition in place. The sense of movement results from the strips having been organized into quadrants whose direction alternates from vertical to horizontal. The "barn raising" (black diamond) element seen here, for which this pattern is frequently mistaken, emerges from black strips which have been carefully aligned to follow the direction of their background section. It is interesting to compare this variation with figures 3.26 and 3.121, where the pattern is developed more traditionally using triangles, squares, and strips to generate the concentric diamonds. (*Photo courtesy Darwin D. Bearley.*)

FIG. 3.62. Joseph's Coat pattern pieced quilt, dated 1893, Pennsylvania. Initialed E.G.G. 88″ x 80″. Cotton. This spare, classic quilt appears to be bent at the ends, as if it has been photographed draped on top of a box. It looks like an isometric projection, rather than the flat surface of a simple quilt. This optical whimsy has been created through the quilter's innovative decision to align the colors in the top and bottom borders so as to extend the colors of the bars within the quilt body. Traditionally, the border is set out diagonally around the body without coordinating the colors, to show a clear separation between those areas. (*Collection of Susan Parrish Antiques.*)

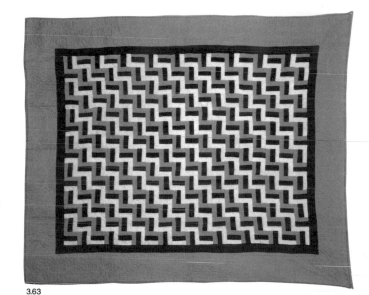

3.63

FIG. 3.63. Fence Rail pattern (Endless Stair variation) pieced quilt, Amish, dated 1927, LaGrange County, Indiana. Maker unknown. Dimensions unavailable. Cotton. Stair steps in light and medium shades alternately pop and sizzle down the quilt surface, casting dark shadows that underscore the illusion of depth this pattern suggests. It appears as if an unseen light source has activated this composition, which is based on the simple construct of making square blocks of three strips in contrasting tones, then rotating the direction of every other one. The Fence Rail pattern usually reads like interwoven striped ribbons, but here the limited palette and the use of black generate a constantly switching three-dimensional illusion. (*Collection of David and Eva Wheatcroft.*)

FIG. 3.64. Unnamed design pieced quilt, c. 1875, Pennsylvania. Maker unknown. 85″ x 75″. Cotton. Looking more like an engraving or etching than a construction in fabric, this maze of pattern may be the quiltmaker's personal artistic vision of an eight-pointed star or of spoked wheels. The octagonal shapes do not remain distinct in the viewer's perception for very long, because the diagonal "spokes" direct the eye through an intricate network of pattern comprised of thousands of narrow strips of Victorian printed fabric. Between the octagons, forms like Celtic crosses also advance and recede. This visual illusion has been achieved solely with line, rather than light and dark tonal contrasts. It is most unusual, sharing its dramatic, graphic originality with Snail's Trails (fig. 3.59), another turbulent masterpiece. (*Photo courtesy Darwin D. Bearley.*)

3.64

Log Cabin Variations

SIX PRINCIPAL VARIATIONS of the Log Cabin pattern are commonly found in quiltmaking, but even two identically named quilts, using the same methods of construction, can appear quite different because of the color and fabric groupings chosen by the quilter who created them. Several examples of some variations are included here to demonstrate the optical variety that is the hallmark of this format.

In the Barn Raising variation, the surface reads as diamonds of light and dark tones radiating concentrically from a central, solid diamond core. The log cabin blocks have been bisected diagonally into triangular light or dark areas and then combined. The successively larger tonal outlines that result convey the illusion of movement.

A different juxtaposition of blocks produces alternating diamonds which appear as solid light and dark shapes. Typically, the Light and Dark variation is composed by first grouping four blocks, in each of which the tones are arranged in triangular areas. When joined so that the lights or darks meet to create corresponding diamonds, and then united with further groups of four blocks, diamonds of the opposing tone emerge at the intersections.

A rotation of the Light and Dark scheme produces the Straight Furrow variation, in which the contrasting triangular halves abut and vary to generate diagonal swathes across the quilt surface. With another twist, the Straight Furrow becomes the Streak of Lightning or Zigzag variation, in which the bands of contrasting shades turn back and forth.

When the log cabin block is divided by lights and darks horizontally and vertically, rather than diagonally, a different variation called Courthouse Steps emerges. The illusion is of strips of decreasing length leading up to a center square.

In the Windmill Blades or Pineapple variation, the strips within the log cabin block can be arranged either in a cross or X fashion. The ends of the strips are clipped at an angle to suggest motion. Because its execution entails difficult and precise piecing and assembly, this variation is perhaps the most dynamic and unusual of the Log Cabin patterns.

Many of these intriguing variations are difficult to decipher, because the structural log cabin blocks are sublimated to the bold visual imagery of the light and dark shapes that form the illusions. By focusing on the central hearth square and following the strips outward from it, the viewer can understand how the groups of log cabin blocks were juxtaposed and maneuvered to create an unusual quilt design. Sometimes two or more block variations were employed in one quilt to produce a dramatic, unusual composition.

FIG. 3.65. Log Cabin (Light and Dark variation) pattern pieced quilt detail, c. 1880, locale unknown. Maker unknown. Dimensions unavailable. Silk satin. The construction of log cabin blocks proceeds differently from other designs. A method known as "press piecing" is used, in which the strips are sewn to and through a foundation cloth block. The pattern is built up around a central square, which represents the hearth. The first log strip is sewn face down to the square, then folded and pressed back. The quilt block, typically from 10" to 14" square, progresses as each piece is attached in the same fashion, perpendicular to the previous strip. One block can contain as few as nine strips or as many as fifty. The placement of light and dark strips within each block and the juxtaposition of the blocks as they are joined makes possible almost unlimited variations of the Log Cabin pattern. (*Photo courtesy The Main Street Press.*)

FIG. 3.66. Log Cabin (Barn Raising variation) pattern pieced quilt, c. 1875, Pennsylvania. Maker unknown. 88" x 82". Cotton. In this pristine classic example, approximately 5,000 quarter-inch strips of patterned Victorian cottons have been coordinated in concentric diamonds of light and dark which vie for attention as they expand to the edges of the quilt surface. The tiny prints are so harmonious in scale that nothing breaks the pattern's symmetry, yet each is clearly legible within the larger contrasting graphic design. (*Collection of Steven Gross; photo courtesy of the author.*)

Fig. 3.67. Log Cabin (mini-Barn Raising variation) pattern pieced quilt, c. 1875, locale unknown. Maker unknown. 90″ x 75″. Wool challis. The familiar large-scale Barn Raising variation has here been pieced in miniature and repeated thirty times across the quilt surface to create a geometric puzzle whose design seems to overlap its boundaries. This effect has been achieved through the placement of the diagonals in relation to the outermost strips which frame each square and through tonal contrasts which heighten the illusion that small diamonds have been set atop square backgrounds. When the strips are close in value, they seem to radiate at their centers. Others, pieced of contrasting fabrics, are boldly outlined. (*Photo courtesy Darwin D. Bearley.*)

Fig. 3.68. Log Cabin (Straight Furrow variation) pattern pieced quilt, c. 1925, locale unknown. Maker unknown. 80″ x 75″. Cotton. Designs are perceived on several planes simultaneously in this unique variation. A checkerboard-like pattern of gray squares alternating with split green and yellow squares seems to surmount the classic imagery of the Straight Furrow pattern as it courses diagonally beneath in bands that are predominantly yellow or gray. Try as we might to fix our focus on one or the other pattern, those designs surface equally in a compelling illusion whose vintage colors and pattern emerge as a strikingly contemporary geometric wonder. This one-of-a-kind quilt seems deceptively simple to make: a square block has been divided in half diagonally by light and dark, alternated with a solid block, and united by a white sashing that appears as a light overlying grid. (*Photo courtesy Darwin D. Bearley.*)

3.68

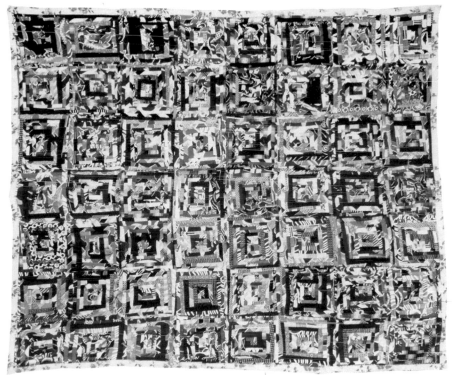

3.69

Fig. 3.69. Log Cabin (unpatterned variation) pattern pieced quilt, c. 1940, Ohio. Maker unknown. 86″ x 72″. Rayon. Pieced of strips from men's ties in wonderful Art -Deco and Moderne designs, this funky variation has been compiled with no regard for the light and dark tonalities that when organized generate an overall graphic pattern. It is included to demonstrate how Log Cabin variations depend for their illusionary impact upon the contrast of tone and value. Even without a scheme, however, this unusual quilt can still be enjoyed for its aesthetic similarity to such movements of modern art as Italian Impressionism or Abstract Expressionism, and for its own excitement. (*Author's collection.*)

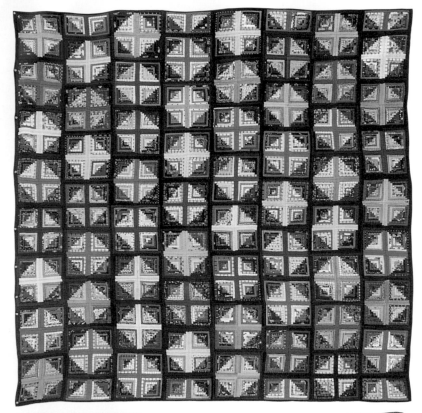

FIG. 3.70. Log Cabin (Streak of Lightning variation) pattern pieced quilt, c. 1850, New England. Maker unknown. Dimensions unavailable. Wool challis. Shadowy zigzags undulate around light diamonds centered with slender crosses in this unusual Log Cabin variation. Achieved through the skillful manipulation of light and dark tones in patterned fabrics, this illusion seems to be woven, rather than pieced. Although thousands of fabric strips are incorporated in the quilt, they are sublimated to the zigzag, diamond, and cross shapes which compete equally for the viewer's attention. (*Photo courtesy Judi Boisson Antique American Quilts.*)

FIG. 3.71. Log Cabin (Streak of Lightning variation) pattern pieced quilt, c. 1920, locale unknown. Maker unknown. 82″ x 80″. Cotton. Resembling an antique Navaho blanket or Indian serape or other woven textile, this pieced Log Cabin quilt has a graphic vigor and sophisticated design emphasized by its restricted palette (blue and white). The central design seems to reverberate, with the light and dark outlines conveying a reversible illusion. Although the quilt surface appears to be constantly in motion, the viewer can locate the square blocks from which the design was built by seeking out the tiny dark squares at their centers. (*Photo courtesy Esprit Quilt Collection.*)

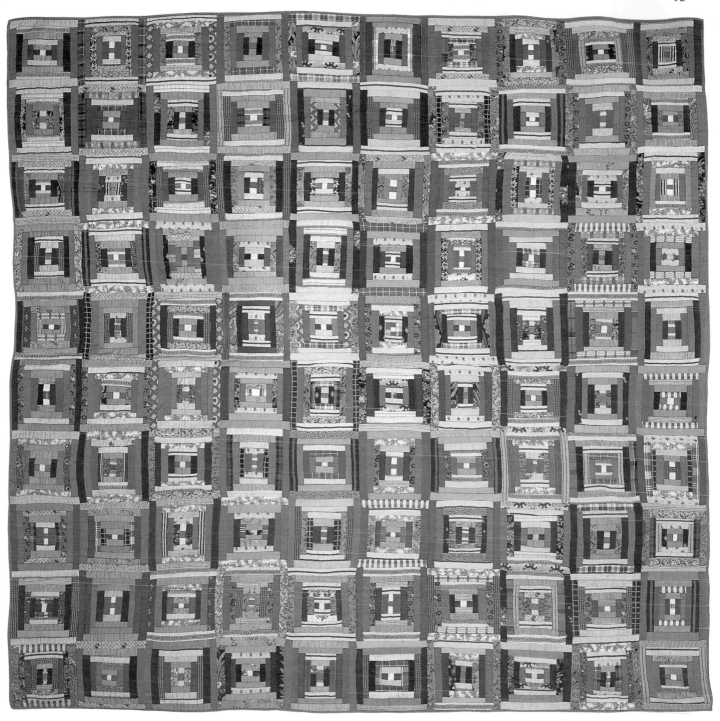

FIG. 3.72. Log Cabin (Court-house Steps variation) pattern pieced quilt, c. 1875, locale unknown. Maker unknown. Dimensions unavailable. Wool. Tesselated diamonds in light and dark tones vie for attention as they pop out of and back into a richly patterned and intricately pieced surface.

In this classic variation, thousands of scraps from Victorian gowns were joined in square blocks with the lights and darks set out on opposite sides, rather than to one side as in a Barn Raising (fig. 3.66) or Light and Dark (fig. 1.14) variation. The "serrated" edges of the diamonds sometimes

merge in our perception as diagonal woven lines, adding to the optical illusions this unusual quilt produces. (*Collection of Tewksbury Antiques.*)

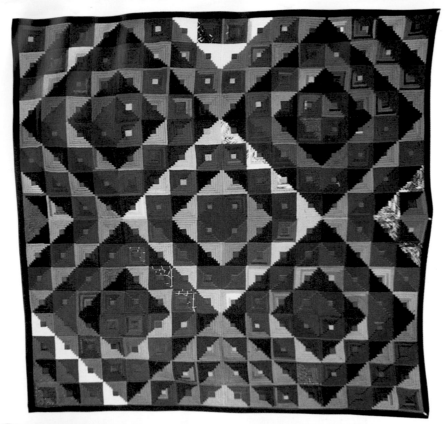

FIG. 3.73. Log Cabin (Barn Raising variation) pattern pieced quilt, c. 1900, locale unknown. Maker unknown. 74" square. Wool. Shadowy, pulsating layers of pattern convey a great kinetic sense in this unusual variation. Rather than presenting sharply defined lights and darks, the elements here are treated like triangles (as in the Delectable Mountains pattern, figure 3.30) to produce large overlapping diamonds which veil underlying colors. In this mysterious, almost architectural, composition, the central area with its red diamond seems to move out and back as it competes with the four surrounding areas for visual dominance. The pointed edges of all design elements serve to keep the surface in motion. (*Photo courtesy Darwin D. Bearley.*)

FIG. 3.74. Log Cabin (Pineapple variation) pattern pieced quilt, Amish, c. 1925, Ohio. Maker unknown. 82" x 75". Cotton. In the typical Pineapple configuration, the perceived pattern switches from light to dark four-pointed forms, but this unusual version presents additional graphic images. Pale diamonds with dark outlines, stars, and circles are visible in addition to the four-pointed Pineapple forms. All the curves, points, and extensions of the pattern keep the surface in motion. (*Photo courtesy Judi Boisson Antique American Quilts.*)

3.75

Fig. 3.75. Log Cabin (Barn Raising variation) pattern pieced quilt, c. 1875, locale unknown. 86″ x 78″. Wool. Outlined diamonds in light, medium, and dark shades appear successively to frame a central pale diamond and then to terminate beyond the borders of this classic variation. At the same time, the little dark squares at the center of each structural block seem to float independent of the quilt surface, as if photographed in 3-D. (*Photo courtesy Darwin D. Bearley.*)

Fig. 3.76. Log Cabin (Courthouse Steps variation) pattern pieced quilt, c. 1875, locale unknown. Maker unknown. 78″ x 72″. Cotton. In this unusual variation, the large-scale image has been transformed into an elongated, interlocking chain rather than a squared-off design. The lights and darks on opposite sides of the blocks are so uniform in color that they exaggerate the sense of dark links advancing toward the viewer, but from another perspective they recede while white Chinese lantern-like forms seem to take center stage. (*Photo courtesy Darwin D. Bearley.*

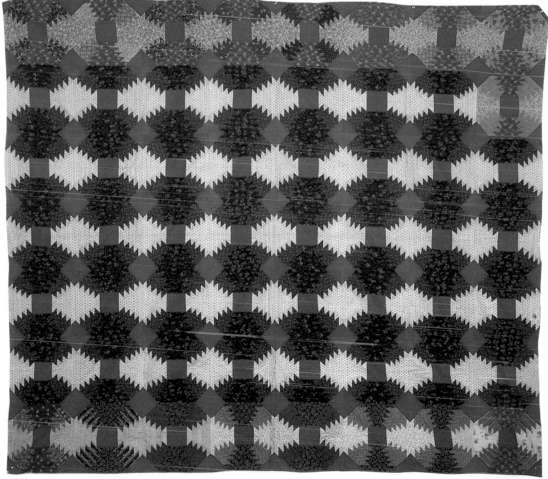

3.76

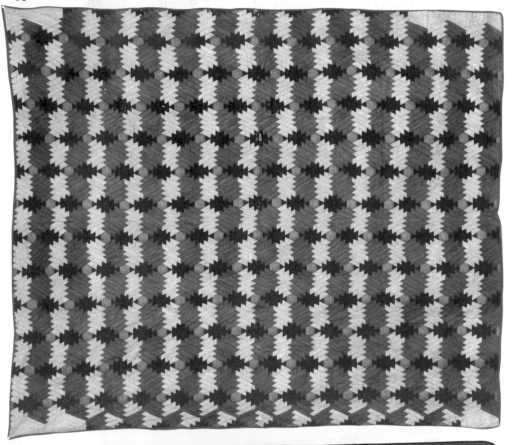

FIG. 3.77. Log Cabin (Church Steps variation) pattern pieced quilt, c. 1860, Tennessee. Maker unknown. 86″ x 74″. Wool challis. Log Cabin quilts are typically two-toned—composed of light and dark fabrics. In this variation, the quilter has introduced a rare third tone to her choice and arrangement of fabric strips to create a complex composition. Horizontals and verticals read simultaneously. Stripes of pale- and medium-toned fabrics alternate in one direction and seem to be woven in the other direction through a "clasp" of black. These visuals emerge because the composition is based on a structure of three: each pattern block is a hexagon rather than a square, divided into three colors (either rust-black-rust or camel-black-camel). In this unusual quilt, the center of each segment is truly three-dimensional: a pale (blue) scrap has been stuffed, giving the quilt tactile as well as visual surface intrigue. (*Author's collection.*)

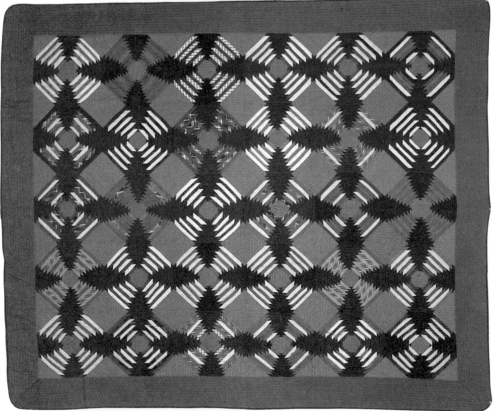

FIG. 3.78. Log Cabin (Windmill Blades variation) pattern pieced quilt, c. 1875, locale unknown. Maker unknown. 89″ x 79″. Wool. Black "propellers" emerging from bull's-eye targets on a dark field elevate this variation into an extraordinary graphic original. All aspects of the traditional pattern have been touched by this quiltmaker's creativity. The blocks have been set on point; the strips alternated by light and dark as well as opposed at the block corners rather than the sides; and the intersections filled in with diamonds. As a result, the quilt's images operate on several planes in intriguing complexity and endless appeal. (*Photo courtesy Darwin D. Bearley.*)

FIG. 3.79. Log Cabin (Barn Raising variation) pattern pieced quilt, c. 1890, locale unknown. Maker unknown. Dimensions unavailable. Cotton. The ripple effect of a pebble tossed into a pond may have been all the inspiration needed for this reverberating design. While great waves of light and dark echo from the center diamonds (as in figures 3.66 and 3.75), rotating the outer log-cabin blocks breaks the light and

3.79

dark continuity and produces an innovative graphic. In addition, the careful alignment of light and dark strips within each log-cabin block expresses a subordinate zigzag pattern beneath the lighter, ripple-like elements. (*Photo courtesy Darwin D. Bearley.*)

FIG. 3.80. Log Cabin (Straight Furrow variation) pattern pieced quilt, c. 1880, Pennsylvania. Maker unknown. Dimensions unavailable. Wool. Shadowy diagonals appear either to veil, or to emerge

from, a design of repeating outlined squares in this unusual illusion. The diagonals have been created by alternating light and dark strips at one half of the structural blocks (on the diagonal) and alternating medium and dark strips at the other half, then aligning those complementary tones on the diagonal. The dramatic outlines of the pieced blocks suggest mazes spiraling in toward the black center squares from which each small block has been built. (*Photo courtesy Frank Ames.*)

3.80

Curvilinear and Hexagonal Forms

THE QUILT EXAMPLES grouped in this category feature patterns where the predominant line is curved, arched, or circular, even when composed of narrow strips or small patches. Hexagons, the six-sided figures, essentially read as rounded forms in illusionary quilts.

The curvilinear form that is probably the most familiar to quilt aficionados the world over is the Double Wedding Ring pattern. Curved edges are featured in all the narrow strips used to piece the rings and in the ground or field (typically of solid color) which centers the rings and forms the ellipses between their arcs, making such quilts more difficult to sew than those whose pieces have straight sides.

The Amish and other Wedding Ring examples featured here were chosen as quilts of illusion because they present either a sense of depth or of motion, due to their incorporation of highly contrasting colors or of solid fabrics darker than those typically seen in this pattern. (The classic implementation of this design uses sprightly pastel-patterned pieces with a light ground.) Our examples show that an innovative quilter with the courage to deviate from the norm can add spatial and kinetic dimensions to the most common pattern.

The hexagonal patch was most typically employed in the nineteenth century in an allover mosaic design sometimes referred to as English patchwork, which joins equal-size patches together without benefit of an organizing grid or other device, as is usually seen in American block work or square-patch designs. In the twentieth century, hexagons were most commonly grouped in a block of seven, where six hexagons of one color or fabric surround a seventh of different, usually solid, color which is kept consistent throughout the composition of the quilt surface. We know these as variations of the Grandmother's Flower Garden or French Bouquet patterns.

Because of the construction process necessary to create hexagonal designs, which employ hundreds or thousands of patches of identical size, there is little possibility for pattern variation. Consequently, there are far fewer examples of optical illusion quilts based on the true hexagon than of any other geometric form. The same observation holds true for most curvilinear designs. It is the straight-sided pieces, offering limitless possibilities for combination with other patches varied in size and shape, that have the greatest potential to become quilts of illusion.

FIG. 3.81. Rainbow (New York Beauty variation) pattern pieced quilt, c. 1890, Hickman County, Kentucky. Made by Ann Johnson Armstrong. 73" x 68". Cotton. Because this quilt masterpiece suggests curving gears and clockwork motion, it is included as an example of curvilinear forms despite its saw-toothed spikes and triangular elements. Each block has been constructed with a fan shape of many points filling nearly half the structural square from one corner. A magical optical effect has been created by varying the background colors and strategically coordinating the rotation of the blocks. The organization appears to be groups of double four patches, arranged by color and direction, which taken together read like cross sections of machinery gears. Through the perceptual phenomena of interrupted systems and closure, the viewer wants to mentally connect the rings. The owners call this quilt "Pull and Change of the Moon." (*Photo courtesy The Kentucky Quilt Project.*)

3.82

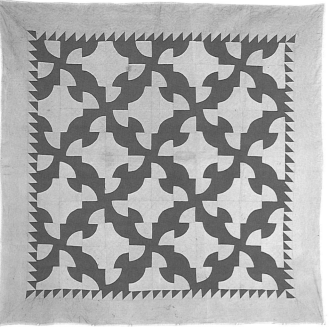

3.83

Fig. 3.82. World Without End (Drunkard's Path variation) pattern pieced quilt, c. 1885, locale unknown. Maker unknown. 80" x 75". Cotton. A variety of sophisticated graphic designs emerges in this carefully orchestrated composition. The viewer perceives a meandering diagonal interwoven grid, a four-leaf effect at some intersections, either a dark or light concave diamond-in-a-square at other areas, and a line of sinuous dark X's dancing repeatedly across the quilt surface. The quilt is a captivating puzzle that is a challenge to decipher. (*Photo courtesy Darwin D. Bearley.*)

Fig. 3.83. Drunkard's Path pattern pieced quilt, Amish, c. 1915, Wisconsin. Maker unknown. Dimensions unavailable. Cotton. This quilt's maker chose just two fabrics—one light (green), the other dark (red)—to create a constantly shifting optical puzzle. The dramatic figure/ground illusion confuses the viewer as to whether the dominant image is a dark diagonal grid or paler four-pointed forms. (*Photo courtesy Judi Boisson Antique American Quilts.*)

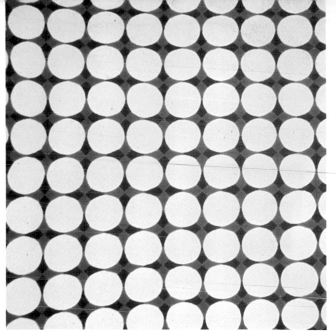

FIG. 3.84. Snowball (Four-Point variation) pattern pieced quilt, c. 1940, Sevier County, Tennessee. Made by Alice Parton. 74¼″ x 57″. Cotton. Tiny concave diamonds of four patches of dark cottons are united as stars whose points touch, forcing the eye to read great white dots as they intersect. The quilt's appearance varies, at once looking as if the maker had taken a hole punch to patterned fabric or laid white dots on top of a patterned ground. Many other names are given to this pattern, including Hummingbird, Kite, and Job's Troubles. (*Collection of Dell Reagan Compton; photo courtesy Quilts of Tennessee.*)

FIG. 3.85. Dolley Madison's Reel pattern pieced quilt, c. 1860, New York. Maker unknown. 96″ x 82″. Cotton. It is virtually impossible for the eye to assign any of the narrow, elliptical leaf forms to a particular hexagonal surround because all are shared by pattern areas. The side of one is the center of its neighbor, and on and on. At times the quilt looks more like white cloth, symmetrically slashed in circles of six lines to reveal dark areas beneath. The eye never stops searching for the beginning, that point at which to focus on the intricate network of lines to determine whether white triangles on dark cloth or dark six-pointed stars on white predominate. (*Author's collection.*)

3.84

3.85

3.86

FIG. 3.86. Double Wedding Ring pattern pieced quilt, Amish, c. 1930, Ohio. Maker unknown. Dimensions unavailable. Cotton. While most examples of the Double Wedding Ring pattern have a circular formation, here the somewhat squared dimension of the rings causes the viewer to perceive bow-knot forms, or four-leaf extensions, caught at their centers with pink and purple squares. Simultaneously, the black concave diamonds surrounded by the touching leaf forms advance as a distinct figural element vying for attention with the multicolor areas. (*Photo courtesy Judi Boisson Antique American Quilts.*)

FIG. 3.87. Double Wedding Ring pattern pieced quilt, Amish, c. 1930, Holmes County, Ohio. Maker unknown. Dimensions unavailable. Cotton. An illusion of never-ending revolution has been created with strips of intensely colored pastels, some of which are so close in value to the hot turquoise field as to dissolve or recede while the ringed fields advance. Classic versions of the Double Wedding Ring pattern, incorporating pretty printed pastels against a white field, are static in comparison with the vitality of this Amish example. (*Photo courtesy Judy Boisson Antique American Quilts.*)

FIG. 3.88. Pickle Dish (Double Wedding Ring variation) pattern pieced quilt, c. 1925, locale unknown. Maker unknown. 75" square. Cotton. The traditional ring shape has been altered here, leaving the thinnest black ellipse between most of the squared-off curves of the visually interlocking rings. The maker restrained the prints and palette, either alternating light and dark strips or choosing fabrics so close in value that they merge as solid areas. This lovely, painterly illusion reads in places like overlays of transparent shading, sheer here and built to deeper tone there. In areas where the tonal contrasts are greater, those elements advance and fan out as spidery forms. (*Photo courtesy Darwin D. Bearley.*)

3.89

FIG. 3.89. Double Wedding Ring pattern pieced quilt, Amish, c. 1940, Holmes County, Ohio. Maker unknown. Dimensions unavailable. Cotton sateen. In this intensely contrasting example, the rings actually appear to be in endless linkage, like a puzzle ring or Romanesque guilloche. They seem to loop through each other, reading both over and under, rather than simply connecting to the four-patch intersection as is characteristic of the Wedding Ring design. This visual phenomenon is caused by the closeness or distance in value of the strips adjoining the intersections. (*Photo courtesy Judi Boisson Antique American Quilts.*)

FIG. 3.90. Wheel of Mysterie pattern pieced quilt, c. 1930. Virginia. Maker unknown. 80″ x 68″. Cotton. Although the main elements of this quilt are curvy triangles set out as four-patch-type blocks, the design's effect is so decidedly curvilinear that the viewer perceives constantly overlapping circles. The structural blocks alternate medium and light tones within and are then arrayed in alternating sequence so that the overall image is of a positive / negative kinetic illusion where shadows of circles keep drawing the viewer in. (*Photo courtesy Stella Rubin.*)

FIG. 3.91. Pincushion pattern pieced quilt, c. 1920, New York. Maker unknown. 76″ x 62″. Cotton. This quilt's maker adapted a very early pieced pattern and updated its impact by coordinating (not quite perfectly) the direction of the strips in the light-colored elliptical areas so that they read as concentric diamonds spreading in succession beneath the black grid. The result is that an almost medieval tracery of attenuated four-pointed stars seems to have been cut from black cloth and placed over a background of pale strips. In addition to the multi-layered effect, the light and dark areas alternate in visual dominance. (*Author's collection.*)

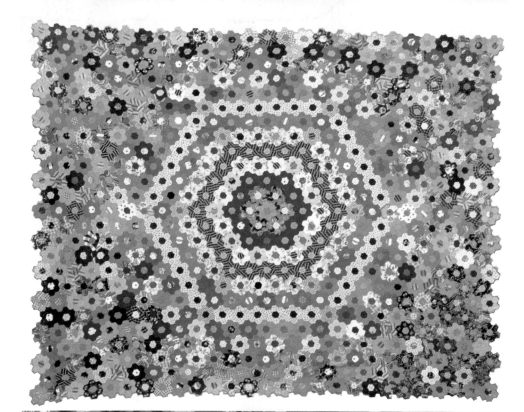

Figs. 3.92, 3.93. Honeycomb (Mosaic variation) pattern pieced quilt top and detail, c. 1860, Pennsylvania. Maker unknown. 92″ x 76″. Wool challis. To convey the illusion of large hexagons expanding concentrically, the tonalities of the central area of the quilt have been aligned and orchestrated in contrast, just as in the straight-edged examples of figures 1.12 and 3.66. At the outside edges, this tonal contrast has been abandoned in favor of the more classic format, where hexagonal "rosettes" or "cells" appear independently. The lighter groupings pop up from the densely patterned surface; the darker ones recede or even merge and sometimes disappear where the fabrics are close in tone. The detail shows the nickel-sized hexagons organized in their familiar "rosettes" of seven patches (six hexagons surrounding a central hexagon). In it, both the tonal alignment that has created the larger scale dynamic graphic effect, and the tonal diffusion that has produced random effects of light and dark upon the retina, are revealed. (*Author's collection*.)

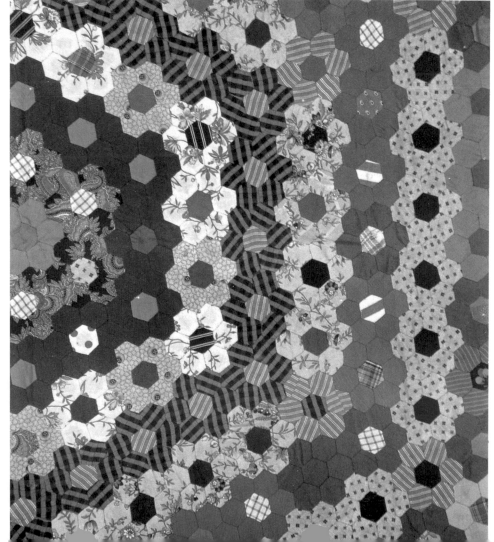

FIG. 3.94. Hexagon (Crazy Quilt variation) pattern pieced quilt, dated 1886, locale unknown. Signed "To Louise from Grandma Crory." Dimensions unavailable. Silk and velvet. Nearly kaleidoscopic hexagons in shimmering gold, beige, and rose advance and recede in relation to the surrounding black hexagonal forms. These dark elements unite as trilobed forms, pointing up or down, lying over or under, the lighter hexagonally shaped areas. As in a crazy quilt, the pattern pieces are imprecisely aligned by size and shape, yet the result reads as multiple hexagons in the viewer's perception. (*Photo courtesy Judi Boisson Antique American Quilts.*)

FIG. 3.95. Mosaic (Hexagon variation) pattern pieced quilt, c. 1890, locale unknown. Maker unknown. Dimensions unavailable. Cotton. This micro-mosaic composition looks as if it has been photographed with a depth-of-field distortion that cause pale "dots" to float up from the crowded quilt surface. The darkest and lightest shades advance from a field of thousands of hexagons because of the specific optical interaction of their contrasting tones with the retina of the eye. (*Photo courtesy Darwin D. Bearley.*)

FIGS. 3.96, 3.97. Milky Way pattern pieced quilt and detail, c. 1870, Whitlock, Tennessee. 84″ x 71″. Cotton. In this rarely seen composition, dark hexagonal sections appear simultaneously as distinct elements on a patterned background and as the background of an intricate six-pointed star made from Log Cabin strips. Executing this design to achieve a consistent result required skillful attention to the length of the strips and the placement of the fabrics. As the detail illustrates, the quilt has been cut and pieced like a Log Cabin Windmill Blades variation, with the diagonally clipped strip ends arranged around a dark "hearth." (*Collection of Brenda F. Fuller; photo courtesy Quilts of Tennessee.*)

Fig. 3.98. Star Medallion pattern pieced quilt, Amish, c. 1910, Elkhart, Indiana. Maker unknown. 77" x 73". Cotton. Similar in construction to the Tumbling Blocks pattern (figs. 3.49 and 4.2), this harmonious composition reads like an illuminated field of stars. The eye simultaneously perceives black stars advancing from a pale field, while light-colored hexagonal dots drift up from a dark surface. This continual shift in perception makes for an intriguing, rich composition. (*Photo courtesy Judi Boisson Antique American Quilts.*)

Fig. 3.99. Honeycomb (Mosaic variation) pattern pieced quilt, c. 1880, Henry County, Kentucky. Made by Sophronia Ann Bruce. 107" x 92". Cotton, wool, and silk. The configuration of this unique ten-pointed star is so complex and atypical that it seems more like an architectural rendering of a three-dimensional star that has been dissected for inspection than a quilting motif. The rosettes or concentric hexagonal "cells" traditionally arrayed in an allover pattern most familiar as Grandmother's Flower Garden take on unusual dimension here. The maker seems to have attempted a "tinker toy" construction in this grand-scale image, and in the process has conveyed a spatial illusion of breadth and shallow depth. The resulting bedcover, certainly kept as a "best" quilt rather than used on a daily basis, has true three-dimensionality, for the field is filled with elaborate stuffed work and padding. (*Photo courtesy Kentucky Quilt Project.*)

Combinations, Representational Forms, and Eccentric Designs

THE QUILTS ILLUSTRATED IN THIS SECTION include examples in which two or more distinct geometric shapes are joined in the pattern blocks—thus qualifying them as combinations. Also shown are quilts whose patterns combine two or more different pieced blocks to develop an interlocking, graphic, and illusionary composition.

The representational forms include images such as a flower, a tree, or other clearly pictorial elements. These are among the least common forms of illusion, because even though they may have been pared down to their essential geometric bases in the manner of abstract art suggestive of naturalistic elements, they will still read as pictorial images unless some form of block rotation is used. For example, the Tree of Life quilt illustrated in Chapter 4 (fig. 4.4) looks nothing like that classic pattern until the viewer can locate its primary block. By rotating the blocks so that the angled elements abut, the Tree of Life quilt's maker created a large-scale, dynamic graphic whole that completely subordinates the pictorial image to geometric illusionary forms.

The eccentric examples given here are so unusual and out of the ordinary that they defy ready categorization. The Depression-era Target quilt (fig. 3.112), for example, is a highly original composition whose inspiration appears to have come from no readily identifiable source. The compelling graphics of the much earlier Diamond in a Square variation (fig. 3.113) are alive with movement.

FIG. 3.100. Touching Stars (Crazy Quilt variation) pattern pieced quilt, dated 1896, Schoeneck, Lancaster County, Pennsylvania. Made by Lizzie Rock Edwards. 81″ x 80″. Wool. Two distinct geometric designs —a series of two- and four-patch blocks, along with a series of octagonal spoked wheels—seem to float on a field embellished with Victorian embroidery stitches. In reality the field is the quilt's primary structure, a format of touching eight-pointed stars. The random, mostly tetrahedral-shaped patches that form the arms seem to submerge in competition with the solid-color blocks. The network of intricate stitchery is so like an overlay that it obscures the piecing beneath. Wheels emerge from the triangular centers of the stars because they are outlined and embroidered. It is remarkable to find this intricacy and delicacy in wool in an era in which such piecing and needlework would usually have been reserved for silk. (*Photo courtesy M. Finkel & Daughter.*)

3.101

3.102

3.103

FIG. 3.101. Foundation Rose and Pine Tree pattern appliqué quilt, c. 1915, Ohio. Maker unknown. 70″ square. Cotton. Floral appliqué quilts with illusionary qualities are rare, particularly when striking geometric forms arise from the precise appliqué work. This example reads more like interlocking circles and four-pointed stars than the blossoms and clusters of pine trees which were the quiltmaker's intention to depict in fabric. Its nine repeat blocks were organized so that the points of the conical trees nearly touch, drawing the viewer's attention from the blossom centers to the other emergent designs. The appliqué block here is similar to figure 1.23, but it conveys different graphic impressions because of the relative areas between pattern and field. (*Photo courtesy Darwin D. Bearley.*)

FIG. 3.102. Cockscomb and Currants pattern appliqué quilt, c. 1880, Pennsylvania. Maker unknown. 78″ x 76″. Cotton. The close juxtaposition of the appliqué elements has transformed the field into a prominent design element which competes for attention with the representational motifs. The near union of the extended elements of leaves, currants, and blossom tips has created an illusion which outlines a square element of appliqué and a cruciform bordered with inwardly curving leaves. Both field and pattern advance and recede as the eye shifts focus, revealing how the abstraction of a naturalistic form generates unanticipated geometric designs. (*Author's collection.*)

FIG. 3.103. Spice Pink pattern appliqué quilt, c. 1870, Tennessee. Made by Mary Adams Heaton. 103¾″ x 85¼″. Cotton. A sprightly, delicate allover geometric surface has been fashioned through the repetition of thirty floral appliqué blocks. The slender stems which join buds to blossoms consequently outline varied geometric forms in white. The phenomenon of closure oper-

ates here as in other designs where elongated pattern elements "touch," causing imaginary linkages in ways the quilter probably never could have conceived. (*Photo courtesy Quilts of Tennessee.*)

FIG. 3.104. Spider's Web pattern pieced quilt, Mennonite (Horse and Buggy Sect), c. 1920, Ohio. Maker unknown. 82″ x 74″. Wool. Each square pattern block creates an illusion within itself, as well as larger and dif-ferent illusions when the blocks are linked. Eight elongated triangles composed of wool strips of deeply saturated solid hues comprise each block. Every other triangle bears an identical color se-quence of strips, from which the viewer perceives four-arm windmill-like geometrics that pulsate above striped octagons which appear through the illusion of closure. (*Collection of M. Finkel & Daughter.*)

3.105

3.106

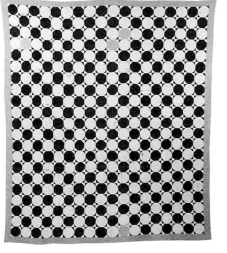

3.107

FIG. 3.105. Arabic Lattice pattern pieced quilt, dated 1931, Ohio. Maker unknown. 70″ square. Cotton. In this rarely attempted pattern, the pointed elements, like perky caps, convey a sense of rollicking motion. The figure/ground illusion switches back and forth in the viewer's perception between the identical light and dark shapes. As in its optical counterpart, the Indiana Puzzle (figs. 1.4 and 3.115), the diamond-shaped pattern pieces are here linked with tiny four-patch segments that visually entwine the figures and delightfully distort perception. (*Collection of Michael Council.*)

FIG. 3.106. Bowknot (Farmer's Puzzle variation) pattern pieced quilt, c. 1910, Fayetteville, Tennessee. Made by the Ladies' Missionary Society of the Cumberland Presbyterian Church. 78″ square. Cotton. Lines that sizzle like a cartoonist's rendition of radio waves draw simultaneous attention to the images of a four-pointed star caught at each corner by a rosette and of a fleur-de-lis centered with a rosette. The angles imply constant tension and motion in this simple yet effective composition of dark strips with white triangles and diamonds. (*Collection of Michelle Johnson Rowe; photo courtesy Quilts of Tennessee.*)

FIG. 3.107. Robbing Peter to Pay Paul pattern pieced quilt, c. 1915, Ohio. Maker unknown. 80″ x 76″. Cotton. A checkerboard-like surface of apparent dots vies with the actual composition of tiny Broken Dishes blocks and larger solid areas. These patches, when joined with the diagonal sides of the solids, create the illusion of circular rather than angular shapes through the phenomenon of closure: the mind perceives curves where none exist. In addition, the small-scale patches seem to merge and disappear as background as the dots surface in our view. (*Photo courtesy Darwin D. Bearley.*)

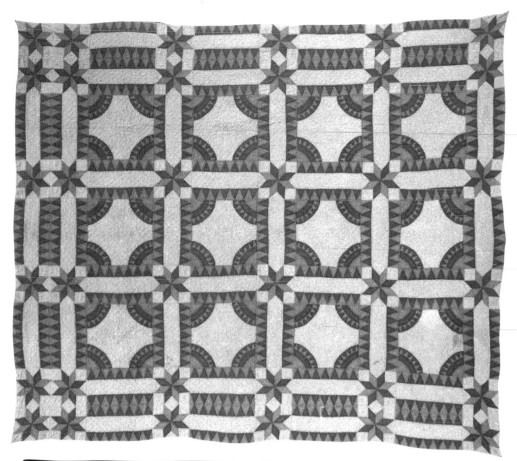

FIG. 3.108. New York Beauty pattern pieced quilt, c. 1930, Ohio. Maker unknown. 83″ x 80″. Cotton. Graphic designs operate here on several planes. A white squared grid seems to anchor shaded pieced disks beneath it; four-pointed white forms within the openings of the grid advance toward the viewer in spite of the extensiveness of the patterned areas. The eye perceives the shaded areas as "beneath" the grid and as whole, rather than as the sawtooth, fan-shaped segments which they really are. The pointed elements which permeate the quilt surface communicate a sense of movement as if they were the teeth of mechanical gears. (*Photo courtesy Darwin D. Bearley.*)

FIG. 3.109 Steeplechase pattern pieced quilt, dated 1883, Brooklyn, New York. Inscribed on back "Made by Old Ladies in the Old Ladies Home." 55″ x 41″. Cotton. In this aptly named design the eye cannot chose what to focus on. Darks and lights race on the diagonal; strongly contrasting squared circles (or are they curvilinear squares?) seem to arise from the kinetic surroundings in this two-tone composition of triangular and arrow-like forms. This intriguing confusion is known as a figure/ground illusion. (*Collection of Paula Laverty.*)

Fig. 3.110. Rabbit's Paw (Goose in the Pond variation) pattern pieced quilt, Amish, dated Jan. 22, 1930, Middlebury, Indiana. Made by Mrs. Amanda Yoder. Initialed "J.D.F." 55" x 48". Cotton. One dozen red and blue pieced blocks have been joined with intersecting blocks of red eight-pointed stars to convey a larger interconnected pattern. The eye shifts between the pattern block and its link. Because of the similarity in color between paw and star, fiery hot X-shaped "brands" appear to hold the paw blocks in place. Their radiant glow is so intense as to read like the absence of color, making the blue areas advance as if transparent above the red squares. (*Photo courtesy Esprit Quilt Collection.*)

Fig. 3.111. Tulip Bud pattern appliqué quilt, c. 1915, Ohio. Maker unknown. 80" x 75". Cotton. Blocks of four yellow tulip buds set with their bases pointed inward toward a center square are repeated thirty times without separation, becoming an abstract geometric design. The tulips almost disappear as the eye perceives a cross set within four-pointed concave stars set within a circular framework. The cross and star designs share elliptical sides with the neighboring blocks, an effect similar to figure 1.21 (Robbing Peter to Pay Paul). The structural block is identifiable if the surface is read from a corner within the pale inner border, showing how each block lends a bud to the overall curvilinear effect. (*Photo courtesy Darwin D. Bearley.*)

FIG. 3.112. Target (Quill variation) pattern pieced quilt, c. 1930, Kentucky. Made by Hattie McWilliams. 86″ x 76″. Rayon and cotton. This Afro-American bedcover is the only quilt in this book whose entire surface is actually three-dimensional. Its fundamental illusion, however, comes from the manipulation of color rather than layering. Thousands of one inch "prairie points" or "porcupine quills" (the folded triangles of fabric which are the patches) combine in a scheme of great drama and energy. The central image of a vortex or comet draws the eye in, while the rays of light and dark extending from that oval area simultaneously direct the eye beyond the quilt's borders. The tactile surface results from sewing the points only at their bases, leaving the tips free to overlap the previous rows. The points face inward and are aligned by color to enhance the sense of a tumultuous vortex. (*Author's collection.*)

FIG. 3.113. Unnamed pattern (Diamond in a Square variation) pieced quilt top, c. 1875, Massachusetts. Maker unknown. 90½″ square. Cotton and chintz. This stunning graphic knockout is unique in its organization of small squares, strips, and triangles. Activity is suggested on many planes—in the foreground and background, at the center, and bursting out to the sides. An array of points, diagonals, and interrupted borders leads the eye deep into and out of the flat surface. The quilt's explosive imagery is reminiscent of Op Art, but its execution predates that art movement by nearly a century. A refined palette of solid, warm earth tones and mauves has here become a work of art daring for its era. (*Collection Museum of American Folk Art; gift of Cyril I. Nelson.*)

3.114

FIG. 3.114. Lily pattern pieced quilt, c. 1865, Trigg County, Kentucky. Made by a member of either the Burgess or Stewart family. 88″ x 72″. Cotton. The stylization of the flower heads, and their arrangement in a group of three whose stems touch, generate a design in which realistic representation takes a back seat to the illusion of a composition of triangles and six-pointed stars. Even though the quilt is pieced of twenty-eight full- and eight half-lily blocks, triangles seem to be outlined by the sashing and are prominent in the field surrounding the lily clusters. (*Photo courtesy The Kentucky Quilt Project.*)

3.115

FIG. 3.115. Indiana Puzzle pattern pieced quilt, c. 1920, Ohio. Maker unknown. 78″ x 74″. Cotton. Intertwined forms mirror each other in this positive/negative figure/ground illusion. The reversible imagery is related to figure 1.4, but here the figures have been elongated and exaggerated in their curvilinear interconnectedness by the three different geometric patches that corner the squares. This rolling graphic resembles the textile designs by Kolomon Moser for the Wiener Werkstätte, which were becoming known at about the time this quilt was made. (*Author's collection.*)

FIG. 3.116. Fly Foot pattern pieced quilt top, Amish, c. 1880, Belleville, Pennsylvania. Maker unknown. 72″ x 69″. Wool. Square blocks in two colors (red and black), bisected either vertically or diagonally, are alternated to create a design of positive/negative illusion. From one perspective, large, skewed, dark X's shift in and out of view; from the other, a network of shaded alternating brickwork dominates. (*Author's collection.*)

FIG. 3.117. Double Hearts pattern appliqué quilt, c. 1935, Missouri. Maker unknown. 92″ x 90″. Cotton. This unique appliqué uses geometrics rather than florals to achieve an optical illusion that is totally reversible in impact. A dark clover-like element, composed of four hearts whose bases point in toward each other, vies for attention with a starry eight-pointed white element. United, the darks form a horizontal/vertical grid, while the attenuated diagonal points of the white elements unite to form an attention-getting diagonal grid. The eye constantly shifts between the two strong designs. (*Collection of The Fosters.*)

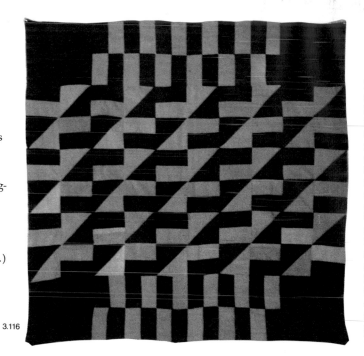

3.116

3.117

3.118

FIGS. 3.118, 3.119. Chimney Sweep pattern pieced quilt and detail, c. 1940, Vonore, Tennessee. Made by Lois Hall. 87" x 67". Cotton. X marks the spot, or, more precisely, the block from which this multilayered kaleidoscopic design emerges. The crisscross form employs one cotton print per block, united by a white center diamond. By adding two black diamonds within the print's right angles, the quiltmaker perhaps unwittingly created a bold, black octagonal grid beneath the light print latticework grid. Where the print and black are closest in color, splashy dark clusters seem to pop out from a pastel field. Diagonals, points, and tonal contrast convey a strong sense of movement by perceptually linking up grids. (*Collection of Lois Hall; photo courtesy Quilts of Tennessee.*)

3.119

3.120

FIG. 3.120. Hayes' Corner pattern pieced quilt, Amish, c. 1925, Mifflin County, Pennsylvania. Maker unknown. 80" x 75". Cotton. Concentric diamonds and an overlying yet seemingly transparent grid emerge from this simple ninepatch variation of squares and triangles. The whole composition seems the reverse of what we would expect to see. A boldly contrasting diagonal image should dominate the surface, as in the Log Cabin Barn Raising variation, rather than operating as if beneath a lighter visual element. This spatial illusion extends even to the quilt's borders, where we imagine that the outermost diamonds become complete. (*Photo courtesy Darwin D. Bearley.*)

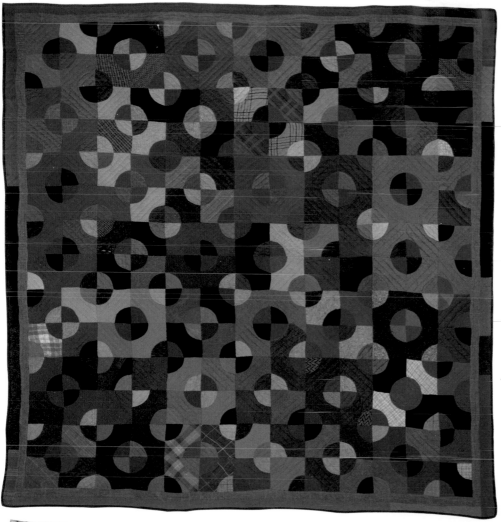

FIG. 3.121. Mill Wheel (Steeplechase variation) pattern pieced quilt, Mennonite, c. 1890, Ohio. Maker unknown. 74" square. Wool. Depending upon the juxtaposition of colors alone, whole and quartered dots appear to float above solid or fragmented blocks in this intriguing composition. In reality, the construction is based on small squares from which quarter circles have been cut on opposing corners. The vacant quarter circles are then pieced in with different colors. When four blocks are joined with these quarter circles abutting, circles of contrasting or complementary colors result. This masterpiece, made from suiting scraps, is similar to the broken overlapping circles present in twentieth-century works by Frank Stella and Sonia Delaunay. (*Author's collection.*)

FIG. 3.122. New York Beauty pattern pieced quilt, c. 1930, West Virginia. Maker unknown. 80" x 75". Cotton. This exuberant version of an always bold graphic design features elements that appear to spin gaily throughout a densely patterned surface. The grid-over-circles illusion in typical variations of the New York Beauty pattern is here almost subordinated by star bursts that sometimes appear through the tonal proximity of patches to the white field. Adding a folksy appeal to an often formal composition, these accidental stars go off in every direction, while the fan shapes merge like a patterned ground. (*Photo courtesy Darwin D. Bearley.*)

4.

HOW TO CREATE QUILTS OF ILLUSION

t is probably safe to say that no quiltmaker ever lacks challenges: most probably have more ideas waiting to be translated into cloth than there is ever time—or fabric enough—to complete. However, on the theory that readers of *Quilts of Illusion* may wish to attempt some of their own illusionary designs, this chapter features a quartet of traditional patterns—Eccentric Star, Tumbling Blocks, Three-Dimensional Fans (a Tumbling Blocks variation), and Tree of Life—that are anything *but* traditional in execution.

Full-size templates, piecing diagrams, and step-by-step instructions accompany large full-color photographs of each original quilt. Fabric requirements are given for two of the quilts (Eccentric Star and Tree of Life); the other two, because of the number of different fabrics used in their execution, are classified as scrap quilts, making estimates of yardage both difficult and unnecessary. (Either Tumbling Blocks quilt would provide an ideal opportunity for a quilter to utilize the fabric leftovers hoarded for just the right occasion.)

Whether you attempt to reproduce one of these superb bedcovers exactly or use it as a point of departure to create your own contemporary masterpiece is up to you. For instance, it might be interesting to experiment with a block quilt other than the Tree of Life illustrated in figure 4.4. A Log Cabin, a Drunkard's Path, or one of the other block quilts illustrated in Chapter 3 might provide inspiration. If you do choose to attempt your own unique illusion, you might want to begin with a pen and a paper, rather than a needle and thread. By drawing one representative block, photocopying it numerous times, and laying out the copies in various arrangements, you'll arrive at an overall pattern that creates the illusion you're trying to achieve. If you have the time and patience, using colored paper to form multiple blocks will give you an even better idea of what the end results will be. Your choice of fabric colors will be all-important: as is evident from many of the quilts illustrated in this book, color plays a major role in creating optical illusions.

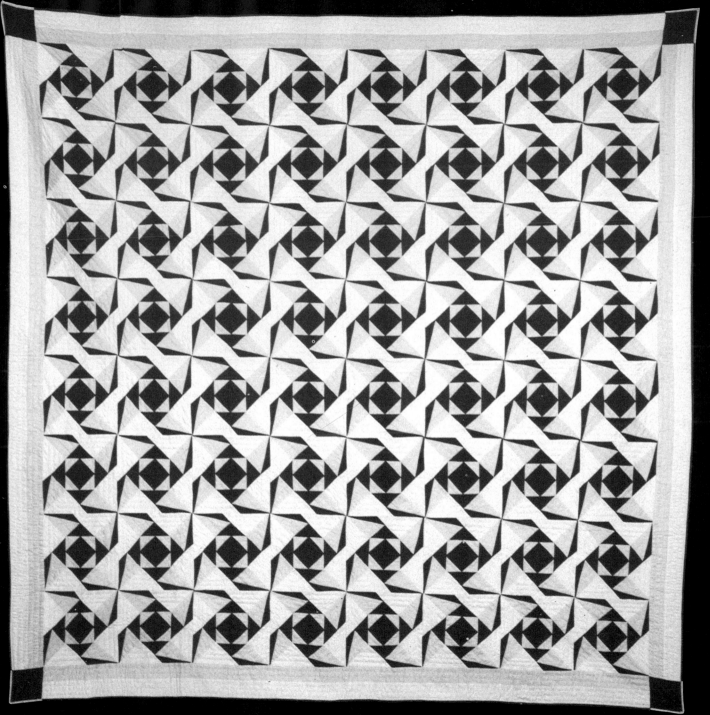

Eccentric Star

BECAUSE THE MAKER of this particular Eccentric Star quilt restricted her palette to three colors, two of which—the yellow and the off-white—give little contrast, the optical illusions that result from the pattern are more subtle than they would have been had more vibrantly colored fabrics been chosen. Sixty-four identical blocks, each 8½″ square, comprise the basic quilt. Each block is composed of six basic pattern pieces—five triangles and a square. While the individual blocks may look complicated to piece, each separate template uses only one color of fabric. Therefore the cutting of the shapes is basically quite a simple procedure, so long as normal care is taken to insure that each piece is accurately measured and cut (add ¼″ seam allowance for each template).

Once you have prepared sufficient pieces for the number of blocks you've decided upon for the quilt, begin the piecing of each block from the center, stitching the four (yellow) triangles to the central red square (thus making a larger square). Then piece the four triangles that make up each side of the outer block, stitching them in turn to the inner square. Once all of the blocks are sewn, it's a simple matter to pin and stitch them together in straight rows, affixing each row to the one above until the main design is completed.

This particular quilt is bordered with strips of the yellow and off-white fabric interrupted at each corner with a red square (twice the width of the strips), the whole rimmed with a contrasting narrow border of red (yellow where the narrow border abuts the outer red squares). You might choose a border of another width, or one pieced of a single color, for a different look.

Fabric requirements (without border or backing): You'll need 2¾ yards of the red fabric, 2¼ yards of the yellow, and 1½ yards of the off-white to complete a quilt of equal size (based on using fabrics that are 45″ wide).

FIG. 4.1. Eccentric Star pattern pieced quilt, c. 1930, Ohio. Maker unknown. 78″ square. Cotton. Although generally considered a star pattern, this complex design appears to combine the Diamond-in-a-Square and Pinwheel patterns. Where the two patterns meet, wispy white Fly Foot shapes emerge to veil the entire composition. Each element seems to twist and extend into the neighboring segment. Even the white "negative" space around the pieced red and yellow areas becomes a distinct geometric shape. (*Author's collection.*)

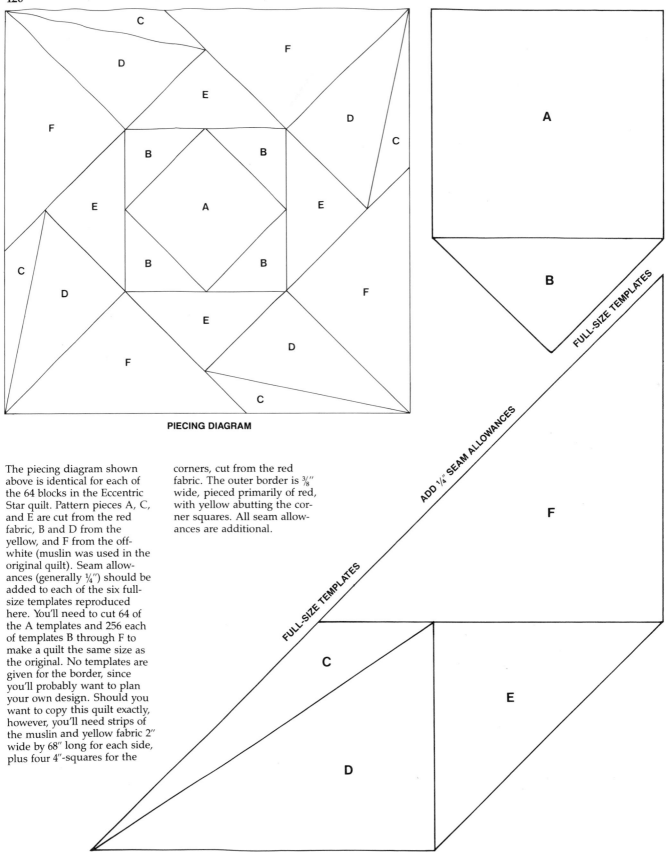

PIECING DIAGRAM

ADD ¼" SEAM ALLOWANCES

FULL-SIZE TEMPLATES

FULL-SIZE TEMPLATES

The piecing diagram shown above is identical for each of the 64 blocks in the Eccentric Star quilt. Pattern pieces A, C, and E are cut from the red fabric, B and D from the yellow, and F from the off-white (muslin was used in the original quilt). Seam allowances (generally ¼") should be added to each of the six full-size templates reproduced here. You'll need to cut 64 of the A templates and 256 each of templates B through F to make a quilt the same size as the original. No templates are given for the border, since you'll probably want to plan your own design. Should you want to copy this quilt exactly, however, you'll need strips of the muslin and yellow fabric 2" wide by 68" long for each side, plus four 4"-squares for the corners, cut from the red fabric. The outer border is ⅜" wide, pieced primarily of red, with yellow abutting the corner squares. All seam allowances are additional.

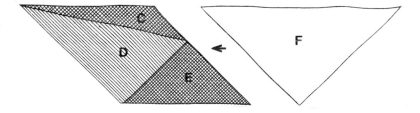

Begin each block by piecing the four B triangles to the central A square. When this is completed, you'll have formed another larger square in which the center has been rotated to become a diamond.

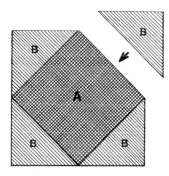

The trapezoids formed of the C, D, E, and F templates are next sewn, in turn, to the central diamond-in-a-square formed of the A and B pieces.

Begin at the top and move in a clockwise direction, using great care in the joining of the final trapezoid. (See piecing diagram, below.)

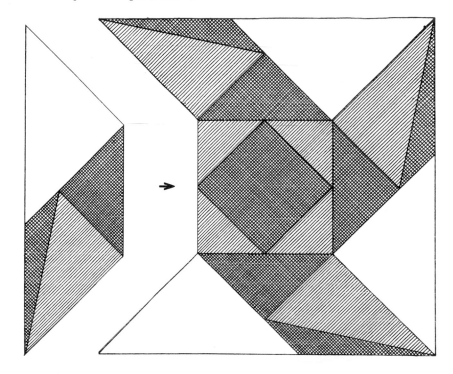

Piece the outer triangles of the block: C to D, then E to D (as shown below) and, finally, F to the diagonal formed by the C, D, and E triangles (see piecing diagram, upper right). Once you have repeated this step four times, you'll have four identical trapezoids.

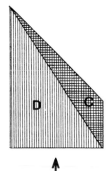

Once you have completed the sewing of all blocks necessary to complete the quilt, carefully pin one block to the next, and sew each in turn until you have a row of eight completed (either horizontally or vertically, as you prefer). Once each row is completed, it will be a relatively easy matter to pin and sew each row to the next until all 64 blocks are joined. The border, batting, and backing are left to your discretion. If you prefer a larger quilt than this, you can add additional blocks to both the horizontal and vertical rows until a desired size is achieved.

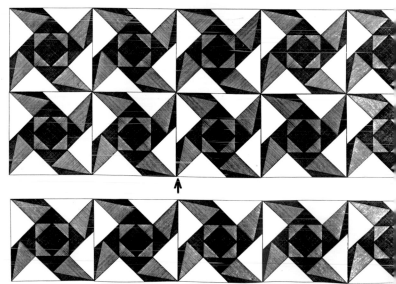

Tumbling Blocks (Seven Sisters Variation)

THIS DAZZLING COMPOSITION, pieced of a wide variety of silk and velvet prints and solids, may at first appear to be a scrap quilt, its basic tumbling blocks or cubes arranged with no attention to the optical illusions that result when they are stitched together. And in terms of the sheer numbers of fabrics employed, it could be classified as such. More careful study of the placement of the diamonds that form each cube, however, shows that the quilter did have a scheme in mind. Most of the cubes were planned in groups of three (in a rough upside-down Y shape), with careful attention given to the arrangement of equal numbers of light, medium, and dark fabric pieces. The majority of the three-block groups were sewn with identical dark fabrics always placed on the outer edges of the cubes and light and medium fabrics alternated to form a six-pointed star when the three blocks were joined. The result, depending upon the brightness of the fabrics used for each trio of blocks, is that in some areas the six-pointed stars are prominent, while in others the lightest of the three fabrics used for the trio forms a dominant three-pointed form.

To emulate the intricate illusions present in the original quilt, the modern needleworker will probably want to cut and piece most of the block trios before beginning to sew the elements together. Those basic elements can then be arranged in various configurations until the desired effect is achieved.

While the original quilt has no border (the edges appear to have been clipped, folded under, and sewn to the backing), a solid-color frame might be effective in containing the exuberance of this blinding composition. Anything other than a solid color, however, would serve only to add confusion to the design.

FIG. 4.2 Tumbling Blocks (Seven Sisters variation) pattern pieced quilt, c. 1880, Ohio. Maker unknown. 68″ x 54″. Silk and velvet. Because of the quilter's attention to the juxtaposition of light, medium, and dark fabrics in the piecing of each cube, together with the light-reflecting properties of the luxurious silks and velvets she used, a variety of geometric forms appears. Among the shapes visible in this vibrant quilt (in addition to the blocks one would normally expect to see) are light and dark hexagons, six-pointed stars, and pale three-pronged elements. It is interesting to compare this mysterious composition with some of the more straightforward Tumbling Blocks quilts illustrated in Chapter 3. (*Author's collection.*)

FULL-SIZE TEMPLATES

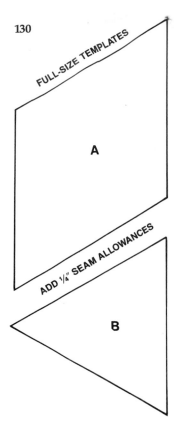

ADD ¼" SEAM ALLOWANCES

A

B

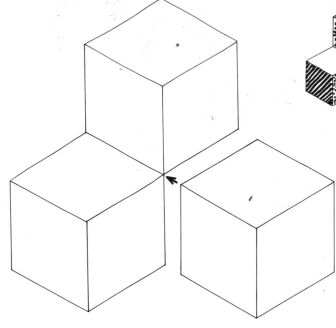

Working in groups of three, join cubes in an inverted Y shape, with the dark fabrics on the outside and the medium and light ones alternated as shown in the piecing diagram below. You'll want to make a majority of the trios in this fashion, using identical light, medium, and dark fabrics for each cube in the threesome, but reserve some odd fabrics for "eccentric" arrangements as shown at the upper right.

Once you've completed enough of the inverted Y's to make a quilt of the size you've chosen (this quilt contains 9 of the trios in width and 11 in length, for a total of 99), try different arrangements until you've arrived at a configuration that gives you the illusions you want. Then number each trio of cubes on the back, from top to bottom. Begin piecing a center vertical strip, as shown.

Three identical diamonds (template A) form each full cube in this Seven Sisters variation. The triangle (B) is used to fill in the sides once the rest of the quilt has been pieced.

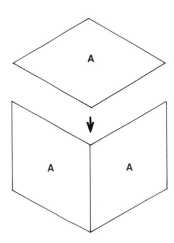

A

A   **A**

Piece each cube by joining three of the A diamonds as shown, using a different fabric for each diamond. Each cube should contain a light, medium, and dark fabric.

Once the central strip is completed, add a row to each side, one trio of cubes at a time, until the bulk of the quilt is completed. (Joining the pieces in this fashion avoids the sewing of difficult right angles.) To finish the top and bottom of the quilt, add double and single cubes, respectively.

To complete the sides, you'll need to make a certain number of wedge-shaped pieces, using one each of the A and B templates. Cut them as mirror images (see the piecing diagram below) and fit in where needed. When you attach the quilt top to the backing, fold over the serrated edges of the top and bottom and pin, then stitch. (You might wish to add a solid border, although this particular quilt does not have one.)

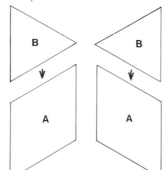

Three-Dimensional Fans

AN INGENIOUS VARIATION of a basic Tumbling Blocks pattern, as is the Seven Sisters quilt shown in figure 4.2, this Three-Dimensional Fans quilt has been intricately pieced of rich silks and velvets. The top of each block—a square, rather than a diamond as in the previous quilt—has been divided into nine pieces to simulate a lady's fan. The profusion of fabrics used in the piecing qualifies this as a scrap quilt. Yet the quilter has arranged the variety of fabrics in a somewhat regimented way. Black velvet forms the base of each fan. The odd-shaped strips connected to the bases are pieced of just two fabrics—one light and one dark—carefully alternated to achieve contrast. The bases of the blocks are always composed of fabrics of contrasting shades. While there is no fixed pattern to the placement of the lighter or darker fabrics, the majority of the darker ones seem to be positioned on the right.

The preliminary cutting and piecing of each block is much more complicated than that of the Seven Sisters block because of the eight wedges that form the top of each fan and the curved piece that forms the base. However, once each block is completed (there are a total of 196 blocks in this composition—14 down and 14 across), they are joined in much the same way as the block trios of the Seven Sisters pattern. A vertical row is sewn together, and individual blocks are attached to each side of it, averting the necessity of piecing right angles.

The border of this unusual quilt is composed of a complex design of velvet triangles and elongated diamonds. The shape of the pieces bears little relation to the quilt's basic design and, in fact, it is obvious that the pieces rounding the corners had to be altered to fit—probably as the top was being completed. Because of the difficulty inherent in trying to size these pieces properly before the quilt top is pieced, no templates are included for the border. It would be far simpler to estimate the number of diamonds and triangles needed once the basic design is completed. The pale green satin backing of this particular quilt creates an outer frame, as the border is sewn to it. A less confusing border might be a better choice.

The finished bedcover is not quilted, but tied with the black silk bows that accent each fan.

FIG. 4.3. Three-Dimensional Fans pattern pieced quilt, c. 1880, Maryland. Maker unknown. 80" x 70". Silk and velvet. The three-dimensional illusion of this Victorian fantasy has been accentuated by transforming the uppermost side of each cube into a miniature fan. Each fan has a base of black velvet tied with a black silk bow; the curve of each base has been embroidered with gold thread. By varying one or two elements of a familiar design, an imaginative quilter can become a pop artist, repeating images dozens of times across a quilt canvas. (*Collection of Marcia Berman and Paul Berberian.*)

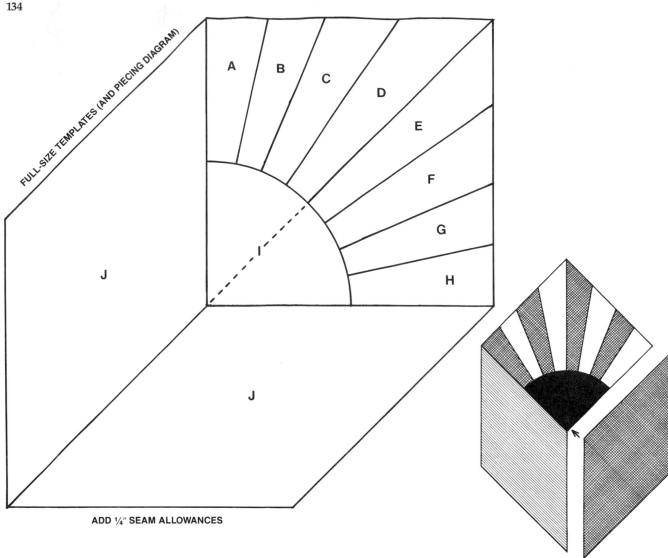

FULL-SIZE TEMPLATES (AND PIECING DIAGRAM)

A B C D E F G H

I

J

J

ADD ¼" SEAM ALLOWANCES

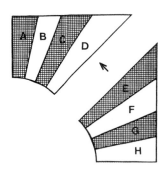

To assemble each full cube, begin by pinning and sewing pieces A through D in sequence, then attach pieces E through H, and join the two sections together as shown below. Then carefully pin and sew the base of the fan (I) to the top. The cube is completed by sewing each J piece to the fan top (see piecing diagram, upper right).

Assuming that you intend to make a quilt of the same size as the Three-Dimensional Fans example illustrated in figure 4.3, you'll need enough scraps of fabric to complete 196 full cubes. In addition, you'll want to make 15 additional fan tops (templates A to H of the piecing diagram) to be fitted into the bottom of the quilt, and 14 half-cubes split vertically (see dotted line in the diagram). Half of these demi-cubes should be made of templates A to D and J; half of E to H and J. The former will be fitted in to the right side of the quilt; the latter, to the left.

Once all cubes are completed, join a vertical row as shown (opposite page, left). The last piece to be added should be the fan top at the bottom. Add to that first (center) row by filling in the indentations to the left and right in a zigzag pattern.

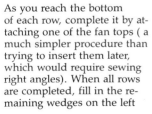

As you reach the bottom of each row, complete it by attaching one of the fan tops (a much simpler procedure than trying to insert them later, which would require sewing right angles). When all rows are completed, fill in the remaining wedges on the left and right sides of the quilt top with half cubes (you'll want 7 for each side). Fold the tops and bottoms, pin, and stitch to the backing in the usual manner.

If you wish to emulate the embroidery used to set off each fan's base, it would be simpler to do so before piecing the quilt. Because of the complicated pattern and the many colors and prints used in the original quilt, the maker chose not to quilt the finished top, but rather tied it with black silk bows that set off the base of each fan.

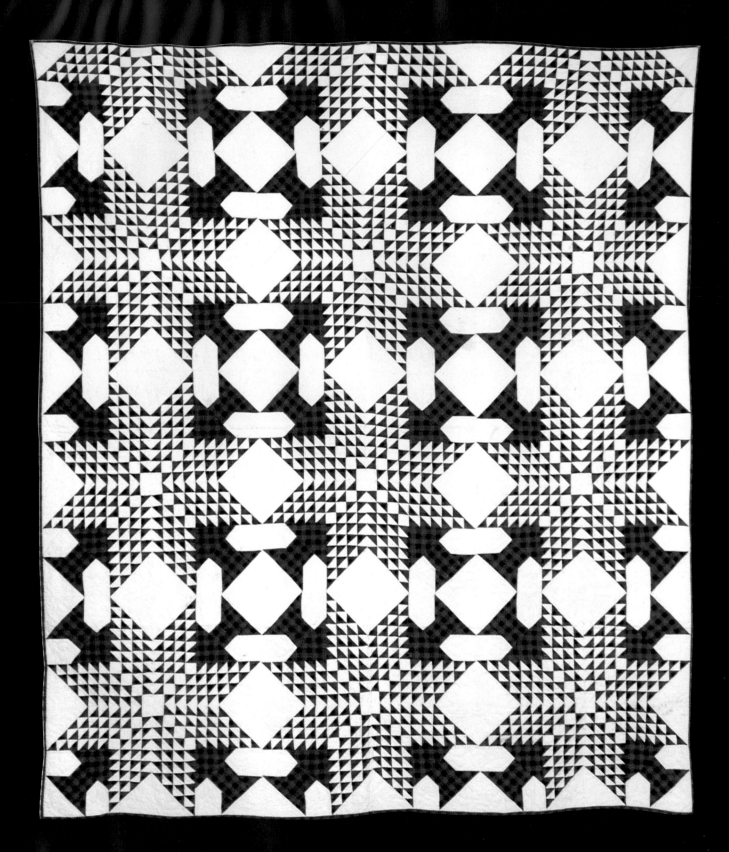

Tree
of Life

THE TREE OF LIFE PATTERN is a familiar representative design that appears often in antique quilts. It suggests pioneer settlement, the importance of the home, and protection. The Tree of Life, or pine tree, is an historic American symbol, seen in flags, coverlets, and political ephemera. As interpreted in this particular quilt, however, it becomes a strong, abstract geometric statement.

Because of the innovative placement of each tree within its block, this quilt appears to be extremely complicated to piece. And because each block is composed of roughly a hundred separate elements, it certainly is not a pattern that a beginner will want to attempt. But once each identical block is dissected and the steps used in the piecing become clear, the task is not as dizzying as it might seem at first glance. Since the quilt utilizes only two fabrics, the job of cutting and piecing is made that much simpler.

Of the 101 pieces in each block, 88 are identical right-angle triangles, 48 cut from the colored (red plaid) fabric, and 40, from muslin. As a first step, 80 of these triangles are joined to make two-toned squares, then the squares attached in rows of increasing length (each row adds one full square) to form the treetops. The balance of the block (the red trunk of the tree and the white background) is composed of larger geometric pieces. If the quilter breaks the basic piecing of each block into three manageable parts, as the piecing diagrams indicate, she should have little trouble in completing each one.

Each horizontal row of six blocks is then sewn in identical fashion, beginning at the left with a block whose treetop is slanted to the upper right, then adding one with the tree turned to the upper left, then right, and so forth until six blocks are joined. Each of the seven horizontal rows is sewn in this manner, then every other row is inverted so that the trees are upside down.

The simple border of this Tree of Life quilt is a ⅜" binding of the red plain fabric which helps to contain the labyrinthine pattern. Not so simple is the quilting design—a complex combination of diamonds and leaves.

Fabric requirements (without border or backing): You'll need 2⅓ yards of the red fabric, and 3 yards of the muslin (predicated on using 45"-wide fabric in both cases).

FIG. 4.4. Tree of Life pattern pieced quilt, c. 1890, probably Pennsylvania. Maker unknown. 80" x 68". Cotton. In the usual Tree of Life pattern, the quilter would align the trees in straight rows within their blocks, giving them the appearance they would have in the natural environment. In this rare example, each tree has been placed on the diagonal within its block, and the blocks positioned in groups of four so that they "touch" at the treetops, creating startling graphic designs. The result of this artistic innovation is a group of geometric motifs that mask the representational aspect of the quilt. The trickery is heightened by the needleworker's choice of a red-and-black buffalo plaid as one of the two fabrics used for the design. (*Author's collection.*)

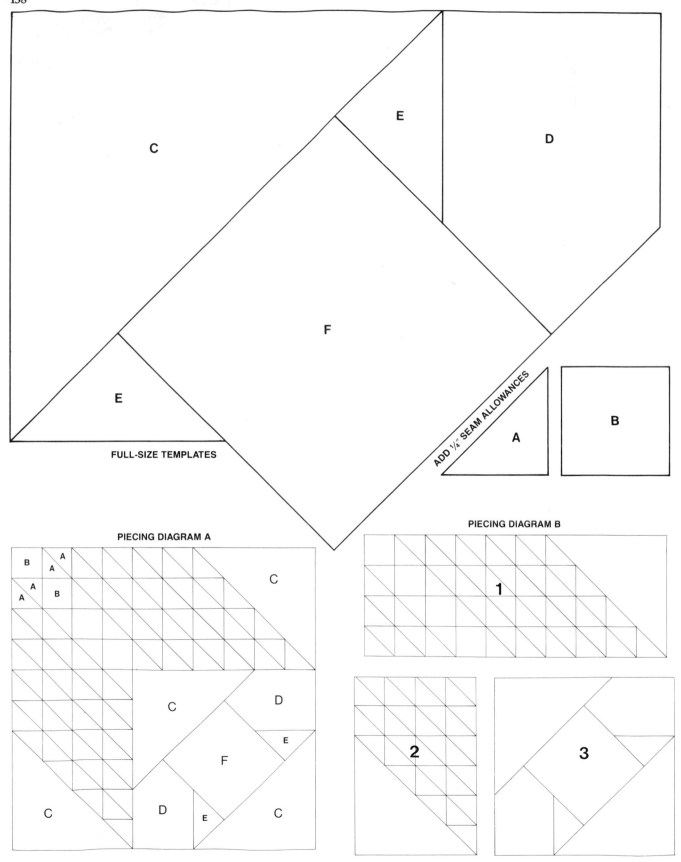

138

FULL-SIZE TEMPLATES

C

E

D

E

F

ADD ¼" SEAM ALLOWANCES

A

B

PIECING DIAGRAM A

B A A
B A
A B
C

C D
E
F
C D E C

PIECING DIAGRAM B

1

2

3

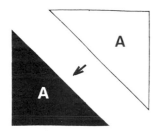

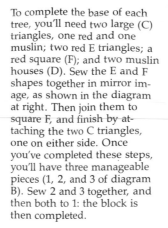

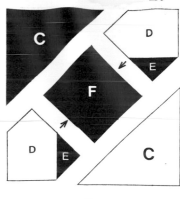

Using template A, cut 88 triangles for each block—48 of the red fabric and 40 of the muslin. Stitch 40 squares using one triangle of each fabric.

To complete the base of each tree, you'll need two large (C) triangles, one red and one muslin; two red E triangles; a red square (F); and two muslin houses (D). Sew the E and F shapes together in mirror image, as shown in the diagram at right. Then join them to square F, and finish by attaching the two C triangles, one on either side. Once you've completed these steps, you'll have three manageable pieces (1, 2, and 3 of diagram B). Sew 2 and 3 together, and then both to 1: the block is then completed.

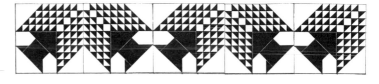

Then join them in rows (see piecing diagram B, steps 1 and 2), adding a square to each row, and ending each with a red triangle alone. Note that four white squares (template B) are needed for the rows in piecing diagram B, step 1.

Once all 42 blocks are finished, attach them in horizontal rows of six blocks each, alternating the diagonal trees from left to right, as shown above. (For reasons of space, only five of the blocks appear here.) When you've pieced seven rows of blocks, invert every other row so that the tips of the trees' bases or the tops will "touch." Sew the rows together, and complete the quilt with a border and quilting stitch of your choice.

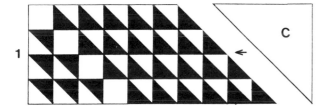

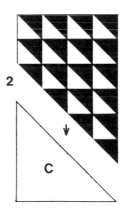

Once each group of four rows is completed and sewn together in the proper order, add a muslin triangle (C) to each group of four, creating two rectangles. You have now completed the treetop.

ACKNOWLEDGMENTS

I WOULD LIKE especailly to thank the many friends who offered unflagging encouragement and sincere interest in the preparation of this book: Marcia Berman and Paul Berbarian for their unbridled enthusiasm; Susan Frame, Susan Freeman, and Susan Gray for their nurturing personal and professional wisdom; Howard Gordon for his scholarly zeal and perfect discoveries; Deborah Harding for her imaginative leads and impressive follow-up; Lynn Lorwin for her good-humored perspective; Rita Rosencranz for her literary secrets; Jane Rosamilia, Rita and Jack Sacks, and Avis Skinner for their warm support and insights; and the twins, the Shandells, and especially the Fishers for cheerleading. And thanks to Larry Grow, Martin Greif, Frank Mahood, and especially Vicki Brooks of Main Street, who shared several lifetimes' knowledge about publishing, and to Lynda Duke for showing us how to re-create optical illusions.

Thanks also to those colleagues and friends who were so ready to share ideas and quilts to make this a rich study: Darwin D. Bearley, Judi Boisson, Susan Parrish, Jolise Kelter and Michael Malce, Michael Council, Sandra Mitchell, Judith and James Milne, Stella Rubin, Barbara Mintz and Rusty Ettinger, Shelley Zegart, Julie Silber, Elizabeth Enfield, Frank Ames, Bets Ramsey, Barbara Janos, Amy Finkel, Morgan Anderson, Tom Foster, Blanche Greenstein and Thomas Woodard, Harris Diamant and Norman Brosterman, and Robert Bishop.

Quilts or photographs have been provided by the following individuals and organizations:

Frank Ames, New York; Morgan Anderson, Frederick, Md.; Darwin D. Bearley, Akron, Ohio; Judi Boisson Antique American Quilts, New York, Westport, Conn., and Southampton, N.Y.; Buckboard Antiques, Oklahoma City; Michael Council, Columbus, Ohio; The Esprit Collection of Esprit de Corp., San Francisco and owner/collector Doug Tompkins, curator Julie Silber, and photographers Sharon Risedorph and Lynn Kellner; M. Finkel & Daughter, Philadelphia; The Fosters, Pittsfield, Ill.; Guernsey's, New York; Barbara S. Janos and Barbara Ross, New York; Kelter-Malce, New York; The Kentucky Museum, Western Kentucky University, Bowling Green and curator Christian Carron; The Kentucky Quilt Project, Inc., Louisville and director Shelley Zegart and coordinator Dorothy West; Paula Laverty, Brooklyn, N.Y.; The Museum of American Folk Art, New York and director Robert Bishop, curator Elizabeth Warren, and photography coordinator Karla Friedlich; Judith and James Milne, New York; Owensboro Area Museum, Owensboro, Ky.; Susan Parrish, New York; The Quilt Digest Press, San Francisco; Quilts of Tennessee, Chattanooga and director Bets Ramsey; Stella Rubin, Potomac, Md.; Tewksbury Antiques, Oldwick, N.J.; Vis-a-Vis, Nantucket, Mass.; and Eva and David Wheatcroft, Lewisburg, Pa.

BIBLIOGRAPHY

ALBERS, JOSEF. *Interaction of Color.* New Haven: Yale University Press, 1963.

ALLEN, JEANNE. *Designer's Guide to Color 3.* San Francisco: Chronicle Books, 1986.

ARNHEIM, RUDOLF. *Art and Visual Perception.* 2nd ed. Berkeley: University of California Press, 1974.

BISHOP, ROBERT AND ELIZABETH SAFANDA. *A Gallery of Amish Quilts.* New York: E. P. Dutton, 1976.

BISHOP, ROBERT, WILLIAM SECORD, AND JUDITH REITER WEISSMAN. *Quilts, Coverlets, Rugs & Samplers.* New York: Alfred A. Knopf, 1982.

BRESENHAN, KAROLINE PATTERSON AND NANCY O'BRYANT PUENTES. *Lone Stars, A Legacy of Texas Quilts, 1836-1936.* Austin: University of Texas Press, 1986.

CARRAHER, RONALD G. *Optical Illusions and the Visual Arts.* New York: Van Nostrand Reinhold, 1966.

COLBY, AVERIL. *Patchwork.* New York: Charles Scribner's Sons, 1958.

DEWHURST, C. KURT, BETTY MACDOWELL, AND MARSHA MACDOWELL. *Artists in Aprons.* New York: E. P. Dutton in association with The Museum of American Folk Art, 1979.

DUKE, DENNIS AND DEBORAH HARDING. *America's Glorious Quilts.* New York: Hugh Lauter Levin Associates, 1987.

DURANT, STUART. *Ornament.* New York: Overlook Press, 1986.

EARLE, ALICE MORSE. *Home Life in Colonial Days.* 1898. Reprint. Middle Village, N.Y.: Jonathan David Publishers, 1975.

ERNST, BRUNO. *The Magic Mirror of M. C. Escher.* New York: Ballantine Books, 1976.

FAIRFIELD, HELEN. *Patchwork from Mosaics.* New York: Arco Publishing, 1985.

FALES, DEAN A., JR. *American Painted Furniture.* 1972. Reprint. New York: Bonanza Books, 1986.

FINLEY, JOHN AND JONATHAN HOLSTEIN. *Kentucky Quilts 1800-1900.* Washington, D.C.: Dicmar Publishing, 1982.

FINLEY, RUTH E. *Old Patchwork Quilts and the Women Who Made Them.* Reprint. Newton Centre, Mass.: Charles T. Branford Company, 1983.

FOX, SANDI. *19th Century American Patchwork Quilt.* Tokyo: The Seibu Museum of Art, 1983.

HADERS, PHYLLIS. *The Main Street Pocket Guide to Quilts.* Pittstown, N.J.: The Main Street Press, 1983.

_____. *Sunshine & Shadow: The Amish and their Quilts.* Rev. ed. Pittstown, N.J.: The Main Street Press, 1984.

HALL, CARRIE A. AND ROSE G. KRETSINGER. *The Romance of the Patchwork Quilt in America.* New York: Bonanza Books, 1935.

HINSON, DOLORES A. *Quilting Manual.* New York: Dover Publications, 1980.

HOCHBERG, JULIAN E. *Perception.* 2nd ed. Englewood Cliffs, N.J.: Prentice-Hall, 1978.

HOLSTEIN, JONATHAN. *The Pieced Quilt: An American Design Tradition.* Greenwich, Conn.: New York Graphic Society, 1975.

HORTON, ROBERTA. *Calico and Beyond: The Use of Patterned Fabric in Quilts.* Lafayette, Calif.: C & T Publishing, 1987.

ICKIS, MARGUERITE. *The Standard Book of Quiltmaking and Collecting.* New York: Dover Publications, 1949.

IRWIN, JOHN RICE. *A People and Their Quilts.* Exton, Pa.: Schiffer Publishing, 1984.

Jones, Owen. *The Grammar of Ornament.* 1856. Reprint. London, England: Studio Editions of Bestseller Publications, 1986.

Justema, William. *The Pleasures of Pattern.* New York: Van Nostrand Reinhold, 1982.

Kile, Michael and Roderick Kiracofe, eds. *The Quilt Digest.* 5 vols. San Francisco: The Quilt Digest Press, 1983-87.

Kobayashi, Kei. *Encyclopedia of American Patchwork Quilts: A Loving Study.* Tokyo: Bunka Publishing Company, 1983.

_____. *How to Make Geometric Patterns by Origami.* Tokyo: Bunka Publishing Company, 1986.

_____. *Shelburne Museum: The Quilt.* Tokyo: Gakken Publishing Company, 1986.

Kolter, Jane Bentley. *Forget Me Not: A Gallery of Friendship and Album Quilts.* Pittstown, N.J.: The Main Street Press, 1985.

Kueppers, Harald. *The Basic Law of Color Theory.* Woodbury, N.Y.: Barron's, 1980.

Lasansky, Jeannette. *In the Heart of Pennsylvania: 19th & 20th Century Quiltmaking Traditions.* Lewisburg, Pa.: Oral Traditions Project, 1985.

Lewis, Philippa and Gillian Darley. *Dictionary of Ornament.* New York: Pantheon Books, 1986.

Lipman, Jean. *Provocative Parallels.* New York: E. P. Dutton, 1975.

Lipman, Jean and Alice Winchester. *The Flowering of American Folk Art (1776-1876).* New York: The Viking Press, 1974.

McKim, Ruby. *One Hundred and One Patchwork Patterns.* Rev. ed. New York: Dover Publications, 1962.

Montgomery, Florence M. *Textiles in America: 1650-1870.* New York: W. W. Norton & Company, 1984.

Nelson, Cyril I. and Carter Houck. *Treasury of American Quilts.* New York: Greenwich House, 1982.

Orlofsky, Patsy and Myron. *Quilts in America.* New York: McGraw-Hill Book Company, 1974.

Rose, Barbara. *American Art Since 1900.* Rev. & exp. ed. New York: Holt, Rinehart & Winston, 1975.

Safford, Carleton and Robert Bishop. *America's Quilts and Coverlets.* New York: E. P. Dutton, 1980.

Stockton, James. *Designer's Guide to Color 2.* San Francisco: Chronicle Books, 1984.

Thiel, Philip. *Visual Awareness and Design.* Seattle: University of Washington Press, 1983.

Tomlonson, Judy Schroeder. *Mennonite Quilts and Pieces.* Intercourse, Pa.: Good Books, 1985.

Walker, Michelle. *The Complete Book of Quiltmaking.* New York: Alfred A. Knopf, 1986.

Wien, Carol Anne. *The Great American Log Cabin Quilt Book.* New York: E. P. Dutton, 1984.

Wong, Wucius. *Principles of Color Design.* New York: Van Nostrand Reinhold, 1987.

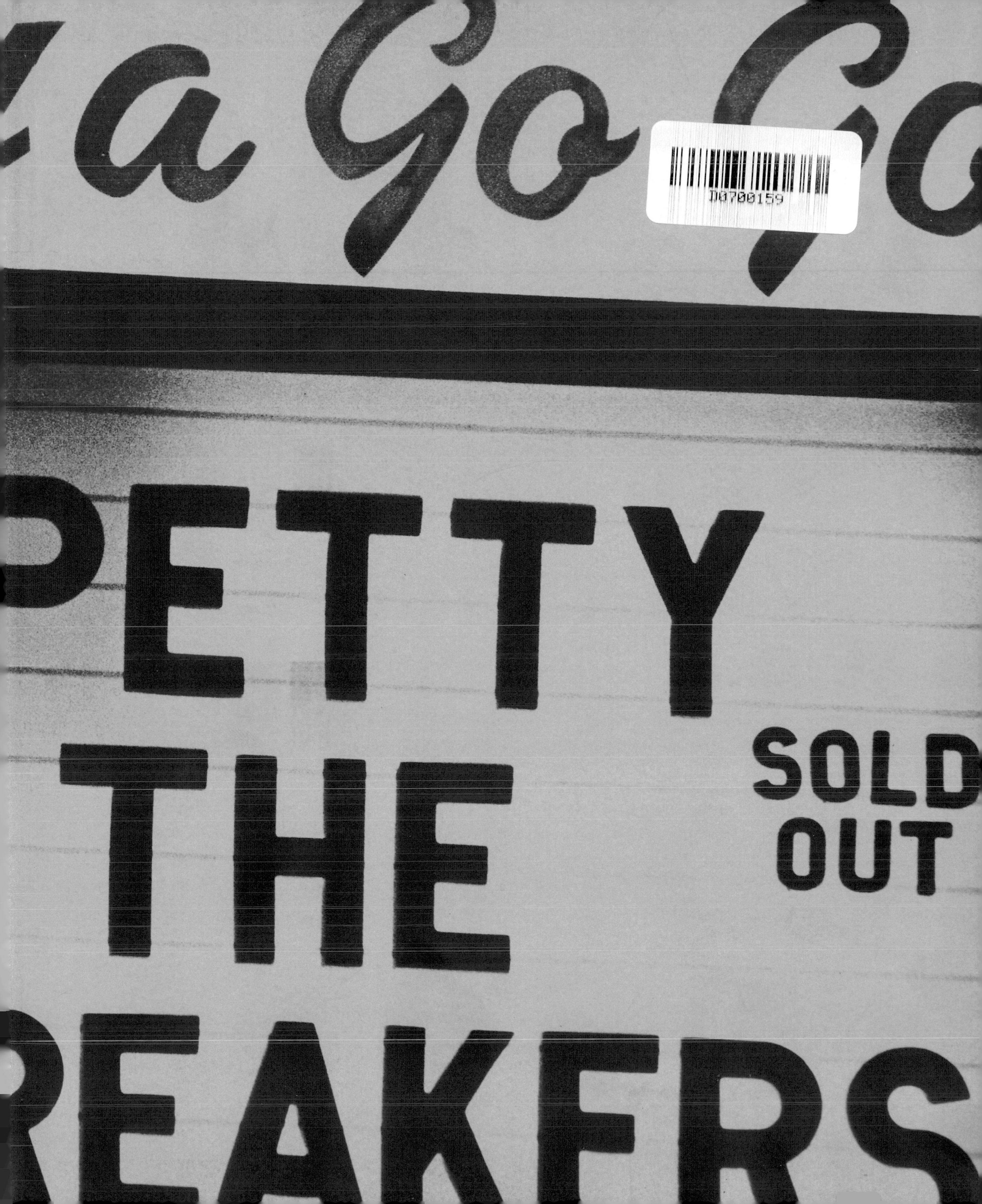
za Go Go
PETTY
THE
REAKERS
SOLD
OUT

TOM PETTY
and the HEARTBREAKERS

TOM and the HE

PETTY

ARTBREAKERS

FOREWORD AND INTERVIEWS BY PETER BOGDANOVICH

EDITED AND ADDITIONAL INTERVIEWS BY WARREN ZANES

CHRONICLE BOOKS

SAN FRANCISCO

Editor's Note

In 2006, Tom Petty was approached with the idea of filming a documentary on the subject of his life and career. The plan was to put director Peter Bogdanovich together with Petty, a meeting of two American mavericks. The project quickly grew in its proportions. Bogdanovich conducted extensive interviews with Petty, the Heartbreakers, and the artist's inner circle of friends, associates, and fellow performers. The wealth of materials that accumulated sparked the idea that a book project would be a natural outgrowth of all the film-related activities. What emerged is *Runnin' Down a Dream*, a volume that puts selected Bogdanovich interview material side-by-side with artifacts and images drawn from the Heartbreakers' archives. Personal, certainly intimate, *Runnin' Down a Dream* takes you straight into the world of one of American popular music's treasures, Tom Petty and the Heartbreakers.

Library of Congress Cataloging-in-Publication Data is available.

ISBN-10: 0-8118-6201-1
ISBN-13: 978-0-8118-6201-1

Manufactured in China

Designed by Jeri Heiden, SMOG Design, Inc.
Front cover photograph by Dennis Callahan

10 9 8 7 6 5 4 3 2 1

Chronicle Books LLC
680 Second Street
San Francisco, California 94107

www.chroniclebooks.com

cast

*(In order of appearance)

TOM PETTY: AS HIMSELF

JIM LENEHAN: MEMBER OF MUDCRUTCH, HEARTBREAKERS' LIGHTING DESIGNER

BRUCE PETTY: YOUNGER BROTHER

TOM LEADON: MEMBER OF THE EPICS, MEMBER OF MUDCRUTCH

BENMONT TENCH: MEMBER OF MUDCRUTCH, HEARTBREAKER

BILL FLANAGAN: MTV NETWORKS EXECUTIVE, AUTHOR

MIKE CAMPBELL: MEMBER OF MUDCRUTCH, HEARTBREAKER

DENNY CORDELL: PRODUCER, OWNER OF SHELTER RECORDS

RANDALL MARSH: MEMBER OF MUDCRUTCH

EILEEN BASICH: SHELTER RECORDS EMPLOYEE

RON BLAIR: HEARTBREAKER, FORMER OWNER OF BIKINI STORE

TONY DIMITRIADES: MANAGER

DAVE STEWART: MEMBER OF THE EURYTHMICS, COLLABORATOR

ADRIA PETTY: ELDEST DAUGHTER

ELLIOT ROBERTS: COMANAGER WITH TONY DIMITRIADES (1979 TO 1987)

JACKSON BROWNE: SINGER-SONGWRITER

DAVE GROHL: LEADER OF THE FOO FIGHTERS, MEMBER OF NIRVANA

JIMMY IOVINE: ENGINEER, PRODUCER, MUSIC EXECUTIVE

RICK RUBIN: PRODUCER, LABEL OWNER

EDDIE VEDDER: MEMBER OF PEARL JAM

STEVIE NICKS: MEMBER OF FLEETWOOD MAC, SOLO PERFORMER

HOWIE EPSTEIN: HEARTBREAKER

ROGER McGUINN: MEMBER OF THE BYRDS, SOLO PERFORMER

STEVE FERRONE: HEARTBREAKER

JEFF LYNNE: PRODUCER, TRAVELING WILBURY, FOUNDER OF ELECTRIC LIGHT ORCHESTRA

SCOTT THURSTON: HEARTBREAKER

JIM LADD: DISC JOCKEY

JOHNNY DEPP: ACTOR

cont

ents

A lot of Tom Petty's songs are like movies. Tight, evocative movies that expand in the mind far beyond the few minutes they take to play. This kind of economy of expression is natural to a poet, and that's what Tom is. One time I commented on the brilliant succinctness of a particular song, and he nodded, "Yeah, I only had two lines for the second act." Actually, Tom's heartfelt obsession with his art and absolute refusal to compromise remind me of some of the great picturemakers I've known over the years, such as Orson Welles and Jean Renoir.

Whether it's the "good girl" from Reseda who loves Elvis and Jesus ("Free Fallin'") or the reluctant waitress who sometimes "used to sing" ("The Best Of Everything") or the "rebel without a clue" ("Into The Great Wide Open") or that American girl "raised on promises," the people in his songs are so real that they resonate down the years. While the lyrics are often very specific, they remain impressionistic enough to be interpreted and experienced in numerous ways. These are songs filled with genuine emotion, without artifice, and deceptively simple. At heart, Tom is a cool romantic, a restless troubadour from the Golden Age.

Having spent nearly two years working with Tom Petty and his associates on a documentary about his work—with and without the Heartbreakers—I can attest to his seriousness as an artist. His dedication to the music he creates, as well as his integrity, is already legendary. It's certainly not an accident that several key musicians of the

last fifty years worked closely with Tom and grew very fond of him, from George Harrison to Bob Dylan to Johnny Cash.

His Heartbreakers are widely acknowledged to be among the very finest musicians in rock history: in particular one guitar virtuoso, Mike Campbell, who also cowrote many Petty hits, and one keyboard virtuoso, Benmont Tench, who seems to know every song ever written. Both men have been with Tom from the start. He also has extraordinary backup from bassist Ron Blair, drummer Steve Ferrone, and Scott Thurston, adept at everything.

It's no coincidence that Tom comes from America's greatest fount of writers, the South, which birthed Mark Twain, Tennessee Williams, William Faulkner, Thomas Wolfe, Truman Capote, and so many others. Like only the best novelists, he possesses a superb visual sense, which helps to explain his major role as a pioneer in the glory days of MTV videos. Uniquely, Petty has an uncanny ability to make his work sound entirely new and familiar at the same time.

As a singer, Tom has a distinctive, edgy sound. This, combined with an unusual sensitivity, creates a potent, ambiguous mixture that is strangely addictive and haunting. Perhaps that's one of the reasons his fans are so devoted, loyal, and diverse in age. At a number of the 30th Anniversary concerts in 2006, we talked to teenagers in the audience, all of whom told us their parents played Petty and the Heartbreakers and they found the songs hip enough to adopt themselves. His popularity now spans three generations. When performing, Petty is remarkably charismatic in a laid-back way, yet he gives a great deal of himself to the audience. His shows build in emotional scope, from an initial sense of intimacy to a larger-than-life experience not unlike what I've felt with soaring grand opera. It's no wonder Tom Petty and the Heartbreakers remain among the most popular and durable concert attractions in show business history.

Petty's courage in the face of malignant authority or exploitation has repeatedly been tested and has repeatedly triumphed, as will be clear in this book. In his bravely honest album *The Last DJ*, he went against the entire dehumanizing corporate society we have increasingly become:

There goes your freedom of choice

There goes the last human voice...

But then Tom has always told the truth in his work—what he calls being "real." That's no doubt why the music doesn't date, why it still sounds so immediate, so fresh.

Peter Bogdanovich

I've worked hard. I've focused my ambitions. All that. But at the end of the day, the most important career turns have been the ones I never could have planned. Guys like Benmont Tench and Mike Campbell came into my life like it was meant to be. I couldn't dream that up. Two of the best musicians in the world just walked right into my life—and completely grasped what I wanted to do. Add to that walking backward into working with Bob Dylan and joining the Traveling Wilburys, becoming allies with some of rock's greatest record-makers, guys like Rick Rubin, Jimmy Iovine, Jeff Lynne, Denny Cordell, Dave Stewart, and George Drakoulias—and not to mention my long-lasting friendships with heroes of my youth like George Harrison and Roger McGuinn. The tangle of coincidences that allowed it all to happen this way is just too much. At a certain point, you can't just file it all under good luck.

Maybe I'm just at that stage in life where I'm beginning to see the faint outline of the whole picture and have started to think of my career as something bigger than me. The music belongs to so many people. And that shift in thinking is very freeing. Things become simpler. I just try to be responsible to a gift I've been given. And that's a job I'm comfortable with. I mean, you won't see me taking all of this down to the pawnshop. I plan on keeping it.

I'm so tired of bein tired
Sure as night will follow day
Most things I worry about
Never happen anyway

It's much more than a job. It's something you have to do. It's like being possessed. Some people get possessed with the lord and have to go out and preach sermons the rest of their lives. We were possessed by rock-and-roll music and, to feel fulfilled, had to go out and play gigs the rest of our lives. It's something you're always going to do. You can quit, but it's really like the sailor and the sea—if he never goes back, he's just going to think about it for the rest of his life, be suspended in a state of longing. I don't think it will ever stop.

PREVIOUS PAGES:

Knebworth Festival, Hertfordshire, England, June 24, 1978. An audience member gave Tom his first top hat.

THIS PAGE:

The Heartbreakers in 1976. From left: Mike Campbell, Ron Blair, Tom, Stan Lynch, Benmont Tench.

We did a session with Annie Leibovitz for the cover of You're Gonna Get It!, *which at the time was being called* Terminal Romance. *We were fans of Annie's work because of the great* Rolling Stone *covers she'd done.*

When we got the pictures back, I remember Noah Shark, our engineer, saying, "No, no, no, no, that's not it." He had an opinion on most everything. But he had good instincts. He felt the pictures were just too bright, that the album was dark and moody and needed a cover that reflected that. After some badgering we were convinced to change it—and by that time Annie was no longer available to do another session. That was when we did the other shoot with David Alexander and got the blue cover.

When I look at Annie's shot, which I really like, I can see that she captured us all pretty much the way we were. She's got Stan laughing. Some sessions can wear on and on and on. But Annie has a way of getting you relaxed. This picture is a real honest document of who we were then.

LEFT:

Benmont, Ron, Tom, Mike, Stan, circa 1977.

PREVIOUS PAGES:

The US Festival, San Bernardino, CA, Sept. 4, 1982. Tom plays cat and mouse with audience.

Chapter One/ Escape

We lived in kind of a low-end suburb. You wouldn't really call it middle class. The kids I knew all had the same type of parents—their dads had been off to the war and had come back. Life was pretty good. It was the fabulous '50s, you know.

THE OTHER FLORIDA

Tom Petty: Gainesville, Florida, USA. A lot of times when I tell people I'm from Florida, they picture Miami. Gainesville was nothing like that. Gainesville is in the north central part of Florida, closer to Georgia than Miami. Closer to Georgia geographically and certainly in spirit. Miami was five or six hours away, but it may as well have been many oceans away, really. I come from the South, not its fringes.

Jim Lenehan: We were all good Florida crackers.

Tom Petty: When I was born, in 1950, Gainesville was a little town. What made it unique was having the University of Florida right there. The school made Gainesville a little less backwater than it might have been otherwise. But there was a farming community still active, the last traces of the agrarian South, I suppose. It was a real mix of people. You could run across just about any kind of person there. And I did.

I had a pretty good childhood in many respects, though my father was kind of strange in some ways. A wild guy. That part of my youth was tough at times. No excuse for nostalgia. My dad wasn't around a lot, tended to come in late at night. I didn't see too much of him.

Bruce Petty: I could tell there was always a friction between the two of them.

Tom Petty: We lived in kind of a low-end suburb. You wouldn't really call it middle class. The kids I knew all had the same type of parents—their dads had been off to the war and had come back. Life was pretty good. It was the fabulous '50s, you know.

COLOR CODES

Tom Petty: My father had a variety of jobs. At one point he owned the only grocery store in the black part of town. I have memories of being very young and going there with him each day. This was before I started school. He'd put me in a little dirt lot behind the store. I would be left out there, eventually finding a group of black kids from the neighborhood who I could play with. They'd try to con me into sneaking candy out of the store and things like that. Then I would go home in the late afternoon and play with the white kids.

Tom Leadon: His family invited me to dinner with them. I was having trouble understanding them because they had such thick Southern accents.

I was a skinny little kid with a weird haircut. But she is talking to me and says, "You're growing your hair, I see." I said "Yeah, I've got a band." And she hires us to play the intermission at her school dance. We struck gold. Word got out, and we found this kid who had already graduated from high school, a bit older than us, and he played the shit out of a guitar. We went to my house, everyone plugged into the same amplifier, and, wham, the heavens split open. It was the biggest rush in my life. We're doing it. We're making this music.

Tom Petty: It was the South, and it was that time before the Civil Rights movement. There would be two drinking fountains, one saying COLORED and one saying WHITE. I guess that's when I first really noticed there was an awful injustice here. By the time I was approaching my teens it had finally become a national issue. A lot of people were asking questions. Life was changing in towns like mine.

Benmont Tench: There's a great misunderstanding about the South. It's always good to remember Tennessee Williams and William Faulkner, Ray Charles, all these people.

Tom Petty: In retrospect, I'm grateful for the experience I had as a child, shuttling between neighborhoods with my dad. I didn't think twice about who I played with in the morning and who I played with in the evening. I just wanted to play, right? But at that age some crucial thinking gets put into place, quietly, there under the surface. I think it's worth remembering that for a musician, for an American songwriter, the movement between black and white music is the most important movement there is. Always has been. That's Elvis Presley's movement, Stax Records' movement, Motown's, the Beatles'. I feel like my travel between neighborhoods probably, in some way, meant something that eventually factored into the music. The South has always been a special place when it comes to music. And the black music of the South is the key ingredient.

VINYL

Tom Petty: My mother worked for the tax collector's office selling license plates. I remember being a very young child and my mother getting us these little children's records that were usually on yellow vinyl, nursery rhymes and such. I liked the whole idea of the record player, of the records. I suppose it was just the feel of them and the look of the player that got me first. I still like to get my hands on vinyl.

My parents listened to a bunch of music. Certainly hillbilly music, country music, was around in the house. My mom liked Nat King Cole. She would have the *West Side Story* soundtrack and *South Pacific*. She also played gospel records.

I remember being five or six years old and hearing "Rock Around The Clock"—"One o'clock, two o'clock, three o'clock, rock." This impressed me. I thought, that's really great. What is this? Then I didn't hear much about it for a while. Later on I made more headway. I had a cousin with a stack of rock-and-roll records, always spinning the stuff. I clearly recall hearing the Everly Brothers for the first time—being confounded because I thought these "brothers" were girls, because they were singing in such a high register. I never heard men sing like that. But I was in love with high harmonies from that day forward.

Those were probably the first strains of music that came in. Elvis didn't arrive on my shores for a while. There was controversy in our house about Elvis Presley. The ladies would all giggle. And it was not a joke, not to everyone. There were some sort of hushed tones about it. No better advertisement to get a young fellow interested, really.

MEMPHIS, LIVERPOOL, GAINESVILLE

Tom Petty: My aunt was married to a really nice guy, a fellow who worked in the film business in Gainesville. From time to time, if there was a feature film being shot anywhere nearby, he would get on a film crew. So my aunt pulls in the drive one day and says, "Listen, Elvis Presley is making a movie in Ocala, and your uncle is working on the picture."

It looked like the Fourth of July parade was in town, just the biggest ordeal I had seen in my young life. Elvis hadn't arrived yet. Then, suddenly, white Cadillacs begin to appear. White, not black, not red—white Cadillacs. Out of every Cadillac, it seems, comes a guy with a pompadour and a mohair suit. Amazing-looking

Lipham's Music was the hub of all of the musician activity in Gainesville. Everyone went there. Lipham's had all the right equipment, all the great guitars and amps. I remember times when I was really young looking at the guitars in the window and just thinking they might as well be rocket ships. They were the most high-tech thing I'd ever seen. Especially the whammy bar. I thought it was some kind of gear shift. It was all way out of my league financially. I was fourteen or fifteen when they gave me a job there because I was around all the time anyway. The manager said he'd put me on commission. But I sold so much stuff in the first week he took me off commission and gave me a part-time job. I'd offer some incredible bargains that the management wasn't too happy with. My theory was just keep slashing the price until the customer bought it. I didn't realize that this wasn't going to go down so well with the owners.

OPPOSITE:

The Epics, circa 1966. From left: Rodney Rucker, Ricky Rucker, Tom, Dickie Underwood.

PREVIOUS PAGE:

Tom playing bass with the Sundowners, 1965.

guys. And I go, "Is that Elvis?" And my aunt goes, "No, that's not Elvis." "Well, is this one Elvis?" I ask. "No. That's not Elvis." And then suddenly she goes, "That's Elvis."

Bruce Petty: At that age we were into cowboys and Indians. We were hoping to get a new gun and holster for Christmas or whatever. But all of a sudden Tom's whole focus changed.

Bill Flanagan: I think that Elvis Presley affected Tom Petty's imagination and gave him entrée into this mythical world of old singles in a shoe box. But it was seeing the Beatles on *Ed Sullivan* that made him actually see a way that he could do it.

Mike Campbell: When the Beatles happened, the next day at school it's like everything had changed.

Tom Petty: There were four guys, and they looked like they were friends. They were playing their instruments and singing. Now you need to remember, the people that the industry was selling us at the time were the Frankie Avalons, Fabians, and Tab Hunters. These guys didn't really have rock groups. Because of them, I imagined that pop stars traveled around with an orchestra and could make music happen on the beach. Magically, the bushes transform into a backing group. When you saw the Beatles, it was very clear that this was something that could happen in the real world, meaning, hey, I could do this. Here is a way out. So, I instantly wanted a guitar. And my dad, bless his heart, threw down $35 and bought me an electric guitar. Probably because I just wouldn't shut up about it. I was in heaven—but I couldn't play a note.

My mom found me a guitar teacher. The teacher showed me one chord. I went home and played it to death. Then I went back the next time. He told me to put my thumb on the back of the neck of the guitar—not to let it go over the fret board, but to keep it on the back the way classical musicians play. As it happened, the Beatles were on TV again that week. They had their thumbs over the fret board. I didn't go back for another lesson.

Jim Lenehan: In those days, longhairs all gravitated toward each other.

Tom Petty: Soon enough, I met another guy with long hair. He played the drums. Next thing you know, we're banging away, the two of us. His drums sort of drowned out my amplifier. I don't think he really knew—or cared—if I could play or not, but I had made a friend. I had an ally now. So, fast-forward a little bit. I'm at the dance hall on Friday night, and the hottest chick in school—you know, the one we all wanted to talk to for some reason—comes up to me.

Bruce Petty: He wasn't very athletic.

Tom Petty: I was not your typical ladies' man. I was a skinny little kid with a weird haircut. But she is talking to me and says, "You're growing your hair, I see." I said "Yeah, I've got a band." And she hires us to play the intermission at her school dance. We struck gold. Word got out, and we found this kid who had already graduated from high school, a bit older than us, and he played the shit out of a guitar. We went to my house, everyone plugged into the same amplifier, and, wham, the heavens split open. It was the biggest rush in my life. We're doing it. We're making this music. Come show day, we got really nervous, showing up to the gig in matching blue shirts. We put our gear up, and the disc jockey took his break. Without even a name for the group, we started to play. We played our three songs. And to our near disbelief, everyone yelled for more. So we played them again.

Eventually we graduated to nice pink jackets with belts on the back. We played frat houses, high school dances, teen clubs, public swimming pools. We called ourselves the Sundowners. The first time we got paid, my mom really thought that I had stolen the money.

THE EPICS

Tom Petty: As happens in bands, the Sundowners experienced a little internal friction. I had a falling out with the drummer. I was quickly offered a job playing bass with a local group called the Epics, older guys. They had driver's licenses—this was the big time. These guys were wild. At about fifteen years old, I was by far the youngest one in the band. I just looked with wonder at what I was seeing, at the girls in particular. These guys were landing babes and getting drunk. It was some heady stuff for a young fellow.

Tom Leadon: When I was in eighth grade a friend took me to Petty's house, and they were there playing. They had the colored lights and the drum riser and everything in this little room. I was quite impressed.

Tom Petty: Even when I was first learning the guitar I tried to come up with my own tunes, likely because I didn't know that many proper songs. I liked to move the chords around and create my own little melodies. Our idols were Lennon and McCartney, people who wrote their own music. So I wanted to figure out how to do that.

Tom Leadon: Right away he was writing good stuff.

Tom Petty: I would take songs to the band, and they would say great. But we didn't get a lot of reaction when we played them in the shows. The Epics just wanted the crowd to dance. It was probably around 1967, when I was seventeen, that a few of us made the decision to play original music and take the punishment related to that—fewer gigs and so forth. A new sensibility was springing up because of hippies—there was more of an audience for hearing originals. That's when Mudcrutch found its way into the world.

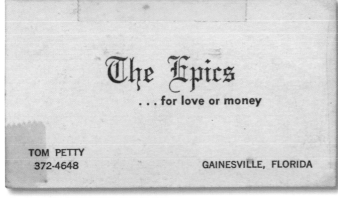

The Epics
. . . for love or money

TOM PETTY
372-4648   GAINESVILLE, FLORIDA

ABOVE:

The Epics in 1967.

From left: Tom, Rodney Rucker, Dickie Underwood, Ricky Rucker, Tom Leadon.

THE EPICS, Gainesville's number one band buys their equipment from the number one music store LIPHAM'S MUSIC CO. 1004 N. Main

4754902

I
1. Good Golly Miss Molly
2. Six Days on the Road
3. Lookin Out my Back Door
4. Sookie Sookie
5. Steve Miller
6. Ride Captain
7. OO Wee
8. Everely Bros ✓
9. Proud Mary
10. Mabelene

II
1. Johnny B. Goode
2. Somethin good at last
3. Honkey Tonk Women
4. Born to Be Wild
5. Long Winding Root
6. Rip it Up
7. Take me Back
8. Los Angeles
9. City Blocks & Country Miles
10. Cruse is Understood

1. Lawdy Mama
2. gy luenti
3. 000 wee
4. Somethigood
5. Flesftock

III
1. Hard Headed Woman
2. She Caught The Katie
3. Hey Lawdy mama
4. get me out of this
5. Empty Bottle
6. Little Wing
7. Mess Ann
8. Whiskey girl
9. you don't have to
10. good golly molly

IV
1. Sookie Sookie
2. Lookin out my Back Door
3.
4.
5. One More Firey Fool
6.
7.
8. Save your Water
9.
10.

ROSE COMMUNITY IS BACK!
Friday & Saturday, Mar. 3-4

MUD RUTH

GAINESVILLE'S NO.1 BOOGIE BAND

AND INTRODUCING AT THE FRIDAY SHOW

RARE BIRD

ROCK-ROLL MADNESS AT THE SHOW

SANTA FE JUNIOR COLLEGE
AUDITORIUM - WEST CAMPUS 723 W. UNIV.
AROUND CORNER FROM THE
SUBTERRANEAN CIRCUS
SHOWTIME 8 P.M. ADMISSION $1

THE EPICS

LOVE YOU!

It was Mike's idea to throw the Mudcrutch Farm Festivals. We figured, really casually, that we'd put on an outdoor show. We put up a few posters and had another group join us. It was just going to be on Sunday—"after church," as Jim Lenehan wrote on the poster—and quite a few people came. It was more than we had ever imagined, over a thousand people. The police turned up, a sure sign of success. It went so well we thought we'd have another one.

The next one we had was just off the map. Cars were parked for miles. After that one, we were kicked off of Mudcrutch Farm. The landlord told us we were being evicted. So, of course, we thought, "Why not have a third one?"

Our name became something of a brand, simply because the event was called the Mudcrutch Farm Festival. After that we were in high demand around town.

MUDCRUTCH

Tom Petty: When I left the Epics, Tom Leadon came with me. Like me, Tom was a teenager who wanted to play originals. The new group's lead singer was Jim Lenehan. Now we needed a name.

Jim Lenehan: Ricky Rucker walked in one day and said, "What do you think of Mudcrutch?" And Petty said, "In relation to what?"

Tom Leadon: The name "the Epics" had become dated. This was the era of the Jefferson Airplane, Moby Grape, the Grateful Dead. And we were called the Epics. Mudcrutch sounded like something adults and straight people wouldn't understand or approve of.

Tom Petty: I was playing the bass. Tom Leadon was playing the guitar. Needing another guitar player and a drummer, we posted an ad at Lipham's Music Store. We got a call from a fellow named Randall Marsh. Randall lived in this rundown farmhouse on three or four acres of land. We went out there to try him out for the band. As we were setting up, somebody made the remark that it's a shame we don't have a rhythm guitar player. Randall says, "Oh, I may have a rhythm guitar player here." And I heard him yell, "Mike, can you play rhythm guitar?"

Mike Campbell: I was just in the back room, listening through the walls.

Tom Petty: Mike's wearing cut-off jeans, which I have never seen him wear since. His hair was fairly short for those days because he had a job at the university library. And he's carrying this $80 Japanese guitar. At that point we all kind of looked at the ground. This guy is bound to be terrible.

Tom Leadon: . . . a toy guitar, worth about ten bucks maybe.

Jim Lenehan: . . . worst guitar I've ever seen. Looked like it was cut out of a door.

Tom Petty: But, one "Johnny B. Goode" later we had a band. Our jaws dropped. This was an incredible guitar player. One snag: Mike is going to college. He seems to be enrolled in the University of Florida. I said to him, "You know, you don't want to do that. Why would you want to do that when you can play the guitar like this?" I can't believe now that I had that much gumption, but I talked him into quitting school. His next concern was, well, what about the army? Vietnam was going on, and you got a deferment if you went to school. I said, "Don't worry, we'll handle that."

DUB'S

Tom Petty: The main club in Gainesville that paid any money was this place called Dub's Steer Room, which later shortened its name to Dub's. The real feature of the place was six topless dancers. Until we were on the stage at Dub's, it hadn't registered to me what topless dancing really was. We went into our first number, and these girls just pulled it off. Nice-looking girls. So we are just playing and watching, and I thought, "I am going to like this professional music thing."

Benmont Tench: After I saw Mudcrutch play in Lake City I became a fan.

Tom Petty: Benmont I knew when he was just a little guy. He couldn't have been more than eleven or twelve when he came into Lipham's one time. Benmont walks in there, sits down, and plays a Beatles album, the entire album, beginning to end. I remember going over and introducing myself and talking to him. He had this weird name, Benmont.

Benmont Tench: If I'm in a music store, I'm going to sit down at the piano until they say stop. And they did. They said, "Kid, enough."

Tom Petty: Years later, I was hanging with this guy who occasionally loaned us his van to move gear. I'm at his place. It's night. The door opens and this guy comes in with an arm full of records. He's got a big, bushy beard and hair down over his shoulders. He's also got all these import records from England. I ask him his name, and he says, "Benmont Tench." I said, "Benmont Tench. You're not the kid that plays the piano?" "Yeah, that's me," he says. "Son of a bitch!" I say. "What are you doing tonight or tomorrow night?" We get him onstage without any rehearsal, and he outplays all of us for five hours.

Ben's dad was a judge. I had to go into his office and talk him into letting his son quit college. One of the more interesting jobs I've ever had. My angle was pretty solid: "Let Ben have a few years of this. And if it doesn't work, he can always go back to college. But he can't always get a record deal and make an album." It was in the judge's living room where we recorded the demos that really got it all started for the band. We cut six or seven songs on a two-track mobile unit at Benmont's house. We thought it sounded pretty good. The next step was to make my first trip to L.A.

DOOR-TO-DOOR SALESMEN

Tom Petty: It was a different time in the music business. Three of us went out to visit the record companies. We packed up a lot of sandwiches and

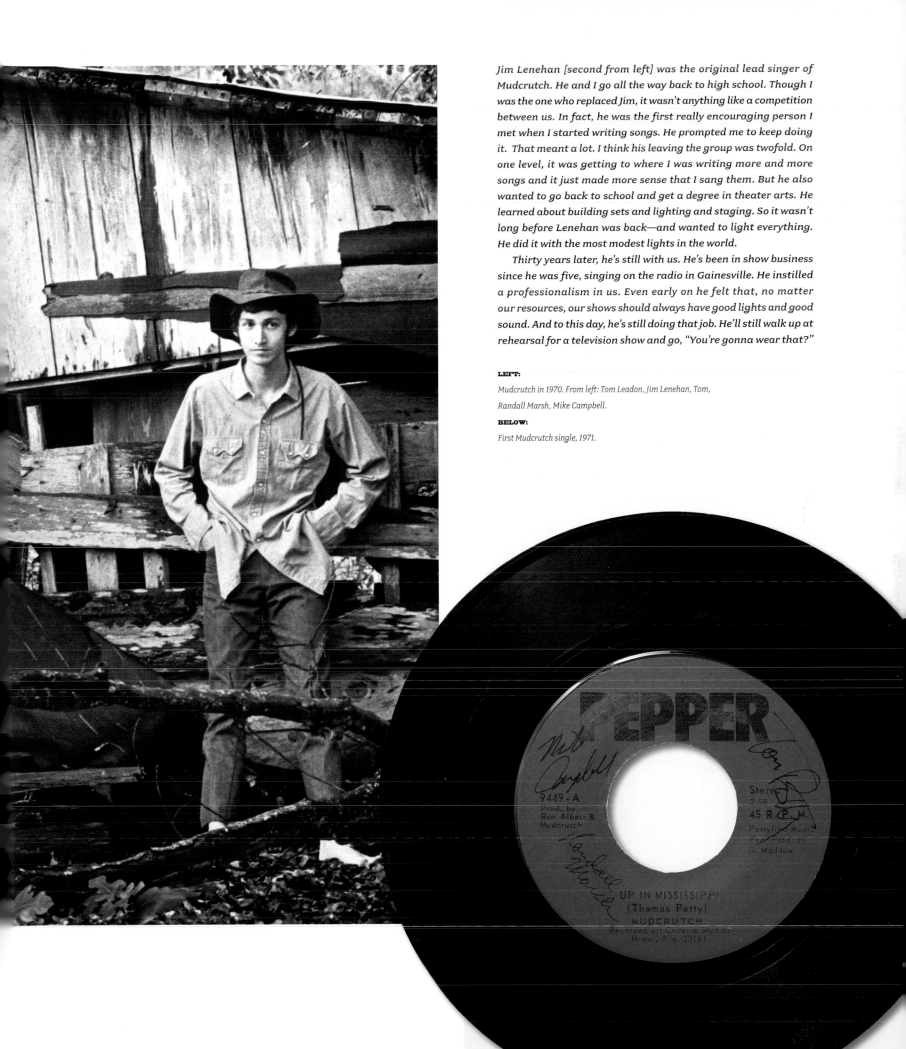

Jim Lenehan [second from left] was the original lead singer of Mudcrutch. He and I go all the way back to high school. Though I was the one who replaced Jim, it wasn't anything like a competition between us. In fact, he was the first really encouraging person I met when I started writing songs. He prompted me to keep doing it. That meant a lot. I think his leaving the group was twofold. On one level, it was getting to where I was writing more and more songs and it just made more sense that I sang them. But he also wanted to go back to school and get a degree in theater arts. He learned about building sets and lighting and staging. So it wasn't long before Lenehan was back—and wanted to light everything. He did it with the most modest lights in the world.

Thirty years later, he's still with us. He's been in show business since he was five, singing on the radio in Gainesville. He instilled a professionalism in us. Even early on he felt that, no matter our resources, our shows should always have good lights and good sound. And to this day, he's still doing that job. He'll still walk up at rehearsal for a television show and go, "You're gonna wear that?"

LEFT:

Mudcrutch in 1970. From left: Tom Leadon, Jim Lenehan, Tom, Randall Marsh, Mike Campbell.

BELOW:

First Mudcrutch single, 1971.

tapes. None of us had been west of the Mississippi. It was a big deal when we started seeing cactus on the side of the road.

Bruce Petty: I remember him sending pictures of cactuses.

Tom Petty: Once we're out there, we drive into Hollywood, down Sunset Boulevard. There were lots of record companies in those days. I said, "Well, this is going to be easy because we will just go to every one. One of them will have to take us."

We walk in—and we must have looked pretty funny, having just driven three thousand miles—and we are quickly told that it's not done this way. We look at the fellow who tells us this and say, "C'mon, we're here and we got the demo and you have a tape deck." He played not quite thirty seconds and stopped the tape, telling us he'd heard enough and to get out of his office.

Change of strategy. Kind of. I had a list of record companies I took from record ads in *Rolling Stone*. I figured we'd make some appointments. I go out to the phone booth, and while I'm on the phone and asking for a number, I look down at the bottom of the booth and there's a piece of paper lying there. On this paper there are twenty-five record companies and their phone numbers. That made me feel good and bad. "Christ," I thought, "how many people are doing this?"

I made an appointment for later in the day to visit Shelter Records. And we went to MGM. At MGM a guy listens to the whole tape. He says, "Who's your lawyer?" We have no lawyer. He says, "Who's your manager?" I point at Keith, the roadie, and say, "I guess he is." The guy says he wants to make a deal to record a single! Our eyes go up. But we're savvy now, right? We said, well, we were really looking for an album deal. We hit the street just leaping in the air. Later we drop a tape at Shelter for Denny Cordell.

The next day we go to London Records. A cute little secretary is in the waiting room, talks to us for a few minutes, and eventually tells us someone will see us. This guy plays our tape, the whole thing. He starts clapping his hands and jumping around going, "This is fantastic. You got a deal." We just looked at him. A deal? He wants to know where we live? Gainesville, Florida. Where? What? What's that? "You're going to have to live here," he tells us. "Go get your band."

CONVOY

Tom Petty: On the way back to Gainesville we swung through New Orleans, went up to Ben's place, and said, "Look. This is it with school. Get your gear. We're going to make records." We started selling anything we owned of value, which wasn't much. One thing we were selling was an old car. We're rehearsing one day, and the phone rings. I put down my bass and go to answer the phone. The band is still playing in the next room. It's loud. I think this person is calling about the car. Talking over the music, I'm saying, "Well,

you know, it's a hundred bucks. It's not that good." The voice on the other end goes, "No, no, no. This is Denny Cordell. I'm calling for Mudcrutch."

When I told Denny that we'd promised a guy at London that we're going to do it with them, he asked if we'd signed the deal. Well, no. Then he says that if we're going to L.A., it's not too far out of our way to stop in Tulsa. We should meet him there and talk a little bit before we sign with London Records.

Denny Cordell: I completely flipped for the whole thing, contacted Tom, and he said he was driving across with his band to various record companies in California. I was desperate, frightened I wouldn't have a chance of getting them. Really, the Tulsa trip was an effort to head them off at the pass.

Tom Petty: We load up everybody and their girls, and a couple of dogs, into three vehicles, including a truck that did fifty miles an hour tops and Benmont's mother's station wagon, which constantly broke down. I got married a couple of days before we hit the road. So we're off on an adventure—on every level.

Jim Lenehan: I have a little piece of silent Super 8 of the wedding. A couple days later we left in a caravan. A truck, a Volkswagen van, and Benmont's station wagon.

Randall Marsh: . . . five cars and a truck.

Mike Campbell: We all got a truck and headed out together.

Benmont Tench: . . . a U-Haul truck, a Volkswagen bus, and maybe something else.

THE PIRATE

Tom Petty: Once in Oklahoma, I remember meeting Denny Cordell in front of the Shelter Studio, which was built in an old church. There was a windstorm, dust blowing everywhere. Through the dust clouds steps this Englishman, who was really something to take in. He had the earring, which you didn't see a lot back then, and a bandana. Some kind of English dustbowl pirate. "Come on over to the diner," he tells us. We immediately hit it off. He tells us we're the greatest thing since the Rolling Stones and that he's going to throw everything he can behind the band. Tells us to go on out to Hollywood and go to his office. Ask for Eileen Basich.

He reaches in his pocket and pulls out a lot of cash, tells us we're going to need some money. He throws it down on the table. There's five grand there. "Will that get you to Hollywood?" I'd never seen that much money in one hand, and definitely not my own.

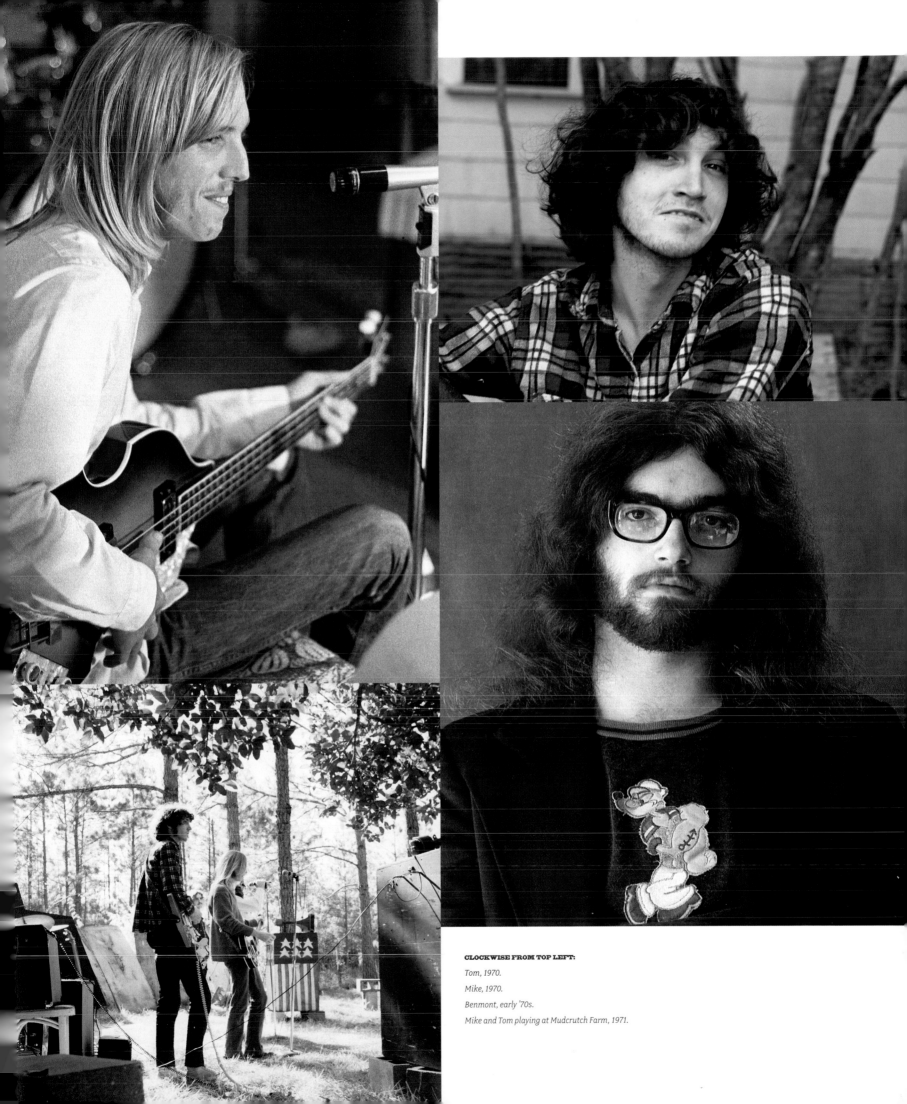

Eileen Basich: There were ten of them. There were so many, and they were so young and excited.

Tom Petty: Within a day or so Shelter Records rented us out a couple of houses, one with a swimming pool. This is heavy stuff for us. We hadn't hardly seen a house with a swimming pool, let alone lived in one. There was no furniture, of course, but we bought lawn chairs so we could sit down. About the second week we were there I learned that I was going to have a baby. It was strange. I didn't quite know what to think. There was so much happening in my life. I just thought, "Well, okay. At least I've got a job now."

I remember Benmont being particularly crazy around this time. He wouldn't let us turn the heat on in the house because he was afraid that the gas was going to blow it up, figured we didn't know how to operate it properly. You have to realize that Benmont didn't even own a pair of blue jeans at this point in his life because he had always been dressed in prep school clothes. He wore blazers all the time.

Benmont Tench: I felt like an alien in this band, anyway, because I was younger than anyone by a couple of years. They were guys that had been in this rock-and-roll band and living on this farm and God knows what kind of stuff. I had been in boarding school in New England. Good lord, it wasn't the same thing. My dad is a judge.

Tom Petty: So, Adria is born. Benmont's wearing jeans. And Denny Cordell figures he's going to teach us how to record. He's going to show us how to trick the mic into doing what we want it to. We learned a lot. He sent us back to Oklahoma for a stint in Shelter's studio, and we also worked in L.A. studios. After what seemed to us like a very, very long time, often waiting for Denny, a Mudcrutch single was released. One side was "Depot Street," and the other was "Wild Eyes," both written by me. It was an overwhelming flop, hit the dirt pretty hard.

We had so many expectations in that time—and then to watch the single disappear. Amidst it all, Mudcrutch breaks up. I went immediately to Mike and said, "You won't leave me though, right? We're going to stick together, right?" It was a hard time. It was really sad because we had been together so long. I felt really terrible about it.

Not much happened for a while. I was still under contract to Shelter and did a couple of sessions as a solo artist, with the best session musicians in town, Jim Keltner, Al Kooper, Jim Gordon. But I didn't like it. I didn't like the feeling of *not* being in a group. I never really wanted it to be that way. I went to Cordell and said, "This is not what I want to do. I really would like to have my own group."

Tom Leadon, Tom Petty, Randall Marsh, Mike Campbell.

Chapter Two/ Tom Petty and the King Bees

I walk in, and I'm sitting in the control room listening to this band play. They sound fantastic. They haven't seen me yet. And I thought, "Whoa, this is it. I have to steal this band." That was my first thought, that this should be my band. God bless Ben for forgiving my subversive intentions. If I hadn't pulled in to do a harmonica overdub, I would have missed the Heartbreakers. That was a pretty big chunk of luck right there.

STEAL THIS BAND

Benmont Tench: I was having a great adventure of being broke.

Tom Petty: About a year after Mudcrutch split up, Benmont, who'd had his own ups and downs being in L.A., was thinking about making a solo record. He was cutting at this place called the Village Recorder, and he called me—asking if I'd play harmonica on his demo. I went down, and there Benmont had assembled in the studio what was essentially the Heartbreakers. He's got Mike Campbell on guitar. There were Stan Lynch and Ron Blair, Gainesville guys transplanted to L.A. He even had Randall Marsh, the Mudcrutch drummer. I walk in, and I'm sitting in the control room listening to this band play. They sound fantastic. They haven't seen me yet. And I thought, "Whoa, this is it. I have to steal this band." That was my first thought, that this should be my band. God bless Ben for forgiving my subversive intentions. If I hadn't pulled in to do a harmonica overdub, I would have missed the Heartbreakers. That was a pretty big chunk of luck right there.

Mike Campbell: It was really Ben's session that put everyone in the room at the same time.

Tom Petty: Even though Mudcrutch had broken up, Shelter Records hadn't released me, hoping I'd make a solo record. The band comes in on a break, and I started my pitch: "You know, you all could throw in with me. I've got a record deal. You wouldn't have to go searching around again trying to get something together. Isn't this the way it's supposed to be?" I tell them that this time I'm going to be the leader of the band—because I'd been with Mudcrutch and come out with nothing, and if I'm going to put all of my effort into this, I want something out of it. And they were up for it. They said it sounds good. Let's try it. I went to Denny Cordell and said I got these friends from Gainesville. Of course, he pretty much knew everyone already.

Enter Stan Lynch. I think he was a little skeptical at first, but that changed. Understand that Randall Marsh was on that demo session of Benmont's, but I felt like I didn't want to go back down that road again. Stan, though, here was something new. Stan had a really big personality. Radiant. He became a great cheerleader and team leader. And—this was important—he was really hungry and wanted to do this thing. All that and he was a great drummer. With Stan I was spoiled for life because he's really a locomotive back there. When he finished playing there would be a pile of sawdust around the drum kit. He kept everyone up, kept everyone laughing.

Ron Blair: Next thing you know we're writing names on a blackboard.

Tom Petty: We decided that we would be a group and needed a name. My choice was the King Bees. The guys didn't much like that. I thought it sounded good—you know, Tom Petty and the King Bees. Where the Heartbreakers came from I'm not sure. It was probably Denny Cordell.

Denny Cordell: Really? I must have nicked it off Johnny Thunders in that case.

Benmont Tench: Cordell and Petty came up with the Heartbreakers. Kind of funny and ironic, isn't it? Heartbreakers? Who are we kidding here?

Tom Petty: The band thought the name had a good ring to it. Later on we were really shocked because there was a band called the Heartbreakers. They were fairly big in New York. But we thought, "We're not changing our name just because of this other group." They thought the same thing. We figured we'd watch and see who wins this contest.

ENGINEERS ON LSD

Tom Petty: By this time Shelter Records had built a studio in L.A., right next door to the office. They let us rehearse in the studio, and we could record when we wanted. That's the moment when we really started to make what I think was pretty damn good music. In that Shelter Studio we did some growing up that stayed with us for a long time.

Denny Cordell fronted us some money to buy gear, so we picked up several Vox amplifiers that we still use today. I'd been writing songs all the while. The band was really locked in, ready for anything I threw at them. Things were starting to get pretty exciting around that time.

Mike Campbell: He was coming out as this amazing writer.

Tom Petty: The folks at Shelter found us two really good engineers, absolutely insane but really good engineers. As people these guys were nice, but no question that they were whack. They took LSD every day. Every day. One's name was Noah Shark and the other one just went by Max. Max was Noah's lieutenant. Noah and Max would get out of bed, swallow some acid, and go, "Alright, let's make a record." Counterintuitive though it may be, they were actually pretty good at what they did.

Benmont Tench: Noah mixed a record by taking a strobe light, flashing it into your eyes so that's all you could see—and then you mix the record. [He'd say,] "We want the cymbals to sound like they're chasing the snare drum, like the bass drum is a big queen grape and the cymbals are mice scurrying after the elephant."

Denny Cordell: They were permanently tripping.

Tom Petty: Cordell would come in and out, in and out, checking to see how it was going. His comments were pretty meat-and-potatoes: "This is good." "You should re-record this." But, for the most part, he actually wasn't there that much. Cordell was a song guy. He taught me so much. His production came in many forms, a lot of them not in the studio. He'd sit me down with records, like— "Alright, let's see. We've got Lloyd Price today. Listen to this, this is Specialty Records out of Los Angeles." There's no manual for what a producer does or doesn't do. I've seen all kinds. Denny's approach often left us to our own devices in the studio. But he was still key. This is when we recorded "American Girl" and "Breakdown," some of the first hits we ever had.

ABOVE:

Benmont, circa 1976.

Stan and Tony Dimitriades, Santa Monica Civic, 1978.

OPPOSITE:

Benmont, circa 1976.

Shelter Records really was a kind of family scene. They had nothing to do with the way most of Hollywood was working at that time. We hung out at Shelter most every day. We'd go down to the grocery store on the corner and get a sandwich, just sit around there every day, in a bad part of town, too. We'd move between the office and the studio. That's where we'd figure out what the night's entertainment was going to be. This photograph was taken at one of the Shelter barbeques.

Because the label was a cool place, on any given day people were stopping by that weren't even Shelter artists. Musicians that had worked with them on this or that project would just drop in. We used to see Freddie King there, J.J. Cale. One day Georgie Fame might be in the studio.

Meeting George Harrison was another Shelter-related thing. Since I was signed to the label's publishing company and Leon Russell [Shelter Records co-owner] was a fan of my work, I would occasionally do some writing with Leon. He had called me one day and said, "I'd really like somebody to help me with lyrics on my next record." I'd go over to his studio, and sometimes we might write some lyrics and a lot of times we wouldn't. It was at Leon's studio that I met Ringo and George, who were both playing the session that day.

Benmont, Tom, Stan, Ron at Shelter Records Picnic, Malibu, 1976.

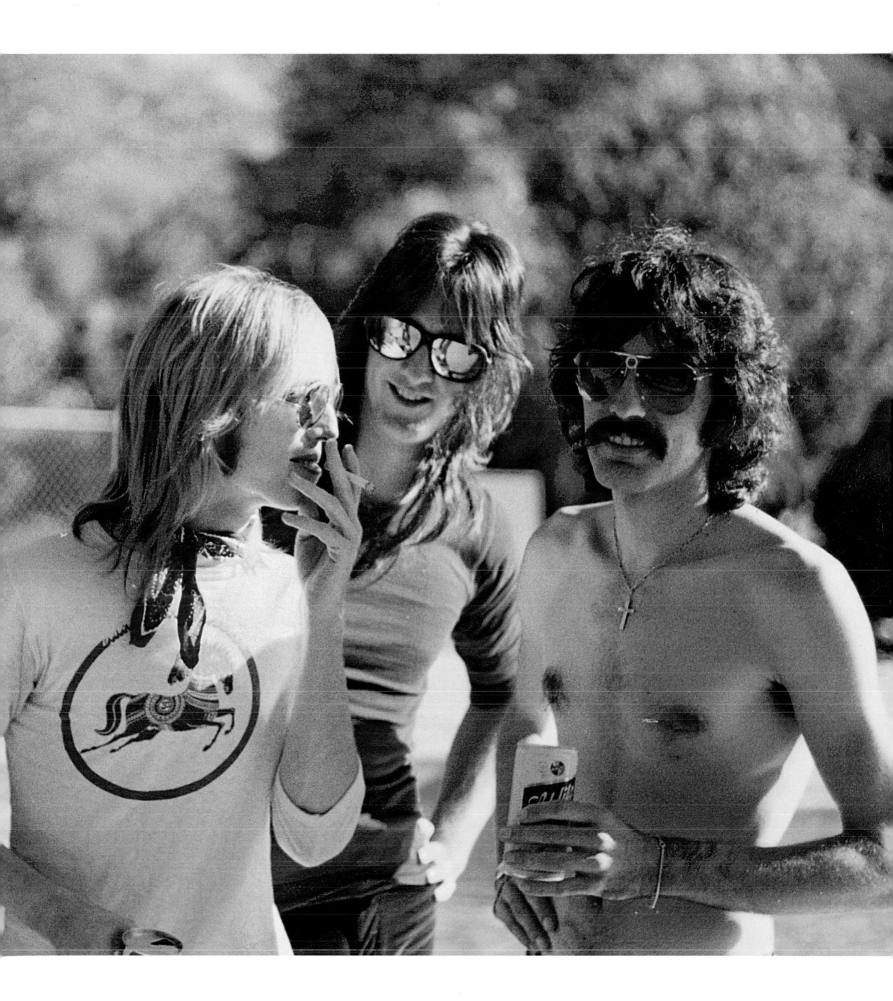

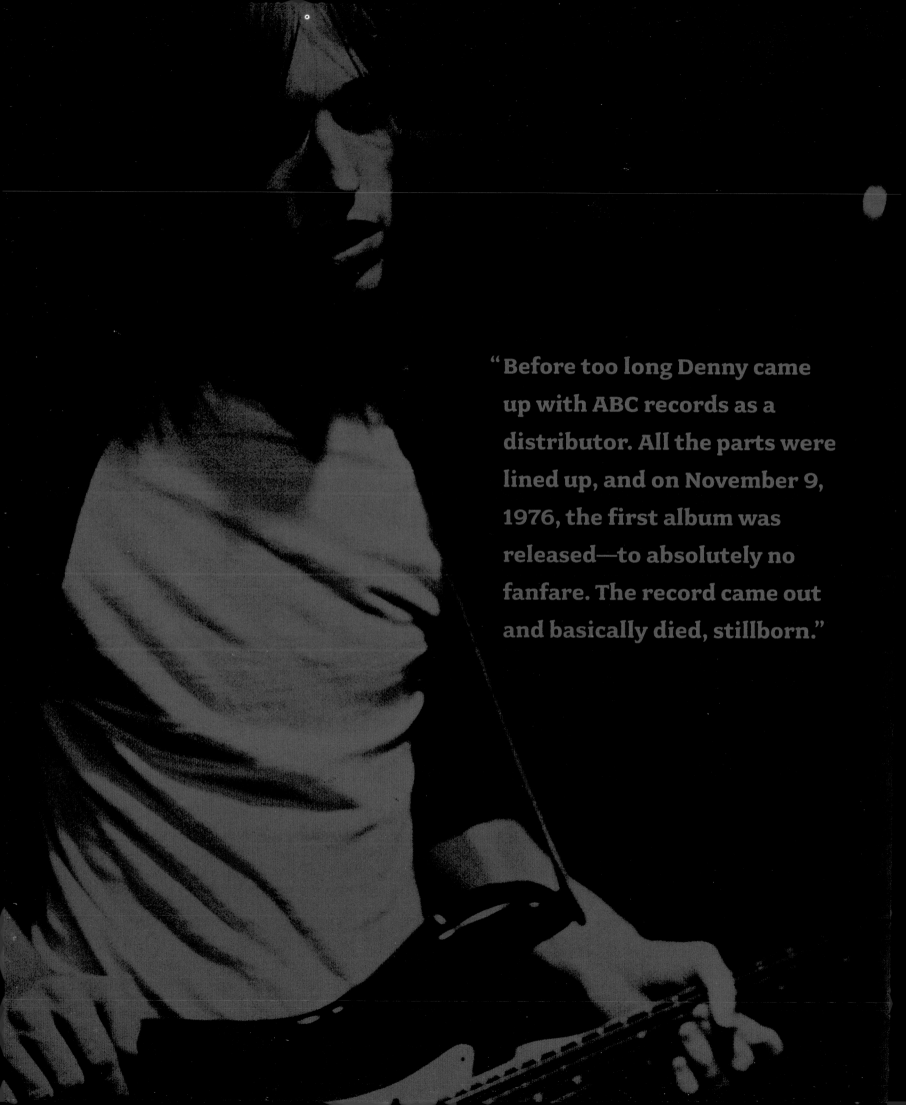

"Before too long Denny came up with ABC records as a distributor. All the parts were lined up, and on November 9, 1976, the first album was released—to absolutely no fanfare. The record came out and basically died, stillborn."

Tony Dimitriades: Denny Cordell helped Tom get this huge education about where it all came from. How rock and roll evolved. Which artists meant something and which ones didn't—which ones were the pretenders and which were the real thing.

Mike Campbell: "Rockin' Around (With You)" was the first song Tom and I ever wrote together, and he wrote most of it. I was just playing a little guitar riff. He goes, "That's cool. Make me a tape." He came back the next day and had put this whole song to it. I was pretty blown away by that. I was like, "Wow! Thanks guy. Let me write some more of those."

Benmont Tench: "Hometown Blues" is Mudcrutch with Duck Dunn from Booker T. and the MGs on bass. "Strangered In The Night" is from Tom's solo record. The rest of it is Heartbreakers.

Tom Petty: The first album feels like it took a long time to complete. I think that's because it had been a long time coming. It really didn't take that long once we were in the pocket. When the album got finished it was very exciting. Unfortunately, at this very moment the record company came to odds with MCA, their distributor. Denny Cordell and Leon Russell had some kind of falling out, ultimately splitting up their partnership. That left Cordell needing a new distributor for Shelter product, meaning us. So we sat waiting, feeling really discouraged.

Eileen Basich: Denny and Leon had their divorce, as such. That caused a lot of problems. For at least a year they couldn't release a record.

Tom Petty: Before too long Denny came up with ABC records as a distributor. All the parts were lined up, and on November 9, 1976, the first album was released—to absolutely no fanfare. The record came out and basically died, stillborn.

Benmont Tench: Our hometown paper said, Don't waste your time on this crap. Go buy the new Grand Funk record.

Tom Petty: But the story didn't end there. You need to remember that radio was very different in that time. There were stations in local markets that had a significant measure of autonomy, that weren't governed by a playlist generated off-premises. To our great surprise, a month or two later, our record starts to get some play in San Francisco and Boston. In fact, it started to get a lot of play. After the initial disappointment, I remember feeling like maybe, just maybe, a dream was starting to come true. It was just two markets playing the record—but they were key markets, music-lover markets. Then, like a bolt of lightning, Bam! —the record hits in England.

GOLD, MINED THE HARD WAY

Tom Petty: The record comes out in England, and it's an enormous success right out of the box. They're writing whole-page reviews and just going mad for it. But before we head over there, we need to play some dates in the States. Al Kooper, known for starting Blood, Sweat & Tears and playing with Bob Dylan but familiar to me from the solo sessions I did, invited us to open his club tour on the East Coast. We accepted.

We needed a manager and a road crew. Every manager in Los Angeles turns us down. No interest whatsoever. Denny Cordell finds a guy, this crazy Englishman named Reggie Locke, who was a friend of his and also Joe Cocker's manager. Reggie came down the studio, loved what he heard, thought that we were the greatest thing since sliced bread. Do I have to tell you that he got the job?

ABOVE:
Denny Cordell, circa 1970.

Sacramento's music magazine **Free**

MUSIC PHAZE

May

TOM PETTY

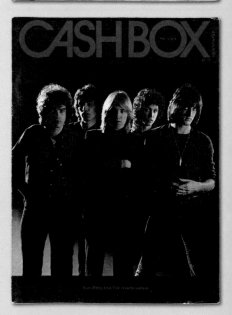

Tom Petty
Freeborn Hall — May 13

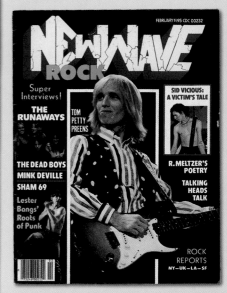

NEW WAVE ROCK

FEBRUARY $1.95 CDC 00232

Super Interviews!

THE RUNAWAYS

TOM PETTY PREENS

SID VICIOUS: A VICTIM'S TALE

**THE DEAD BOYS
MINK DEVILLE
SHAM 69**

Lester Bangs' Roots of Punk

R. MELTZER'S POETRY

TALKING HEADS TALK

ROCK REPORTS
NY—UK—LA—SF

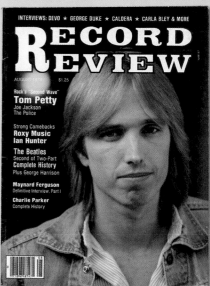

INTERVIEWS: DEVO ★ GEORGE DUKE ★ CALDERA ★ CARLA BLEY & MORE

RECORD REVIEW

AUGUST 1979 $1.25

Rock's "Second Wave"
Tom Petty
Joe Jackson
The Police

Strong Comebacks
**Roxy Music
Ian Hunter**

The Beatles
Second of Two-Part
Complete History
Plus George Harrison

Maynard Ferguson
Definitive Interview. Part I

Charlie Parker
Complete History

CASH BOX

"To our great surprise, a month or two later, our record starts to get some play in San Francisco and Boston. In fact, it started to get a lot of play. After the initial disappointment, I remember feeling like maybe, just maybe, a dream was starting to come true. It was just two markets playing the record—but they were key markets, music-lover markets. Then, like a bolt of lightning, Bam!—the record hits in England."

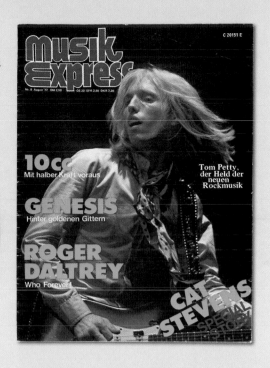

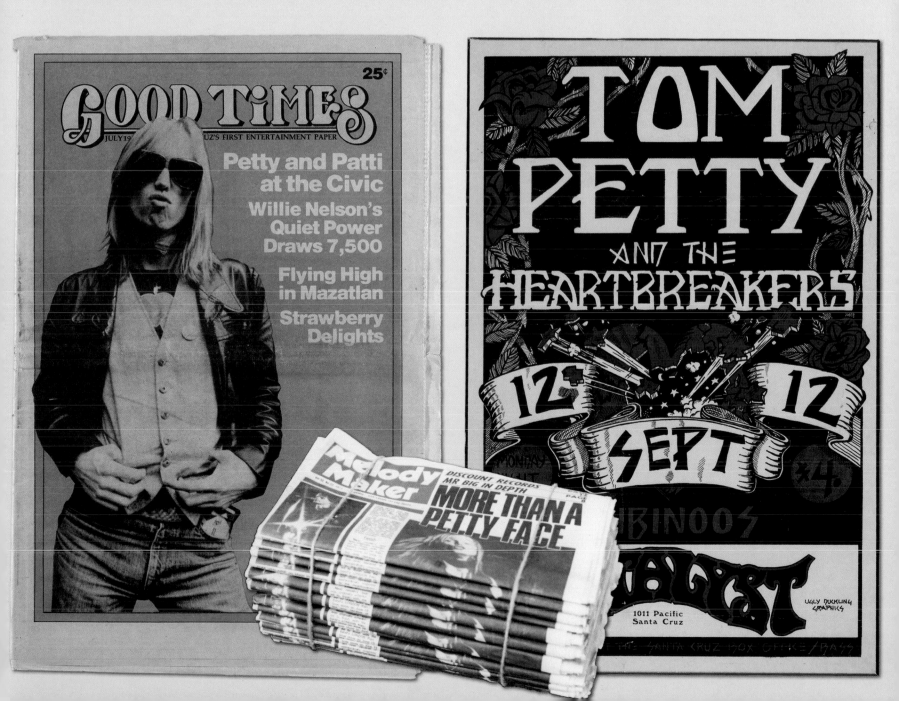

Tony Dimitriades: Denny Cordell played Reggie and me some of the album. It had "American Girl" and "Breakdown." We stepped into something really good and became the managers of the group. Reggie went on the road while I stayed home and took care of business.

Tom Petty: Reggie was a great cheerleader, made us feel like a unit. He fit right into the Heartbreakers-against-the-world mindset. Even if we were going onstage in the littlest shithole bar in Florida, he made us feel like it was Madison Square Garden. It was an attitude that was good for us, and one that we kept. In Reggie's view, every night mattered. We got this tour with Al Kooper that was named after Al's current release, the Act Like Nothing's Wrong Tour. The name couldn't have been more perfect, because no one came out to see the shows. Reggie's philosophy that every night mattered got its most rigorous test on the Act Like Nothing's Wrong Tour.

Immediately before the Al Kooper tour, we did a few club shows in south Florida and opened for Kiss in South Carolina. This was a time when no one knew who we were, so why not have us open for Kiss? But the band was cooking. We'd assembled a crew comprised of Bugs Weidel and Jim Lenehan, former lead singer of Mudcrutch, both of whom are still with the Heartbreakers today.

Jim Lenehan: The first arena was with Kiss. Nobody in the audience had a clue who Tom Petty and the Heartbreakers were. But they would go out there like they were the headliners. They would demand that people pay attention. And they did it. Boy, it worked.

Tom Petty: When we hit Boston, where our record was being played a lot, it was a really good feeling. I think it was the fourth night of the tour when we recorded a live broadcast that went out over WBCN in Boston. That recording was bootlegged—*Live at Paul's Mall.* I listened to it not long ago, and you hear this big crescendo of music followed by a handful of people clapping. There's nobody there. Things came slowly for us. Level by level. When we finished out that tour, it was time to go to England.

THE FIRST TIME YOU FEEL IT

Tom Petty: We went to England as an opening act for Nils Lofgren. From the moment we got off the plane, there were journalists to meet us, photographers taking our photos. We were on the covers of the weekly music magazines. This was big time for us. We were impressed. None of us had ever been to England, but all of us viewed it as a mecca. In our minds, this is where all of that music came from—Beatles, Stones, Animals, Yardbirds, Kinks.

We had a single called "Anything That's Rock 'N' Roll." It was never released as a single here, but it was moving up the British charts when we got there. We performed on *Top of the Pops*, the BBC weekly television show that, at least then, governed the charts. The first night of the tour was in Cardiff, Wales.

The label set us up with an English road manager, Mike North, who told us we were going to be traveling by bus. I remember us all standing in the hotel room, looking out the window to see our bus like excited schoolchildren. We don't see it. "Where's the bus?" we ask the road manager. He goes, "Right there," pointing to a little bread truck. In the back it had nothing but two wooden benches. So we sat in this little van, on wooden benches, facing each other, shuttling toward Wales. Then, at that first show the audience went insane. They rush the stage. For us it was the biggest mainline shot of adrenaline you can imagine. At that moment, bread truck or not, we thought, "Hey, we're really going to make it. This is going to work." It was an amazing time. Nothing will ever again feel like it did when it first started to happen. Nothing.

We did some more television, including *The Old Grey Whistle Test.* The more television we did, the more records we were selling in England. When that supporting tour ended, we stayed on in England, this time going out as the headliner. During this time we got to know Reggie Locke's partner, Tony Dimitriades, a bit better. The first thing he did for us was change our London hotel because we thought it looked too much like a dungeon.

Tony Dimitriades: There were some issues with Reggie's use of the money the record company had allocated for touring. It made for a lot of fun for the band, I'm sure, but it also made the money disappear rather quickly. Reggie kept calling me for more tour support. Finally Tom told me that I could be the manager if I would fire Reggie. So I had to fire Reggie.

Tom Petty: The tour winds its way through England, and it also hit Holland, Belgium, France, and Germany along the way. Touring with the Heartbreakers in those days, anything could happen day to day. It was high adventure. Everything was new. Everything was exciting. We were meeting lots of nice foreign ladies and trying to extend as much American hospitality to them as we could. We were thrilled.

Dave Stewart: Tom was probably the only American music that was acceptable in Britain—you know, when he came out with "American Girl."

Tom Petty: Then the tour ended. Next thing you know we're back in L.A. taking out the garbage.

Adria Petty: We were very poor. My parents rented our TV. They were always worried about money.

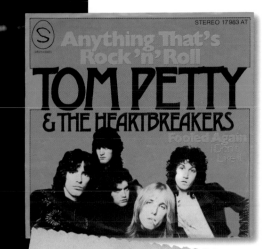

Anything That's Rock 'n' Roll

TOM PETTY & THE HEARTBREAKERS

Fooled Again (I Don't Like It)

POP MUSIC REVIEW

S.F. Smitten by Heartbreakers

BY ROBERT HILBURN
Times Pop Music Critic

SAN FRANCISCO—It's only two blocks from the Miyako Hotel to Winterland, where Tom Petty and the Heartbreakers shared the bill Sunday night with Bob Seger. The limousines that Petty's record company, Shelter, ordered were an obvious luxury. But Shelter's Denny Cordell figured a toast was in order.

After 10 years in rock 'n' roll bars and back streets, Petty, 24, could be on the threshold of something big. His growing radio airplay, strong concert response and glowing reviews make him a hot new property in a field whose vitality depends on finding new attractions.

Petty, who drew two standing ovations at Winterland,

TOM PETTY
. . . on the rock road since 15.
Times photo

begins a two-day stand tonight at the Whisky in L.A., then heads for England where one major pop newspaper called his LP the best debut by an American band in 1976.

Petty's album, which sold only 6,500 copies its first three months, has sold seven times that figure in recent weeks. A new single, "American Girl," could multiply it more. If so, Petty will be viewed by the rock industry and audience as another one of the lucky, unexplainable "over-

Please Turn to Page 12, Col. 1

We played the Marquee Club in London in 1978, around the time You're Gonna Get It! was released. We saw the Marquee as this great shrine. We associated it with bands like the Yardbirds and the Who and all those R&B-based rock bands of the mid-'60s.

The band thought it would be a fantastic place to play. God, it's a hot and sweaty place. It's very small, and it was really packed. I remember wondering if I was going to pass out from the heat. It certainly felt kind of triumphant, but there was very little oxygen.

We'd just played the Knebworth Festival to 100,000 people. Dealing with that size crowd takes a bit of learning. I think the Marquee show came about because we wanted to balance things out by playing a club. But our show worked in both places. We didn't really have any act except the one we did wherever we went. We did the same show at Knebworth that we did in clubs, and felt really good that it translated.

ABOVE:

Playing the Marquee, London, June 27, 1978.

ABOVE RIGHT:

Mike, circa 1978.

RIGHT:

Tom, circa 1978.

PREVIOUS PAGES:

Recording at the Shelter studio with engineer Max Reese and Stan, 1976.

FOLLOWING PAGES:

Knebworth Festival, Hertfordshire, England, June 24, 1978.

A CHANGE OF HEART

Tom Petty: Coming home was like going from pop stardom to "Welcome back, you really don't mean much in these parts." But, slowly, the press we got in England started to drift back here. The critic at the *L.A. Times*, Robert Hilburn, wrote a very nice review of us. He'd actually written about the album prior to that and given it a so-so review. Then he wrote a second one saying that he was wrong, that our record is actually really great. In a rare and wonderful instance of critical humility—we need all of that we can get, right?—he wrote a second review because he changed his mind. Then he did an interview with me, a nice piece. That got us a weeklong stand at the Whisky. By the time the shows happened, we were seeing lines around the block.

Randall Marsh: I didn't see them for a while, but then they played the Whisky. And it was like I'd never heard anything like that. It was like seeing the Beatles. I just went, "Shit!"

Denny Cordell: I remember when he played the Whisky. It was just . . . it was a red-hot band. The place was packed. They came on and they did everything perfect. That was a day that the tide turned.

Elliot Roberts: I saw them at the Whisky. Tom had the best collection of new songs by a new artist that I had heard up to that point.

Tom Petty: At one of these shows this fellow comes up to me in the dressing room—there wasn't much security in those days—and says, "You ever hear yourself on the radio in L.A.?" Then he said, "Remember my name when you hear yourself on the radio." Jon Scott. Another crank coming out the woodwork, I figured. Two days later I heard us on KROQ. Jon ended up being a key member of the Heartbreaker team. On a handful of stations like KROQ you could hear Elvis Costello, the Talking Heads, Blondie. Punk rock had loosened the ground a bit. As a result, the Heartbreakers were grouped with the acts that were a short, sharp reaction to the big, bloated seven-minute exercises of bullshit that you heard everywhere those days.

You've got to remember, there were other artists our age who still remembered when music was much more vital, who remembered Chuck Berry, James Brown, and the Beatles. Quite a few bands emerged at the time.

Maybe because I had a leather jacket on the cover of the first album, maybe because our songs hovered around three minutes or under, maybe because we had a raw edge to our production—whatever the case, we were labeled as punk rock by a lot of people. This meant that they didn't always listen to what was inside the record jacket. They just said, "Oh, punk rock," and dismissed it. Eventually we started to cross over to the mainstream radio stations. Add to this the fact that ABC was marketing us in funny ways, getting us into teen magazines like *Tiger Beat* and *16*. We did every-

thing we could to discourage that, worked at making sure we weren't cute. Then, to confuse the message further, we were opening up shows for bands like the Doobie Brothers one night and the Ramones the next. But, however odd the formula at the time, the music was cutting through. The music was our passport to a lot of places. By the end of that year we cracked the top forty with "Breakdown." As far as we were concerned, in 1977 we were sitting on top of the world.

Jackson Browne: I don't think anybody knew exactly what they were.

Dave Grohl: What I love about Tom Petty is that he was so hard to get a hold of. He was like a fish slipping out of your hands. Like wait a second, is he . . . they're a rock band, right? Yeah, but they wear those skinny ties . . . they're not new wave, are they? But he kind of screams like a punk sometimes. A blues band? You couldn't really tell because their range was so wide and the songwriting was so unique. I can't think of any band that sounds like Tom Petty and the Heartbreakers. He's just a bad ass. All of us loved him.

WANTED: SONGS FOR YOUNG ROCK-AND-ROLL BAND

Tom Petty: The second album dilemma is that you have most of your young life to write the first album and a year or less for the second. Add to that the fact that there's pressure to show the world that the first wasn't a fluke. I'd kept writing even after the first album was done. I was pretty vigilant in that respect. So we had some of the material ready when we went in to do the second album, and we made it really quickly. It went on to sell more than the first one, but, honestly, we didn't really need to have a new album out when we brought it out. Because the first one had been a sleeper hit—it took a good year for the first one to really saturate the marketplace—there was no rush. But what can you do with young men on an adventure who want fresh material for their live shows, right? We weren't businessmen, at least not yet. We were a rock-and-roll band.

You're Gonna Get It! marks the first time I took a production credit. I guess I realized that I was already doing the job of a producer in some respect. Cordell told me that any artist worth his salt is a coproducer. That made me think, "Well, okay, then I'm coproducer." For the first album I wouldn't have dared assume the title because I didn't know a thing about making records. By the second one, however, we'd spent more time in the studio, and Cordell was actually there less than he was on the first album. It was more like he'd come in every week and sum up what we were doing. He was definitely involved in the material. But for the day-to-day, it was me and the engineer, Noah Shark, and, of course, Mike was quite helpful. We were experimenting with sounds a little more on that record. It's a funny little record. Very short because we wanted the songs themselves to be short. I like it when I hear it.

Bill Flanagan: You listen to "No Second Thoughts" and you realize that that impulse of Tom's, that very artistic impulse, was always there along with the meat-and-potatoes rock and roll.

Tom Petty: We went in and worked good six-day weeks, and it was done before you knew it. There's a song called "Hurt" that has always been one of my favorites. That's where we first learned about loops; about how to make a tape loop. We did a percussion track where we're all playing percussion and then we had the loop going. We cut the track playing to this percussion loop. We were really pleased with that one. It was that kind of record. Lots of experimentation. We used a loop on another track, in fact. Maybe it was "Baby's A Rock 'N Roller." We did a lot of sound effects and were squishing vocals with compression and putting whatever else we could on them. A lot of tape delay. There's another good song on there, "No Second Thoughts," another one where we made a tape with percussion and played along with the tape. "I Need To Know" and "Listen To Her Heart" are on that record and became Heartbreaker staples.

"I Need To Know" was based on Wilson Pickett's "Land Of 1,000 Dances." I was trying to do something like that, though I clearly couldn't do anything like that—but that's what I was thinking of and it came out like "I Need To Know." That's how we were at the time. We were listening to anything we could get our hands on. It was a great educational phase. Because we were on a big record label, all of a sudden we got free records. So many records at our disposal. I could go down to Shelter and say, "God, you know, I really want to hear Wilson Pickett." And Cordell would give me ten Wilson Pickett records. He'd just order them and give them to me.

We were at a feast, listening to things we hadn't been able to hear because we didn't have the money. I got really caught up in wanting to write songs like what I was hearing, wanting to capture the feel of what I was hearing. It was really helpful. Just like "I Need To Know" was in a Wilson Pickett bag, "Listen To Her Heart" was really like a Searchers kind of song. It was a gumbo. What was going on in our heads then is we were trying to get every record we ever liked into what we were doing. That will always make something interesting. There are some out-there tracks. It's almost a little psychedelic at times.

After we finished *You're Gonna Get It!*, I got a letter from Elliot Roberts, who managed Neil Young and Joni Mitchell, and later the Cars and Devo. We were still running Heartbreaker business out of Tony's bedroom, with one assistant helping him out. I was thinking we needed more people on the case because the business was growing, the demands were greater and greater. In Elliot's letter he mentioned that if I ever need any help with management, he would love to be involved. Turned out he and Tony had worked together before, back when Tony was Graham Nash's lawyer. That was when Elliot entered the picture, partnering with Tony. The business moved into Elliot's offices on Sunset Boulevard. Elliot is kind of a mix of Gene Wilder and Woody Allen, but exactly what we needed to make that next step up the ladder.

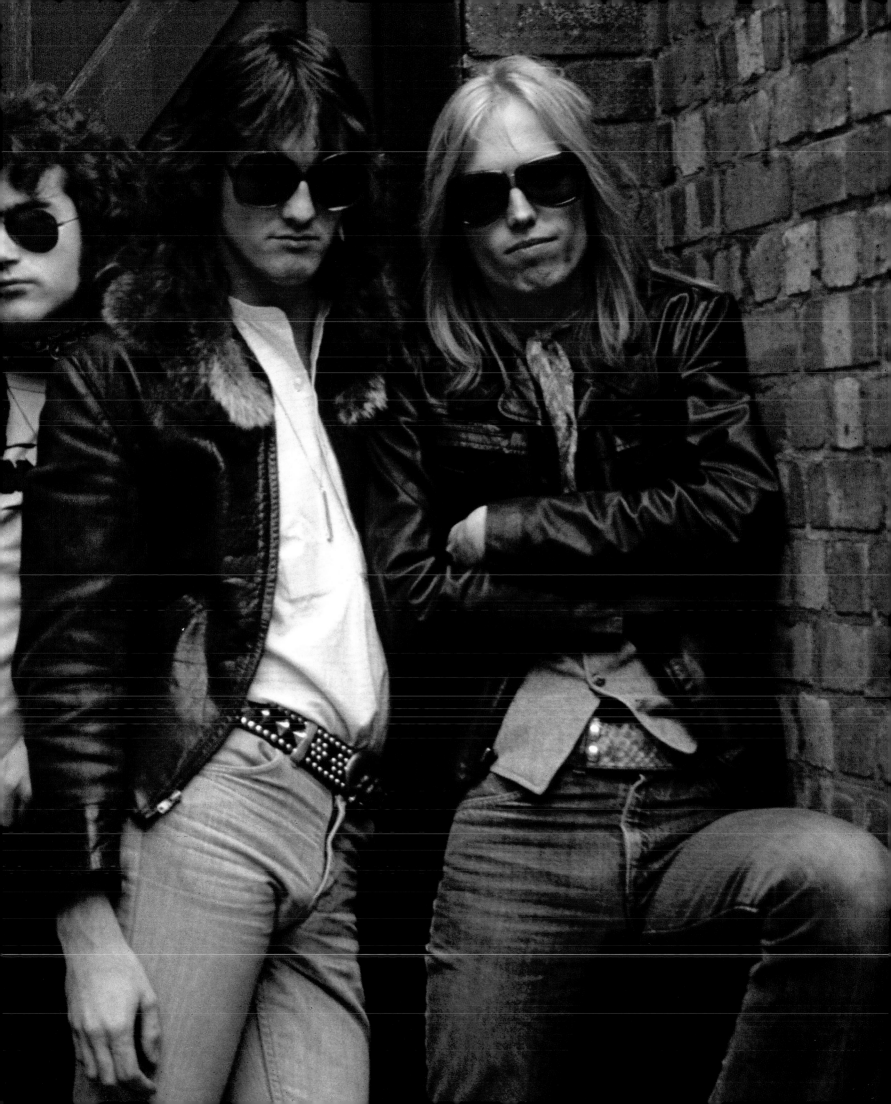

Chapter Three/ It's Just the Normal Noises in Here

Bigger personalities than Jimmy's are hard to come by. These days Jimmy . . . well, it seems like he owns the whole record business. He's a mogul, a kingpin. But in those days we knew Jimmy from his work as an engineer and producer. He'd engineered Bruce Springsteen's Born To Run. *He'd worked with John Lennon. But the thing that caught our attention was something he'd done with Patti Smith, a song Springsteen cowrote with Patti that Jimmy produced: "Because The Night."*

IT CAME FROM HELL'S KITCHEN

Tom Petty: I started the serious writing for *Damn The Torpedoes* as soon as we got off the road from supporting *You're Gonna Get It!* I think it was around early 1978, and we began recording some time that same year. I wrote "Refugee" and "Here Comes My Girl" with Mike. And that's where the recording process started.

Damn The Torpedoes was the record that kicked us up into the stratosphere. Initially in our career, success had come in stages. It seemed that for every leap forward there was a lesson in humility waiting just around the corner. We stayed grounded as we grew. We'd gone from playing clubs to playing theaters. The vehicles we toured in got a little bigger, a little more comfortable each time we went out. With every passing tour it was harder to remember a time when we shared hotel rooms. But when *Damn The Torpedoes* came out, the pace really picked up. I think we toured from late in '79 to almost fall of the next year, nearly ten months of work. So much changed in this period. A lot of significant things went down, things that were defining for me as an artist. But why not begin with a positive one, eh? Jimmy Iovine comes into our lives.

Denny Cordell: I know I can take some people only so far. Jimmy had made a record with Patti Smith that really impressed us all.

Tom Petty: Bigger personalities than Jimmy's are hard to come by. These days Jimmy . . . well, it seems like he owns the whole record business. He's a mogul, a kingpin. But in those days we knew Jimmy from his work as an engineer and producer. He'd engineered Bruce Springsteen's *Born To Run*. He'd worked with John Lennon. But the thing that caught our attention was something he'd done with Patti Smith, a song Springsteen cowrote with Patti that Jimmy produced: "Because The Night."

Denny Cordell had become too busy with his label to produce records. He wanted to oversee things but didn't really want to do the day-to-day work. So we started discussing who we might want in the studio with us. When Iovine's name came up, I thought, "Well, we can try him and see if he's interested." As it turned out, he was very keen to do it. He made plans to come to Los Angeles. "Don't worry," he tells me, "I'm going to come out and we will get going on this thing."

Now I'm about the same age as Jimmy, and we both come from humble backgrounds, but he's Hell's Kitchen and I'm the American South. We run at different speeds.

Mike Campbell: I think Jimmy sometimes got frustrated because we were, you know, from the South, a little slower.

Ron Blair: He was a guy that was a little more, uh, New York about it.

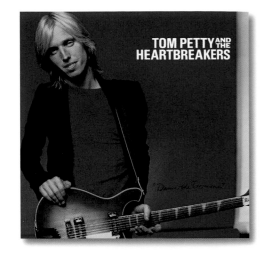

Jimmy Iovine: I was very confident. Overly confident. I broke up with my girlfriend to make that album. I had to come to California. I was so dedicated. I didn't care about anything. I didn't care about my shit or anybody else's shit.

Tom Petty: The fit was exactly what was needed. For the next several years I was, in many ways, closer to Jimmy than I was to anyone else on the team. We got very close.

So Jimmy comes out to L.A. Surprise number one? He shows up that first night with an engineer. I thought I was hiring him to be an engineer and a coproducer. He's no longer doing that, he tells me. Okay. Got it. I'm not going to make this a sticking point. He wants to hear what songs I've got, to know where we're going to start. He tells me he liked our first two records, so what have I got for this one. I play him "Here Comes My Girl" on my guitar. And I see he's looking kind of excited, and he goes, "Just that one? What else do you got?" I play "Refugee," again just me on the guitar. Jimmy looks around at everybody in the room and goes, "We're all going to be millionaires!" We liked him right away.

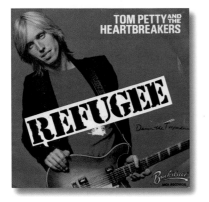

Jimmy Iovine: It's the first and last time I've ever said to anyone that they don't need any more songs. I've never said that to anyone since. Tom is one of the great songwriters of the rock era.

ONE MORE TAKE

Tom Petty: Jimmy worked like a dog on that record. We all did. We worked so hard. Eighteen-hour days. "Refugee" in particular. I think we did over a hundred takes over a period of time. The arrangement kept evolving, and we would keep hitting it.

Benmont Tench: Elvis cut fifty-six takes of, I think, "Hound Dog."

Rick Rubin: That's the way all the great records were made in the olden days.

Tom Petty: We chased the perfect take with a level of obsession that I have never repeated, not like that. We got so hypnotized with working on it that we never knew when to quit. But we got it. Jimmy probably still doesn't think so. For all I know, he may still be sitting there complaining about the drummer. But I think we got it, that our efforts paid off. That song became our calling card.

The process of recording "Refugee" wasn't just about getting the perfect take with the perfect feel. That was a big part, chasing that one special performance that really did the song justice. But we were also developing a drum sound that was much bigger than what we captured on our first records. We were going after a huge sound. What Jimmy did in that regard changed the way drums were recorded. For years that sound was imitated by a lot of people. To achieve it, we tuned the snare drums so low that the stick had no bounce back— usually the snare drum is very tight, and when you hit it with the stick, it bounces right back. This drum was tuned so low that there was no bounce back. Hit it and you had to pull up. This made it very hard on the drummer because he didn't get that expected response from his drums. It was like throwing a drummer into unfamiliar territory and expecting him to know his way around right away. And, frankly, Jimmy didn't always have the best bedside manner with Stan Lynch. Not that Stan always made it easy. The two of them were sometimes a pretty potent cocktail.

Mike Campbell: We wanted to make great records. Not just average records. Naturally, in a recording session the drummer is going to get most of the pressure.

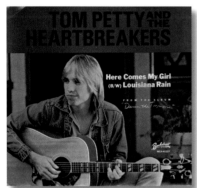

Benmont Tench: I don't think Jimmy liked the way Stan played . . . [but] Jimmy isn't the villain of the piece.

Jimmy Iovine: I had problems with drummers in general. Nothing ever sounded in time to me, the way Stan's backbeat lay slightly behind. . . . I was probably overreacting and being neurotic, you know? It was before Prozac. Before any of that shit. And being broke. The combination is tough.

Tom Petty: Once we got the right performance and the drum sound was in the vicinity of what we were after, the next step was to get the right sonic blend between the organ and the guitar and the drums. And the bass. We got there only through the principle of subtraction, meaning what we *didn't* play ultimately meant as much as what we did. Initially we were all trying to do those verses together, with guitars running through the whole thing. But the secret was to let the organ do it alone. Just have the guitars drop out and allow the voice and organ to carry it. That allowed a focus on the intensity of the lyric. That lyric carries a lot of the song's weight and needed space.

Jimmy Iovine: I learned so much from Tom. He has a dedication to writing that you rarely see today. He will never bring in a bad song.

Tom Petty: "Here Comes My Girl" was another song that we needed to play with in order to make its essential power come forward. The first key to achieving it came when we extended the verse. I couldn't get the right feeling with the short verse. We needed to let the tension build. Then the real breakthrough came when I started talking the vocal line. Do you remember how the girl groups sometimes did this, like the Shangri-Las on "Leader Of The Pack"? "Is she really going out with him? Let's see." By the time Mary Weiss sings, "I met him at the candy store," there is a remarkable emotional energy that's released. Very powerful stuff in that song. Elvis also did it in the song "Are You Lonesome Tonight?" There's that section where he breaks it down, goes "Someone once said the world is a stage." I stumbled on the idea because when we first extended the verse, the length felt right but you were tired of the guy singing before you got to the chorus.

I thought, well, what if he started talking? I got really excited because that gave me these two levels of emotion, and the chorus came as a huge release. It really worked. But, frankly, it took a little bit of courage to stand up there and talk the verse. It was a little bit like acting. I had to sell it without any notes.

I can't tell you how satisfying it was, as a creative process, to really understand the needs of the song, first, and then to answer them. We made some choices at the level of production that were crucial to how the song was heard and how the character, the guy singing, was perceived. We really understood how important character development was going to be with this song. And we got it right. We needed a lot of room to build that character. Iovine said it best, "At first you don't know if you like this guy—and then you suddenly love him." It's that build from the kind of shifty person speaking the verse to the guy singing in the chorus. It's a love song, a big love song.

Bill Flanagan: *Damn The Torpedoes* made radio stations realize that rock and roll still had some teeth left.

Tom Petty: With the record finished, we still had to mix it. The craziness carried over into that process. Jimmy never felt like we nailed it and was saying, "I don't know. I think we just have to mix it one more time. Let's go to New York and see what it sounds like there." So we did. Jimmy and I flew to New York with the tapes. We were crazy. I don't know why would it sound different there. I can't imagine he knew. He just thought, "Let's take it to the Record Plant in New York, mix it again, and see what happens." So we got into mixing it. We were in the studio when the engineer finally turns to us and says, " I don't know, you guys. I don't think I can

"I put myself into a situation where I wasn't simply in a battle with one record company—I was in a battle with all of them. I got tangled up in a legal situation that put a lot of what we were doing as a band at risk. Life went crazy for a while."

beat what you already have. I can't. What you've got here is pretty amazing. I don't think you should mix it anymore." And that's when we finally threw in our towels.

Jimmy Iovine: For a minute there we thought the album sucked. So we go into the studio and get the masters that we cut. And we put them on. And we realized, "Whoa, this shit sounds bigger than life!" I remember that moment. We both looked at each other. It was the greatest feeling in the world. That moment of doing something with your friend like that and having it become such a great record, such an important record at the time, there could never be anything to top that. Nothing. Nothing could ever beat that feeling. It's the most magical thing in the world. It's not like a movie where there's forty-five people involved. The record is you and this guy. Your family and his family.

PENNIES FROM HEAVEN?

Tony Dimitriades: Tom's first record deal involved a very low royalty rate.

Bill Flanagan: Like so many artists, Tom signed a bad deal. But he did what very few artists do, he actually stood up on his hind legs and said I will go to war for this.

Jimmy Iovine: We made the record under the pressure of the lawsuit. Extreme, extreme pressure.

Tom Petty: During the time that we recorded *Damn The Torpedoes* I learned a lot about the Heartbreakers as a band and about myself as a songwriter, producer, and bandleader. But it was also a defining moment in terms of me learning about the limits of my principles.

Jackson Browne: This is one of the first ways in which Tom distinguished himself. Everybody has had problems with their record company, but he really took it to the wall.

Tom Petty: I put myself into a situation where I wasn't simply in a battle with one record company—I was in a battle with all of them. I got tangled up in a legal situation that put a lot of what we were doing as a band at risk. Life went crazy for a while. Every night Jimmy and I were talking on the phone about how we were going to get the album out. We were in such deep water with the law at that point. We were hiding the tapes because they were threatening to take them.

It all began with the fact that I had a low royalty rate. But I had also signed away my publishing many years before, without understanding what that meant. I got my education along the way.

When Damn The Torpedoes *hit it was incredible. There was a great feeling of accomplishment, like we got something that we'd all been pulling for for years. I'm sure the lives of everyone in the band were changing so rapidly that they were just trying to hang on to this thing wherever it was going.*

Later on I could see it as the beginning of a lot of problems. You can't really bitch about it because, well, that's what you wanted, it's what you were trying to do. But that level of success brings with it the beginning of a certain amount of isolation. I focused more on the positive side. I thought it was fantastic that we'd broken through. We had a lot of hit songs on the radio, and this was in the glory days of FM rock. Damn The Torpedoes *was just made for that era. It really did well for us. The band didn't talk about it much among ourselves, but we all knew things were changing.*

Success seems very unreal. You work so hard and, when success comes, you've almost forgotten what you're doing. It's very hard to believe that things are going that good. You're waiting for the other shoe to drop. Your impulse isn't to assume it will go on like that for a long time.

ABOVE:

Mike in the dressing room, circa 1979.

PREVIOUS PAGES:

Tom, Mike, Stan, Ron, Benmont, NYC, September 1979.

Tony Dimitriades: He made a point of knowing what was going on in the business right from the time I started working with him. But when the lawsuit happened, I guess that's when he really got his education in business.

Tom Petty: When we first signed with Shelter Records, MCA was our distributor. Then somewhere in there we were moved over to ABC distribution. Because our first record took off, we were able to renegotiate the deal we had with ABC. When we did that renegotiation we were so nervous about things changing all the time that we had a clause added that said if our contractors sold to anybody else that they would need our consent and—this part is important—that we would have the right to leave or reach an agreement with whoever they're selling the contract to. ABC said okay to this. Next thing we know, they've sold the whole company to MCA. No one got our consent. I was furious. I felt like they sold us like we were groceries, frozen pork or something.

We went to MCA and said, "Well, wait a minute. You're going to have to let us go because of the clause in the contract." At that point we were told that we just had to forget about that and go along with what they had in mind for us. Of course, we were not in a position to fight a big corporation, which MCA was at the time. It was astounding to see a company of that size act like they were above the law—or, worse yet, to realize that they might just be. It could make you crazy.

Elliot and Tony said, "Well, there's a way around this. The royalty rate that they have you at goes all the way back to the deal Mudcrutch signed with Denny Cordell. It hasn't changed since then. You're making pennies on a record." They also said that on those terms we hadn't yet made enough to cover our debts to the record company. Understand that when a record company gives money, it ain't free. They're expecting it all back. At that moment, if you ran the numbers, we were not in the black. Until the band made enough royalties to pay back the cost of the recordings, we were in debt to the label. The common knowledge in the industry is that a label will float you, as long as you float. "Technically," my managers said, "you're bankrupt."

Here we are, thinking our ship had come in—we've had hit records, you know? And I'm told we're bankrupt. The point? If we're bankrupt, all contracts are void. Add to this the fact that ABC sold our contract without consulting us. It looked like we could walk. But, why stop there? Let's go on. We could also make the case that the publishing deal was not fair because it had been signed under duress. They had said, "You sign the publishing deal, or we won't sign the recording deal." I signed my songs away without even knowing what publishing was. This is, of course, a common practice in the business. Happens all the time. But I asked myself, "*Should* this happen all the time?" Boy did I open a can of worms for myself. I was a small figure, an ant, going at a very big issue that affected some very big people.

Mike Campbell: I'm happy to be the second seat to this guy because he doesn't take any shit.

AN INDUSTRY POWERED BY DREAMS

Tom Petty: I love the music business. It gave me a way out. But I also hate it. Here's an industry that would be nothing if it weren't for young people, typically outsiders, who have a dream they can't let go of—and then they sign bad deals. The hopes-and-dreams factor can give businessmen one hell of an advantage. From the artist side it's often, "Give me that contract." A head full of dreams, a whole lot of nerve and ambition, and no legal background. I was exactly what they were looking for. There's a lot of money to be made off of fellows who fit this description.

Jackson Browne: The record business is founded on thievery. It's robbery. From the beginning to the present it has been like a systematic ripping off of the artist. It's a deal with the devil when you make this agreement. What was that song from *The Last DJ*, with that line, "You get to be famous, I get to be rich"?

Tom Petty: I was being ripped off just like the black artists in the '50s and '60s, just like the innocent rock-and-rollers who were making the music that got me started. This industry has always taken in the hungry, talented youth and exploited them to its own advantage. I'm hardly unique. I just started thinking, "Here's this huge corporation, and they want to take my songs away from me? I wrote them. I should own them." When I signed that paper, I thought publishing was songbooks, I swear to God. I didn't know that when I signed that contract they owned the copyright to my songs and I would never see a dime for them. When I found out that was the case, I certainly knew that was wrong. So I figured I'm just going to fold my hands until somebody does something about this, until the label lets us go.

Tony Dimitriades: We refused to deliver an album.

Tom Petty: No more music. Then it turned into a big deal because, apparently, were I to prove myself bankrupt it would set an industry standard that would allow lots and lots of people to use the same argument and leave their contracts. For this reason, more and more lawyers were showing up on the scene. Lots of lawyers.

MCA brings me to this big lawyer. But before he comes out—they're doing this like a real show—he has an opening act, a few lesser lawyers who try to talk legalities. I didn't really understand what they were talking about. Then the big guy comes out. He says, "Let me tell you something, kid. You're going to forget this whole thing. You're going to make your records and shut up. You don't have a leg to stand on here. You don't have

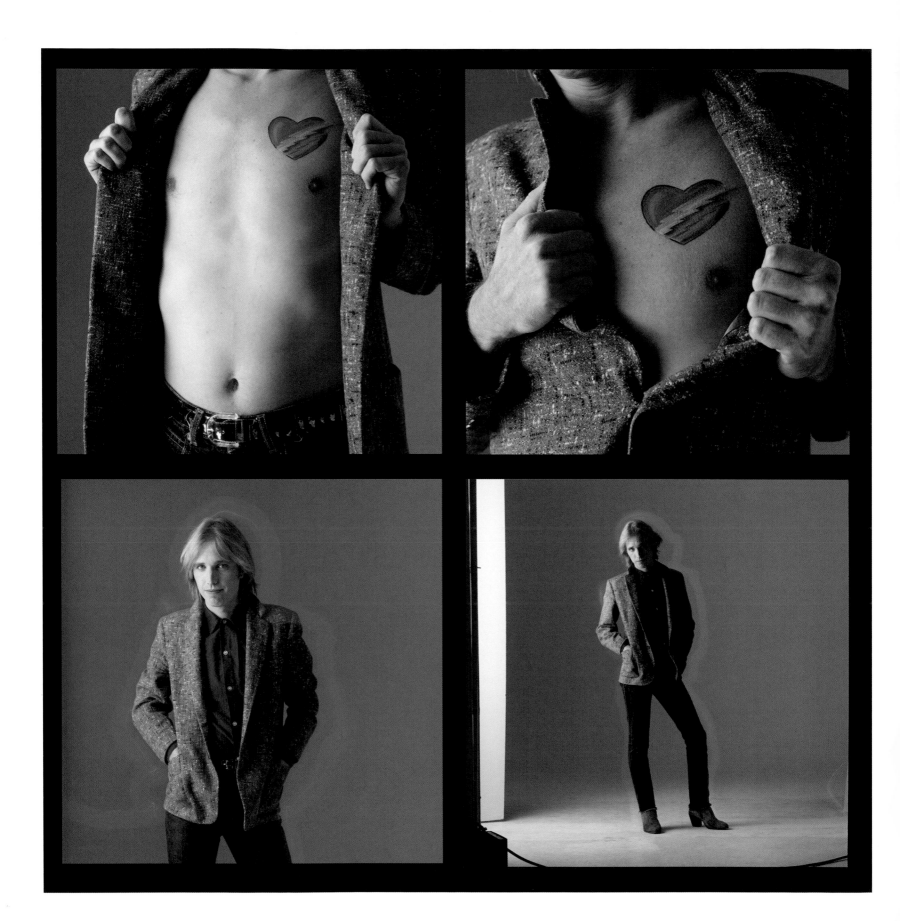

near the money you would need to pull this off. Do you see what I have here? Do you see this office? You think I got this because I don't know shit? You shut up and go make your records."

Now, you can imagine my personality, especially in those days. He was as good as baiting me. I said, "Look, I will sell fucking peanuts before I give in to you. You can break me, but you can't make records, can you? You can't sing. And I ain't going to buckle, not until you let us go. I will file for bankruptcy and take it all the way to the Supreme Court if I have to." It was a standoff. It made me mad. I wasn't going to be talked to that way. For me, this was just another giant to throw stones at. I wasn't buying it that this corporation was so powerful that they could just tell us what to do.

So Elliot Roberts bankrolled us, paid for all of the attorneys and the recording. And I filed for bankruptcy.

Tony Dimitriades: There was an audible gasp around the music business.

CHAPTER ELEVEN

Tom Petty: It wasn't a pleasant experience at all. I was never found bankrupt. Understand that I had plenty of dough in my pocket. It wasn't that. The bankruptcy case was based on the premise that we couldn't possibly pay back the money we "owed" the label under the terms of the record deal. But then—and here is where it gets cold—they took away our right to perform. They put an injunction on us. I had to go to the court and show just cause that we needed to perform. The judge says, okay, you can play a tour. That was what we called The Lawsuit Tour. We had shirts that said "WHY-MCA" on the front.

We finally went to court. The case is being heard and witnesses are being called. And at the last minute MCA buckles. They realized I'm not going to give up, which I wouldn't. What did I have to lose? I'm going to see it all the way through. Even if I did lose, what are they going to do? Take my songs away from me? That had already happened. The tide started going my way in the courtroom. At the end of it all, what they did was give us our own label at MCA and give me my publishing back. MCA would be the distributor. We started a record label called Backstreet Records. Our first release was *Damn The Torpedoes*, the title of which came from that whole tumultuous experience.

Bill Flanagan: He'd been involved in a lot of legal battles. He was out of the spotlight for a while. People didn't know if the band was going to break up or if they would ever be back. It was a moment of triumph when they came back, like the good guys are actually winning the war.

FOLLOWING THIS I HAD TO FOLLOW THAT

Bruce Petty: I think that's really when we went, "Wow! He's made it. This thing is really going to go."

Tom Petty: *Damn The Torpedoes* took us all the way around the world, from America to Europe back to America to Australia, New Zealand, Japan, and then back for another tour of America. After we got home, that's when it first dawned on me—you're competing with yourself now. You're going to have to give them another great LP. At the same time, I recognized that the artist in me didn't want to do the same thing. A lot of folks do that in the record business, but we always frowned on people that made the same record again with different words or whatever. We were going to try and take it somewhere we hadn't been. And I think we did.

I was already working on *Hard Promises* when I got a call letting me know that my mother had died. The last time I'd seen her was on the *Damn The Torpedoes* tour. She was very sick and was in so much pain that I knew it probably wasn't going to go on. When I got the call that night I almost felt a sigh of relief for her. It was another cloud on that year for me. You can file things like that away, but they're still working on you.

Getting our first Rolling Stone *cover was a very exciting thing for us. It meant you had arrived in a big way. When that issue of* Rolling Stone *finally came out I was lying in a hospital bed. I'd just had my tonsils out. Someone came in and dropped it on the bed. I couldn't really talk. I just looked at it and smiled.*

PREVIOUS PAGES:

The Heartbreakers backstage at the No Nukes concerts, Madison Square Garden, September 1, 1979.

Top right: Tom with Jackson Browne and Elliot Roberts.

FOLLOWING PAGES:

On the set of "Woman In Love," 1981.

My mother could see my success coming. I remember sending her a gold record when the *You're Gonna Get It!* album got there, and she was happy about that. The last time I saw her she couldn't speak well, but she had some newspapers that she had saved and showed me she was aware of what the record was doing. She was really proud. It's a great regret of mine that I could have made her life so much better at that point, but she wasn't there anymore. I think I came back and addressed the loss with *Southern Accents*, but at the time I didn't want to deal with it musically.

Adria Petty: It was sad because it was the first time that he had success, and he didn't get to share it with her. That was hard on him. I remember him . . . it was like some light went out. She really believed in him.

Tom Petty: So I was writing songs for what would become *Hard Promises*. The rest of the band was out chasing women. They're out having a great time and enjoying the fruits of our labor. Really, I remember this as a nice time. We all got nice cars and started buying homes. You would come out of rehearsal, and there would be five shiny black cars—they were all black for some reason. But, for me, most nights and most days my time was spent trying to write songs.

Jimmy Iovine was coproducing again, so this meant we were on the phone a lot, talking about where we might take the recordings. For Mike and me it was all about learning to make records, that whole time of *Hard Promises*. We were very curious as to how you got sound from your head to the tape. It wasn't always as simple as just playing it. It was how you played it, where you played it, what unexpected noise you could get from something, what microphone you used. The whole art of recording became a matter of greater interest. We started to change and experiment a little bit with song style, with sounds. I think *Hard Promises* sounds like we were trying lots of different things.

It turned out good. If not exactly what people expected, it did well.

Eddie Vedder: I waited in line. I skipped class and waited in line, brought the record home at lunch, learned the song "The Waiting," and went back to school with it in my head. Then I was playing it by the time I went home.

Jackson Browne: "The Waiting" kills me.

Tom Petty: "The Waiting" was a big hit and "Woman In Love" was on its way, at least until another song, not from *Hard Promises*, stopped it. But that's a story that requires a little set-up.

NO GURLS ALLOWED

Tom Petty: This was, of course, when we got to know Stevie Nicks better. After this year-long campaign of "write me a song," I finally wrote something for Stevie. She said she was going to leave Fleetwood Mac to make a solo record. Initially the way she put it was this: "I'm going to leave Fleetwood Mac and join the Heartbreakers." We would go, "Well, that's interesting, but there aren't any girls in the Heartbreakers. You can be our friend but you can't be in the band."

Stevie Nicks: I joined Fleetwood Mac on the first day of 1975. I think I started to become a fan of Tom Petty's in 1977. By 1978, a big fan of Tom Petty. By 1979, if Tom Petty and the Heartbreakers had called me up and said leave Fleetwood Mac and come join us, I would probably have left Fleetwood Mac.

Tom Petty: She hung around all the time, and God bless her, she's got some staying power I'll tell you, because we did not make it easy for her. I finally tell her I'm going to give her a song, and it's this really beautiful song

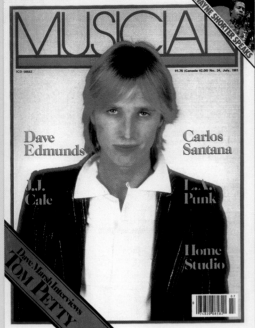

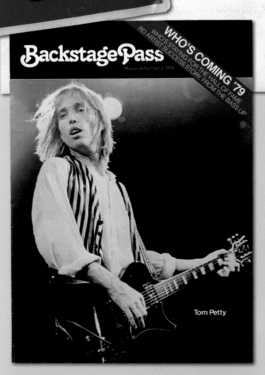

TOM PETTY AND THE HEARTBREAKERS

Expenses - U.K. and Europe - Spring 1980   "Damn the Torpedos"

Trucking:	2 semis (including fuel, tolls, ferries, tax and hotels for drivers)	$25,000.00
Airfares:	Approx. 15 people @ $1,000.00 each	15,000.00
Freight:	Round trip $1.17 per lb. est. at 6500 lbs. + carnet + bond	15,810.00
Pay:	Band - 6 wks. at $500.00 x 5 people	15,000.00
	Crew - 6 wks. at $2,700.00 per wk.	16,200.00
	Crew (perdiem)- 40 days x $25.00 p. day x 5 people	5,000.00
Buses:	2 - U.K. for 20 days @ $260.00 per day	10,080.00
	2 - Europe for 3 wks. @ $1,500.00 per bus	15,000.00
Misc:	Including hire of piano, rehearsal in U.K., cars in London, repair, etc.	10,000.00

(includes band, road crew & bus drivers)

London-	Band- 7 singles @ 11 days x ₤45.00 p. day		7,000.00
	Crew- 5 doubles @ 7 days x ₤50.00 p. day		3,500.00
Provncs.-	Band- 7 singles @ 12 days @ ₤25.00 ea.		7,000.00
	Crew- 5 doubles @ 15 days @ ₤30.00 ea.		4,500.00
	2 bus drivers-singles-(1) 12 days @ ₤25.00		600.00
	(2) 15 days @ ₤25.00		750.00
Europe-	Band-7 singles @ 16 days x ₤40.00 p. day		9,000.00
	Crew- 5 doubles @ 17 days x ₤50.00 p. day		8,500.00
	Bus driver singles (1) 17 days @ ₤40.00		1,360.00
	(2) 16 days @ ₤40.00		1,280.00
Rehears:	Per estimate at Electrasound - including rehearsals		50,000.00

TOTAL $217,780.00

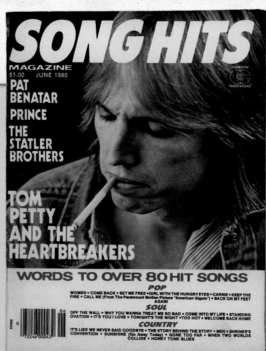

ICD08675   FEBRUARY 21ST, 1980 • ISSUE NO. 311 $1.25 UK 70P

Rolling Stone

Tom Petty

*'Damn the Torpedoes'
and Full Speed Ahead
By Mikal Gilmore*

Henry Kissinger

*The Prince of Power
under Siege
By Tom Wicker*

Hotline to Heaven

*A 'Holy' Housewife
Battles the Church*

McCARTNEY BUSTED IN JAPAN

**CAMBODIA BENEFIT: Wings,
Who, Zeppelin, Rockpile,
Elvis Costello, Clash**

called "Insider." I took it to the studio, and Jimmy was elated with it. He was just knocked out, and said, "I can't believe you're going to give this away."

We immediately sat down, the five Heartbreakers, and started working out the song. Jimmy was there looking over our shoulder. We cut the song in anticipation of Stevie coming down to sing it. She appears the next day—and it's a complicated song, so we played it quite a bit for her—and she likes it. But, as we run the track for her, she doesn't sing the lead on it. She sings a beautiful harmony, really beautiful. But it was me carrying the melody. When we got to the end of the night I said to her, "I'll be honest with you, Stevie. I don't really want to give you this song. I like it a lot. I know I said I was going to give it to you, but I'm not going to give it to you. I'm really sorry." She was great. She tells me it's no problem and says, "To tell you the truth, I was looking for something with a little more tempo."

Stevie Nicks: I wanted to have a solo record that sounded like Tom Petty. I don't know what you would call it, that Florida swamp rock-and-roll, Southern religion thing that Tom has.

Tom Petty: At that point I learned that when you're writing a song for somebody you always tend to write one that you think sounds just like them. But the reason they're asking you to write them a song is they want something that doesn't sound like them.

I felt apologetic about taking "Insider" back. At that point I had four or five songs that had been recorded for the *Hard Promises* album that I hadn't gotten around to finishing, even though they had vocal and track recorded. One of these was "Stop Draggin' My Heart Around," which she liked. I told her she can take it. Then it became a little bit like Spy vs. Spy when Jimmy got involved. I started to think I should finish the song and then decide if we should give it away, because we had done that with the other one. He said, "No, I hear a girl singing this song."

Stevie Nicks: Jimmy really moved the chess pieces to make it possible for me to have a solo career.

Jimmy Iovine: Stevie has even changed the story. I saw her recently. She says, "It's because you were my boyfriend." I mean, she's horrible because she will immediately side with Tom. She will go right there.

Tom Petty: Now I've heard a lot of different people tell me stories about how Jimmy maneuvered to get that track for Stevie and that Jimmy Iovine was kind of shady, that he knew all along that that's what he wanted to do. Convincing stuff. I don't know if it's true or not. From my standpoint, I didn't see him do anything like that. Part of me thinks Stevie was just bound and determined to get the song and got it. There were so many hits we were having at that point in our life that I don't think we were that upset or concerned about it. Stevie did a great job on it. It was a huge record. And I'm sure it bought a lot of bicycles for our kids. The only gripe we ever had about "Stop Draggin' My Heart Around" was that it sort of knocked "Woman In Love" out of the water.

Mike Campbell: I remember Stevie was in New York, checking into the hotel the same time we were checking out. She came running up to me and said, "Did you hear our song? It's a big hit!" And the first thing out of my mouth was, "Yeah, it killed our single dead."

Jimmy Iovine: Now, years later, at my fortieth birthday, Bruce Springsteen gets up and says, "Tom, he stole 'Because The Night' from me, for Patti Smith." These guys tell the stories with absolute fabrication. But they make for great stories.

RollingStone

ISSUE NO. 348 • JULY 23RD, 1981
$1.50 UK 80p

TOM PETTY

ONE MAN'S WAR AGAINST HIGH RECORD PRICES

What everyone leaves out is that Tom and I really, really believed that "The Waiting" was the biggest song he ever cut. And we were wrong. I thought "The Waiting" was five "Stop Draggin' My Heart Around"s. Now I see Tom sometimes, I say you know, I think there were too many words in the chorus. This is fucking thirty years later, and I'm still like, "Why wasn't that song a bigger hit?"

$9.98

Tom Petty: When we were doing the *Hard Promises* album, things got difficult because we wound up in another fight with the record company.

Tony Dimitriades: I walked into a record store and I saw this sign up behind the counter saying, "Coming soon, new Tom Petty—$9.98!"

I called the record company and I said, "What's with this? I saw this thing at a $9.98 list price." They tell me, "Oh yeah, we're going to put it up. We can make more money on this album." I said, "I feel sure that Tom is not going to want that." I called Tom and he freaked out. He said they weren't going to raise their prices on his back. And we refused to deliver the album.

Tom Petty: This was the last thing I wanted, but the record company was looking to use our popularity to increase record prices across the board. I didn't want to land in that briar patch again, but it was deflating. Like a fool, I stood up to them and said, "No, you can't do it to us. That's too much money." It's funny now, but at the time $9.98 seemed like an outrageous amount of money for an LP. So, there I am again in hot water with the record company. And I've made my case so that there is no way to back out or concede the point. It was around then that I started to get a little depressed about the whole thing and thought, you know, this is just more than I signed on for. Once again it became like I was fighting with all the labels, because no one was too keen about me stopping the increase. The press made a big deal of it, but I can't say I ever saw another artist back me up on it. It was more like, "Let him be the sacrificial lamb, and we'll see what happens and if he gets away with it." I did get away with it. I got the record out at a lower price. But I don't think I was the same human after that. I think it beat me up pretty good. It was traumatic.

It went on for months. But they finally backed down. I suppose they figured they'd sneak the higher price on someone else later. The truth is that this really did keep the price of records down for a long, long time. There was nobody that wanted to do it after I was on the cover of *Rolling Stone* tearing the dollar bill in half. I was making statements like, "I don't really need the extra buck. I don't understand why they do." It was a long time before they creeped the price up, and I'm kind of proud of that because I had something to do with it.

Bill Flanagan: Tom Petty has fought a lot of public battles.

Chapter Four/
Between
Two Worlds

I'm proud, really proud, of how long the Heartbreakers have stuck together. Here we are today, traveling with four original members after thirty years. That's an achievement. Not too many bands can make this claim. My feeling is that you'll never really know what a band is, what it can do, if it doesn't have time to reveal its identity.

A BIKINI STORE?

Tony Dimitriades: I don't remember if Ron actually quit. I think he demonstrated that he wanted to quit by not showing up a couple of times, and I had to fire him, is what really happened.

Ron Blair: It just kind of happened, and I was relieved to not be doing that for a year. At the time I had a lot of issues with the music business. I thought that it was a little sleazy and funky and full of people with egos. I was right.

Tom Petty: There was a lot of pressure in the studio on the rhythm section, and he began to be there less and less as I remember it. If he was late, Mike or I would play the bass, and I think that hurt his feelings in a way. He just left. Was he fired? I don't think so, but I think by the time he was going to leave we were all on the same page. He didn't just leave us, he left the music business. Opened a bikini store.

Jim Lenehan: Opened a bikini shop. I would have never called that one.

Tony Dimitriades: Ron was a wonderful, easygoing guy, but the pressures of success were taking their toll on him. On some level, Tom and Ron were at different ends of a spectrum. As the business grew and got more complicated, Tom dug right in, asserting himself as the leader. He was always much more than a great songwriter and performer—he instinctually knew how to lead a band. But Ron, well Ron drifted away as the operation took on more complexity.

Ron Blair: There used to be a hotel on Sunset Boulevard called the Tropicana. I think Tom Waits had a room there year-round. Bowie was staying there. And I just stayed there for months during the lawsuit. Just by the pool or whatever. Just waiting for things to settle up. I could have waited a few more months. It was fine with me.

Elliot Roberts: When you wake up at four in the morning and make notes so that the next morning you don't forget what you were thinking—that's how you live your life when you're on a project. That's how Tom is. That's how Neil [Young] is. That's how Bob [Dylan] is. That's how Joni Mitchell was. Those kinds of artists are twenty-four-hour artists. They're not nine to five.

Eileen Basich: Tom was the one. He wrote the songs. He sang the songs. He had the ideas. I think it was always obvious.

Tom Petty: Playing in a band has been one of the greatest joys in my life. I'm proud, really proud, of how long the Heartbreakers have stuck together. Here we are today, traveling with four original members after thirty years. That's an achievement. Not too many bands can make this claim. My feeling is that you'll never really know what a band is, what it can do, if it doesn't have time to reveal its identity. If you put a group of great players together who share a love for a particular kind of music and allow them to develop, something is going to happen. But you won't know what it is until you get there. The surprises have kept me deeply engaged. But there's no doubt that personnel issues have been among the most challenging issues for me as a bandleader.

BREAKING IN A NEW HEARTBREAKER

Tom Petty: There was a guy named Del Shannon who was sort of a rock-and-roll legend in the early '60s—late '50s. I had always been a big fan of his and ran into him one day in 1978, I think. He was talking to me about producing a record for him. Would I be interested in that? I was very interested. I had never produced a record for anyone except for us, so I took the job. I thought it would be fun, and it was. It wasn't a real hard record to make. At one point we had a few overdubs left to do on it. We needed bass on a couple of tracks. I asked Del if he had anyone. He said, "Oh, yeah, I've got a kid in my band who plays great."

In walks Howie Epstein. He looked really striking, three-foot pompadour all brushed back, a big gold earring, and Cuban heeled boots. He really looked like somebody you should take seriously—and he was really good. What really knocked me out was when they went to do some vocals. Del brought him out, he sang, and I was like, "Wow! This kid is a really good singer." I decided in my mind that I was going to steal this guy and put him in the Heartbreakers. My dream had always been to have a very solid harmony singer.

We had Stan, who was a harmony singer, but I wanted somebody who could get above Stan, with a high tenor voice. If we could do that, we would have three voices. I just wanted one more voice. I made it my business to go down and see Howie. I went down to a rehearsal they were doing, Del and his band, and they were going to play in Phoenix. So I flew into Phoenix to see the gig. I cornered Howie and asked what he would think about joining the Heartbreakers. He was surprised, but quickly said he'd love it. He asked when I wanted him to start. I said, "Well, Ron's leaving, and the other guys will need to see you, but I think you're going to get the job." That meant right away.

Howie Epstein: Sometimes I wondered how it was for them, being together and growing up together, what it would be like to have this new guy in the band? Sometimes I think it was weirder for them than for me. I can appreciate my change in fortunes, though. I know the other end way too well, trudging through the Midwest in vans and U-Hauls in twenty-below-zero weather. I never take it for granted.

Tom Petty: I get home and Del Shannon calls. He's furious and says, "Don't take Howie. You cannot take Howie. I count on him so much. You can have anybody you want, but don't take Howie. Why would you take my guy, we're friends?" I said, "Del, I love you, but I'm taking Howie." And that was that. Del got over it after a while. Howie was a friend for some twenty years after that. He was as crazy about making

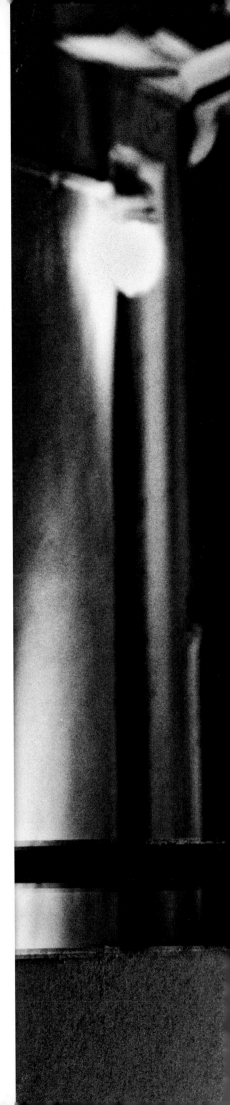

PREVIOUS PAGES:

Tom and Del Shannon, Cherokee Studios, February 1981.
Publicity photograph from the Southern Accents period
(note Tom's broken hand).

records as we were, and he turned out to be a pretty good producer in the end. An unusual guy. He had no interest in celebrity or being famous or anything like that. He never gave an interview that I know of, completely shunned all that, but he was a true musician. His first record with us was *Long After Dark*.

STRAIGHT INTO DARKNESS

Bill Flanagan: I think of *Long After Dark* as being a real band record. It's a record that I really, really loved. It has one of my favorite Tom Petty songs, "Straight Into Darkness." He has this ability to write something that everybody can identify with.

Benmont Tench: Tom was singing so well [around that time] it would blow your mind. My favorite cuts . . . there's an absolutely lovely song called "A Wasted Life." And "Straight Into Darkness." And "Between Two Worlds."

Jimmy Iovine: *Long After Dark* was my third album working with the band. After three albums you should shoot your producer. I mean, except for George Martin. I don't think I was as focused as I was earlier.

Tom Petty: It had a big single called "You Got Lucky." I think it's a good album. The last time I heard it, it was pretty good. The only thing I could say that I didn't like about it was that it wasn't really going forward enough for me. I think it's imperative that you move everything forward with each recording. It was sort of a "tread water" album. We're doing what we're supposed to do here—we're not really going forward.

Tony Dimitriades: I've never seen another artist who judges his or her own work with such scrutiny. He can be very self-lacerating.

Tom Petty: There was some music cut that didn't get on *Long After Dark*, music that I felt would have made it a better record. But Jimmy Iovine and I didn't always see eye to eye on the material. He thought some songs sounded too country. They didn't sound country to me. And I think our choices hurt the album in a way. There was a really good song called "Keeping Me Alive" that I really love. Somehow it was decided it wouldn't go on, and I think it would have made a difference if it had. You live and you learn. Most of the time.

I think we kept setting the bar higher. If we'd come out with a real stinker and then came out with *Long After Dark*, then we might have had it easier. But we're pretty steady. I don't think there are many groups in rock and roll that have had our career. In a way, it makes you a little less appreciated at times because your audience is taking for granted that it's going to be good. There are things on that record, like a song called "Finding Out," that's fantastic. "Straight Into Darkness," a really,

really good song. I think that was a better record than we got credit for at the time. It's like, oh yeah, they've got a hit song on the radio, but it wasn't really applauded. What am I to do? Spoiled and mistreated, right?

BRINGING IT ALL BACK HOME

Tom Petty: We would go on tour and get back from the tour and go straight into the studio. If there was a break of any kind, I had to use it to write because I always needed ten or twelve songs. We didn't like to sit around much: everybody was anxious to keep going. And we did.

Needless to say, it's very hard to try to have a family and do this routine. My kids didn't see as much of me as they would like. I don't know how you could do the conventional family thing. Your life as a performer has got nothing to do with anyone else's. Because of this a lot of your friends become people who are musicians and can relate to how you live your life. This was how I had been living since I was very, very young. If I wasn't playing shows, I was trying to figure out how to. But it was in my mind to find out if I could have it both ways.

So, I get a brilliant idea: put a studio in the house. That's when *Southern Accents* was made. The line between family and work got a little confused in there. I mean, I already had some trouble stopping working. This gave me new territory to explore in that regard. We approached that new situation with some unwritten rules, like if I was home and writing or in the studio, we never let the girls in there. No gals down at the studio, just the band, no distractions.

Adria Petty: They had a recording studio in our house when I was about ten, nine or ten, when they were making *Southern Accents*. That was cool. The music would come up through the vents.

Tom Petty: There were a few things going on with that album. If I felt like *Long After Dark* didn't move things along as far as I wanted, *Southern Accents* was thick with departures. There was a lot of experimentation. One of our experiments on that record came in the form of Dave Stewart. Now, the Heartbreakers were a closed circle, a very tight-knit entity. My immediate joy in bringing Dave's eccentricities into our living room was not matched by the band. They were slow to accept Dave. There had never been anybody from the outside working on our records. I think the fact that I was writing with him made them suspicious or jealous. I don't know what it was. When they got to know him and saw that he was harmless, that he was only trying to make good music for everyone—you know, then it was okay.

Dave Stewart: I think most of his band—and I don't blame them—were going, "What the fuck is this?" It was called *Southern Accents*, and it sounded like we're in India all of a sudden.

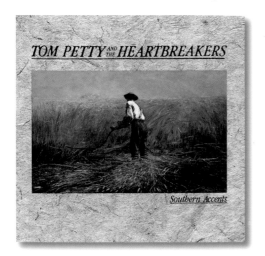

Tom Petty: It was Jimmy Iovine who brought Dave Stewart to me. Jimmy was working with Stevie Nicks again and wanted me to write something for her. He came to me and asked me who I thought was a good songwriter working at the time. I said, well, I think this guy Dave Stewart from the Eurythmics shows a lot of potential. The Eurythmics were just starting to break big. I told Jimmy he should call Dave.

Then I got a call at home one day, and it was Dave Stewart. He told me he was over at Sunset Sound, that Jimmy had called him and said we should get together. Dave said he was supposed to write something for Stevie Nicks and would I help? Iovine at work again, right? I went down to Sunset Sound and Dave was great. We started to hang out every day. It was his first time in Los Angeles. That's like your first time at Disneyland. Dave wanted to go on all the rides.

Truth of it was that Dave was one of the only bright lights in that period. He was sober and funny and crazy. And quite a dresser. Each day he'd arrive in a different outfit. I remember the two of us going to a rodeo tailor and buying expensive cowboy boots and hats, just wearing these clothes and hanging around town. He kept things lively. Once in the studio there was a background singer with a really high part, and Dave was having trouble getting her to hit the note. She's going for the take and he runs in in his underpants—and son of a gun if she didn't do it. He took her mind off it for just long enough for her to nail the part.

The song we wrote for Stevie, or meant to write for Stevie, was "Don't Come Around Here No More." We wrote it and started to record it when Stevie wasn't around. When she finally came in and heard it with my vocal on it, she was put off by it. It was like, "I can't sing that. You've already done it. It sounds good with you singing it. I don't think I could make it better." She took a pass, but it wasn't for her. It was for me.

Jimmy Iovine: I said, "Tom, do me a favor." He says, "I'm not coming." I said, "Tom, just do me a favor. Come here and write the fucking lyrics please." He came down, wrote the lyrics, and took the song. That's the fucking truth. You know it's true, Tom.

Tom Petty: "Don't Come Around Here No More" was a very big song for us. A bit of a breakthrough. Dave Stewart eventually bought some property right around the corner from me, built a house and a studio there, became part of the family.

GOT MY OWN WAY OF TALKING

Tom Petty: I wanted to explore the sense of place that I got growing up in the South. Stereotypes cloud our understanding of what the whole region is. Those Southern accents . . . rock and roll really comes from the South. It comes out of Memphis, Mississippi, Louisiana, Texas. In my mind were all the people that I see as the beginnings of rock and roll and R&B, and all the places they came from, and I just wanted to explore that landscape. Sometimes I look back and I think it was a confusing thing for some people. There were those who could only process this by thinking of us as a Southern rock group, which we're not by any stretch of the imagination. This was another side of the experimentation with *Southern Accents*, that thematic focus that brought the project into the vicinity of the concept album.

You hear this most explicitly in "Rebels" and "Southern Accents," but it's there in a number of the songs— you know, "Spike," "The Best Of Everything," and certainly the B-side of "Don't Come Around Here No More," "Trailer," which I've always really loved. I think that part of my interest in looking at the South, at least at that time, comes from the experience of my mother's death. Events on that scale don't always make it into your writing right away. In this case there was certainly a delayed reaction. She passed around the time of *Damn The Torpedoes*. But this was the period when she found her way into the songs, and she brought her world with her, you know?

ABOVE LEFT:

Benmont Tench and Howie Epstein, poolside.

ABOVE:

Tom, Jimmy Iovine, and Tony Dimitriades on June 6, 1980, leaving the ABC studios.

LEFT:

The Heartbreakers about to take flight on the tour supporting Long After Dark, *1982.*

The song "Southern Accents" is one of my best, I think. It's not the kind of song that will go over as big in, say, Buffalo or Boston as it will in the South, where the emotional connection will propel it. Johnny Cash recorded that song, and he actually told me this could be a better song than "Dixie," that it could replace "Dixie." Few comments have meant as much as that one from Johnny.

It's very personal in so many ways, so I wrote it using characters—one guy is a migrant worker and one is working in the orange fields in Orlando—maybe just to give me a little distance from it. There's nothing wrong with this song, nothing I would change. For my money it's the best bridge I've ever written. It's hard to write a bridge. We call it a middle 8. We used to hear the Beatles call them middle 8s, though they're not always eight bars. It's the part of the tune where you go somewhere else—it's not a verse and it's not a chorus—and then you return, and the song, hopefully, resonates in a new way. I've learned over the years if you haven't written a great bridge, then don't write one. It's got to be as good as the chorus and the verse, or there's no reason to do it. On that bridge, it's almost like the narrator drifts off into a place of very high, even mystical emotion. It provides a kind of road sign to that last, very personal verse.

Bill Flanagan: The song about his mother coming to him in a dream is just some of his most beautiful lyric writing. The guy, the guy could have been Tennessee Williams if he had been born in a different town, with a different sexual inclination.

Tom Petty: Initially I recorded "Southern Accents" with just the piano, Stan playing cross stick on the snare drum, and maybe there was a bass. Very empty. It was so obviously a kind of centerpiece to the album, the thematic and emotional heart of the thing, that I thought maybe instead of putting guitars on it we should bring in an orchestra. The song seemed cinematic, like it needed a score. I was lucky to find Jack Nitzsche, who was available. He had done a lot of movie scores, had worked with Neil Young, had done all the arrangements for Phil Spector back in the '60s. He was my first choice, so he came over and listened to the track, and said, "I can do it." A few days later he showed up with a score.

We went to the Capitol studios. In the basement studio, where Sinatra used to cut, we brought in the orchestra, with Jack conducting. I still think it's one of our best tracks. It was very exciting to see it go down. After one take I said, "Let's overdub it," and Jack whirled around, looked at me, went shhhh, and said, "You'll have to pay everyone again if you say overdub—just say we're going to do another take." So we kept the two takes of orchestra and made it really big.

THE BIG BREAK

Tom Petty: A song called "Rebels" opens that album.

Benmont Tench: "Honey don't walk out, I'm too drunk to follow." It's as good a line as you'll find in any rock-and-roll song, certainly. The whole song is in that line. It's just wonderful, just wonderful.

Tom Petty: The voice belongs to this redneck who's coming to terms with his heritage. I really wanted it to be right, and it was the simplest thing. We worked on it for months. I made a demo track when I wrote it, and we spent all this time trying to get the horn arrangement right and the mix right. It wasn't coming. *Southern Accents* was a damn tough record to make. We were off the road for the first time in years, and there were a lot of drugs around. . . . God, we wreaked havoc. Had nothing to do and a lot of money to get into a lot of trouble. Some really bad behavior. Personally, I think I just got kind of lost. I was making a record, but I couldn't keep up with myself. I started without Iovine, trying to produce it myself. Mike and I were going to do it, and that

CLASS PROGRAM

NAME _Tom Petty_   ADDRESS _EARTH_

SCHOOL _of the Unknown_   CLASS _less_

TIME	FROM TO...		PERIOD 1	PERIOD 2	PERIOD 3	PERIOD 4	PERIOD 5	PERIOD 6	PER
MONDAY	SUBJECT								
	ROOM								
	INSTRUCTOR								
TUESDAY	SUBJECT								
	ROOM								
	INSTRUCTOR								

... cm x 19.0 cm
Wide Ruled
09-9100   The Mead Corporation, Dayton, Ohio

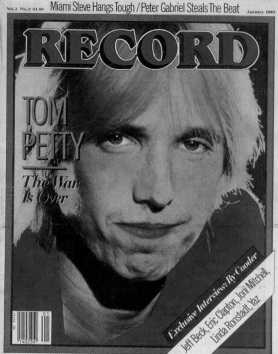

Vol. 2 No. 3 $1.00   Miami Steve Hangs Tough / Peter Gabriel Steals The Beat   January 1983

RECORD
TOM PETTY
The War Is Over
Exclusive Interviews: By Cooder
Jeff Beck, Eric Clapton, Joni Mitchell, Linda Ronstadt, Yaz

WIN A FREE LES PAUL GUITAR!

PAT BENATAR   BOB SEGER   MICHAEL JACKSON   MICK JAGGER
APRIL 1982 $1.95

America's Only Rock 'n' Roll Magazine

CREEM

AFTER *AFTER DARK:*
TOM PETTY
GETS LUCKY!

OZZY OSBOURNE
FROM IRON MAN TO BAT MAN!

BLACK UHURU
NO SPEAK ENGLISH!

LORDS OF THE NEW CHURCH
MR. BATORS IS BACK!

**ROCK 'N' ROLL'S TEN
GREATEST GUITARISTS!**

WHO NEEDS THE
BEATLES?

GRACE JONES
BEAUTY SECRETS

WORST MOVIES OF '82!

KEITH RICHARDS
NEIL YOUNG
RICK OCASEK
SUPERTRAMP
JOHN CALE
BUCK DHARMA
CHIC
YAZ

OZZY OSBOURNE

0 71486 02137   04

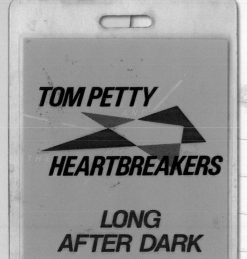

Straight into darkness   Tom Petty

There was a little girl, I used to know her
I still think about her, time to time
There was a moment when I really loved her
then one day the feeling just died

We went straight into darkness
out over the line

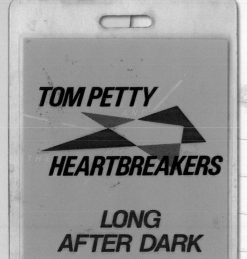 *(City Limits magazine cover)*

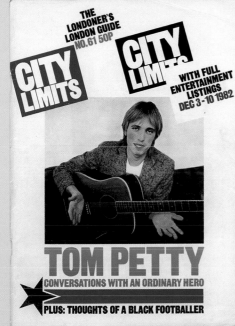

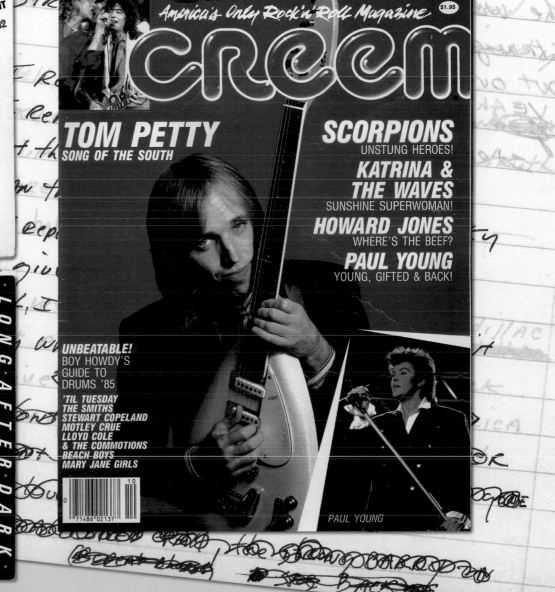

was a joke. We couldn't police ourselves. We would listen to a producer because there was some level of authority there. But without the producer, we lost our efficiency. We were starting to whoop it up.

We're trying to get "Rebels" to sound like it did in our heads. And we're not getting it. At one point I went into the next room and saw the "Rebels" demo tape, put it on, and damn, it was so much better than the version we were working on that I got furious. I was furious with myself. I went walking up the stairs—this was in my home studio—and I went up the staircase just to get out of the house because I was so frustrated. I took my hand and smacked the wall really hard. I don't know what made me do that, but I must have been really mad because I pulverized my hand. I didn't just break it, I powdered it—the bone went to powder. It was very painful. The next thing I know, I've got this Mickey Mouse hand and I went to the emergency room.

Dave Stewart: There was a lot of tension in the house, upstairs and downstairs. I think Tom was getting it from all sides and just exploded.

Stevie Nicks: I know a few guys who have done that.

Jim Lenehan: He got pissed off about something and punched the wall. We all do dumb things like that.

Mike Campbell: I remember the day it happened. It was when I had gotten the mix for "The Boys of Summer," a song that I had done with Don Henley. I brought it to the studio that day and said, "Oh, check this out." He sat there and listened to it. I don't know what was going through his head. But as soon as it was over he went up and put his hand through the wall. It could just be a coincidence.

Elliot Roberts: He punched the wall, okay? The wall deserved whatever it got.

Tom Petty: Eventually, I went through a long operation where they put metal in my hand and rebuilt it with metal and wire and studs. It was really incredible. Nine or ten years ago I cracked my forearm and they had to X-ray it. When they saw my hand, they were bringing in doctors from all over the place, going, "You've got to see this. Come in here and take a look at this hand." The doctors were amazed at how they rebuilt it.

I really sobered up after that. It was a huge wake-up call. My life changed. We all cleaned up, brought in Jimmy Iovine to help us finish the record, and got down to business. I had intended it to be a double album, but Jimmy came in and said there's no way you have a double album here. His suggestion was to make a record out of what we had, which was a good idea. It came out good. I was pleased when it was done. It's pretty typical that once a record is released I really let go of it. I've heard it so much at that point, and it belongs to others by that time. So I haven't heard *Southern Accents* in a long, long time. But people keep buying that one. Something special happened there.

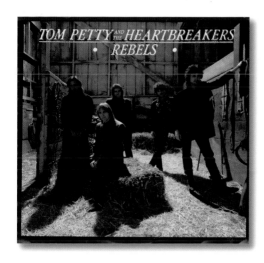

FOLLOWING PAGES:
The US Festival. The Heartbreakers' biggest gig to date, with over 300,000 in attendance.

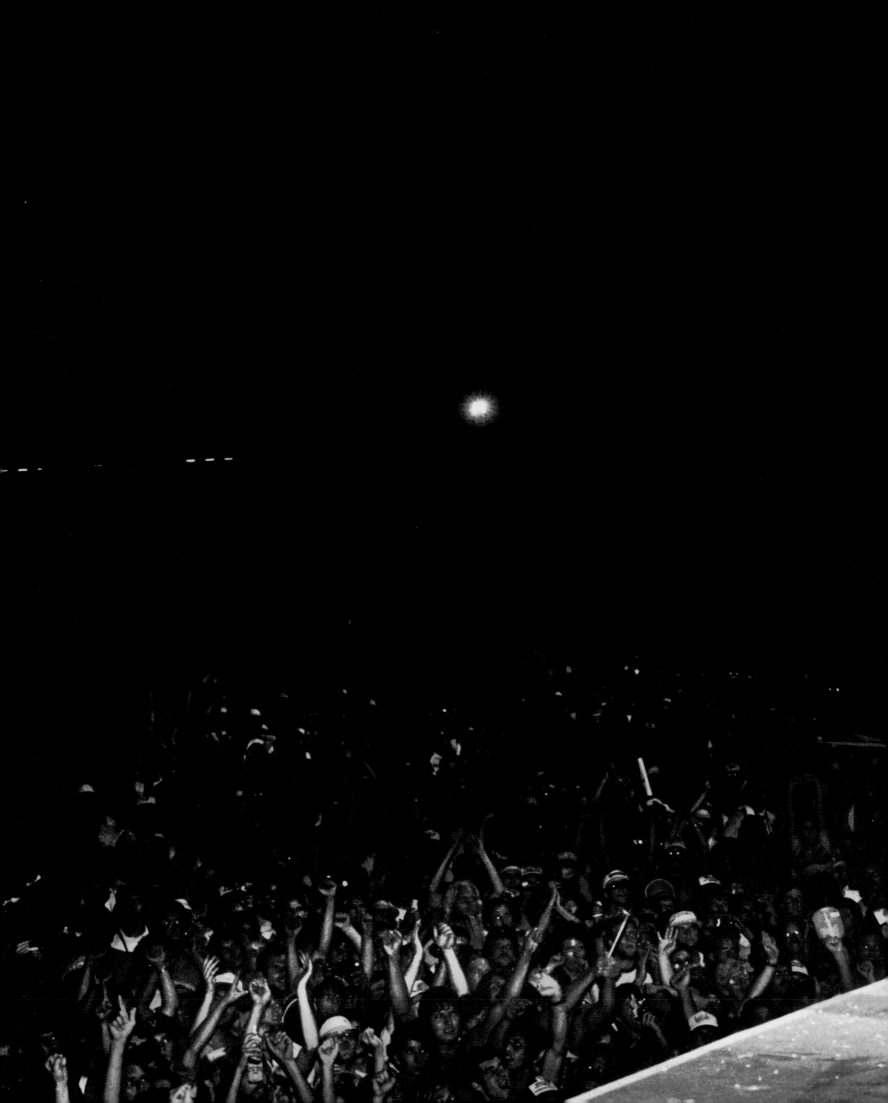

Chapter Five/
Seeing Music

I remember Mad *magazine used to have pictures of a sort of rock-and-roll guy. He had the ornate guitar, the pompadour, and pointy shoes. I thought, "Well, that clearly must be a rock-and-roller."*

Tom Petty: Music has never been simply a sound experience. At least in my time. It's a visual thing, too. Rock and roll without the visual component wouldn't be near as much fun. From my earliest days I had a picture of what a rock-and-roller was. I remember *Mad* magazine used to have pictures of a sort of rock-and-roll guy. He had the ornate guitar, the pompadour, and pointy shoes. I thought, "Well, that clearly must be a rock-and-roller."

The more I listened, though, the more I wanted particulars. I definitely remember when I was young, just starving for photographs of the bands I loved. Whatever I could find. It was all part of trying to get behind the mystery of this powerful music. It's amazing how long we stared at album covers, getting more and more out of them. The Beatles really took the art of it to new places with *Revolver*, *Sgt. Pepper,* and after that. I really absorbed the look of the performers I dug. The music hooked you, but the images deepened the relationship. I've always admired a band like the Rolling Stones with their sophisticated visual sense. Albums like *Exile On Main Street* and *Sticky Fingers* had a real strong look to them. It wasn't that the images answered the questions, they generated more questions. In the best case, the pictures made you want to dig deeper, back into the music.

This isn't to say that music couldn't work without the visual part of the equation. There's plenty of great music, Robert Johnson, for instance, that predates what I'm talking about here. But, for my generation, there's a tremendous amount of image materials that bands need to think about. I really learned about that just by being a fan myself. I used to think that I knew the guys I was listening to, and that I was going through their lives with them. I had a picture in my mind of who I was listening to. I always liked that.

Denny Cordell, once again, did some subliminal work when it came to me thinking more visually. He always wanted us to know more, to have a broader outlook than just the record we were making. Once he took me to an art exhibition in the middle of a session. It was the strangest thing in the world. We took a break and he said, "Come on. I want you to go with me and see these pictures." I thought it was really odd, but I trusted his instincts. We went over to this gallery and looked at these paintings. He was a very cryptic fellow. At all times he was very

cryptic. He said something like, "You know, if you could get these colors into the track—you see how these colors have blended? Well, that's what we want to do with this record. We want to get these particular colors and blend them." I said okay, but I really didn't have any idea how that was going to happen. I'll tell you what, though, I went back to the session feeling a little bit more like an artist. I think that kind of encounter made me take the visual part seriously.

There was never any resistance on my part to seeing what we could do with images, still or moving. It all seemed like, if we did it right, it could be an extension of the music.

Elliot Roberts: Tom was one of the handful of artists I've worked with—Devo comes to mind, the Cars come to mind—who were very open to video when it first started. Tom was in that first class of artists. He was always visually open to it.

Tom Petty: We had made what we called promo clips, three or four of these things where you'd see us lip-synching the song. We sent them out to the *Merv Griffin Show* that we didn't want to do, or some other program. When we made the "You Got Lucky" film, it turned out to be a huge MTV track, though we had not, believe it or not, seen MTV at that time. They didn't get MTV in Los Angeles until, I think it was '82 or '83. I had never seen MTV, just heard about it. Jim Lenehan and I brainstormed the idea one day. We were going to make a promo clip for "You Got Lucky," and I didn't want to lip-synch it. I asked Jim, "What if we made a little movie?" We made this kind of science fiction western for real cheap. In those days you could hustle up something for not a lot of money. It worked beautifully. We had a little intro on the beginning that I scored, and I'm sure that it was the first video that had an intro like that on it. That wasn't common then, though it became common.

Next thing we know, people everywhere are recognizing us. Not just me, but all of us were getting this. People would say, "Oh, we saw the thing with you in the desert," or "I saw you on the motor bike." I started realizing that a lot of people are seeing this. When we finally did see MTV, it all made sense to us.

Jim Lenehan: We looked at it as guerrilla filmmaking. I was into that, you know? I wanted to direct like everybody wanted to direct. I thought—and I still think— that one of the best people to direct a visual representation of a band is somebody who absolutely knows that music upside down, inside out, backward and forward. That's the lighting guy, because he's got to hit those cues live. He's got to know what that song is doing, where it's going. When we started doing it we would get mad if someone called it a video. We didn't shoot this on videotape! This is a film! We are making films. We'd go out and steal locations. Grab it before somebody asked if we had a permit and things like that. We made "Woman In Love," "The Waiting," " Insider," "Stop Draggin' My Heart Around," "Letting You Go." Those were the first ones that I directed.

LEFT:

Making videos in the early 1980s. At bottom, Ron and Stan are joined by Alan "Bugs" Weidel.

Tom Petty: MTV was a different thing then. It was exciting because it was so brand new, and they were starved for product. We sent them old clips, and they played them over and over again. They were never meant to be seen in that way, but they worked. That kicked off our thing with MTV in a big way, and it went on for years and years. Eventually it became a matter of trying to make a clever video for each release. I liked it. I liked the whole idea of being on the set and watching how it was done, how it was lit. I learned about editing. The whole idea of making these little movies was fascinating to me.

Bill Flanagan: A while back Tom was given the Video Vanguard Award at the MTV Music Awards. He was consistently creative in his videos. By the time MTV had been around for, let's say, twenty years, Tom and U2 and Madonna were probably the only three artists who were still around, who had been important young video artists when the channel began and were still important video artists at that time. That's completely unique.

Tom Petty: There are a number of my videos that I really like, but as a songwriter I also recognize the problems that the medium brings with it. It bugs me that these images would get fixed in people's minds. They weren't creating the images themselves—they were getting them from MTV. That was the bind I always found myself in. How could I make a video that had a little ambiguity to it? This wasn't easy. You had to tax your imagination to come up with another four-minute film for another new release. I got frustrated with it after a while—had to ask myself if we really had to put out a video for each release. But we did. Because all of a sudden the biggest radio station was the TV.

Jackson Browne: Tom was very good in videos. He really made great videos and was on MTV a lot. Just in terms of how the business worked, that was a very important thing for him to continue getting a younger audience and for him to keep an audience that was kind of moving into a whole different way of getting into rock and roll. I don't think you can find anybody that has a TV that hasn't seen Tom's videos.

Tom Petty: The key for a rock-and-roll band is to keep changing and to keep moving. With us, we were lucky, really, that that kept happening, because, truthfully, we were just a five-piece rock-and-roll band. There wasn't a lot to be spelled out about it. It was just a five-piece rock-and-roll band. We were really about music but had to learn how to present that in many ways. The videos were one way to keep the image changing or keep the imagery changing. It became a significant part of our process.

FACING AND FOLLOWING PAGES:
The Heartbreakers with Stevie Nicks on the set of the "Insider" video, 1981.

```
                              YOU GOT LUCKY

      ERT - A HIGHWAY - DAY

      E GROUND, WIDE ANGLE shot. The d
           flat and still. The two lane bla
           ight as an arrow, recedes to the
      nd all is silent save for a softl
      CAMERA PANS LEFT across the road
   where we look the desert is fla
      the camera move is completed, a
       vehicle pulls into frame from c
      st fills the frame. For a moment
          extremely out of place on the rug

   g engine whines to a stop. Sudde
       ch side open with a WHOOSH. Again
      nt.

   HE CAR

         teps down into frame. It is
          is exiting from the car.
                                          CUT

      OF DESERT
   ... with a bit of the car roof and gull wing door in the
   foreground. T.P. climbs out of the car and rises int
   frame from below so it becomes a CLOSE UP. We
   is looking off past camera at something i
 5
   MEDIUM SHOT OF MIKE                        CUT TO:
      ... as he exit
   side of th
   over
```

On the set of "Don't Come Around Here No More," 1985.

Alice looks on, a
becomes more awar

Tom's hat is now enormo

The sung
and on the le
reflection is laug
the right side, she's

Tom and Johnny Depp filming "Into The Great Wide Open," 1991.

ABOVE:

From the music video for "I Won't Back Down,"
1989. From left: Ringo Starr, Jeff Lynne, Tom,
George Harrison, Mike Campbell.

OPPOSITE:

Tom with Kim Basinger on the set of
"Mary Jane's Last Dance," 1993.

Chapter Six/
Back There
With the Band

Dylan and I were talking about when he had a band, when he had the Band, and how he felt when he was playing with an actual group and not just a loose affiliation of desperate musicians. And I said that the only band I could think of that might be a band like that for him again would be Tom Petty and the Heartbreakers. (Dave Stewart)

BOB

Tom Petty: Around 1986 we started playing with Bob Dylan. Benmont had been working on a track or two with Bob, and then Mike ended up going down and playing, followed by Howie. A gradual migration of Heartbreakers. Around that time Bob had a show, the first Farm Aid show. He wanted to play with a group, play with an electric band, so he approached us. We were more than happy to do it. Bob hadn't worked with an actual band since he worked with the Band way back when.

The Heartbreakers could cover a lot of instruments. I'd play the bass when Howie played the lap steel. Mike played mandolin. We could pretty much give Bob what he wanted. Every one of us admired him so much. So we got together and rehearsed quite a few songs for Farm Aid, more than we needed for the show. The chemistry was quickly apparent. Elliot Roberts helped set that up.

Elliot Roberts: I don't think the whole thing took more than eleven or twelve minutes. Bob said something to me. I said something to Tom. I called Bob back. It was done.

Dave Stewart: Dylan and I were talking about when he had a band, when he had the Band, and how he felt when he was playing with an actual group and not just a loose affiliation of desperate musicians. And I said that the only band I could think of that might be a band like that for him again would be Tom Petty and the Heartbreakers.

Tom Petty: The show went out on TV and went really well onstage. That night in the dressing room Bob suggests a tour. That was easy. Let's go. We did Australia and New Zealand, and it just kept going on from there. How about America? So we did America. What do you think about going to Europe and Japan? Israel, Egypt? We did all that, and it took us through 1987. We also did a short U.S. tour on our own in that time period and recorded *Let Me Up (I've Had Enough)*. I remember the Dylan period being more fun than we'd had in a while. We were happy.

The Heartbreakers got plenty of time in the Dylan shows to do our own stuff, so we didn't worry about that. We all came on together in the first part of the show, and then Bob would take a break and the Heartbreakers would stay up there. We loved it, just thought it was fantastic and wanted to do our best for Bob. He was a great influence on the Heartbreakers, and we came out of it a better band. It couldn't have hurt that we felt like the hottest spotlights were off of us and onto Bob. A little pressure was released.

For me, as a bandleader there was a lot to be drawn from his approach. The way he'd rehearse, for instance. We adapted a lot of that into the way

The best songs in the folk tradition are kind of there for everybody, meant to be passed around. And Dylan's songs are the same. If the Grateful Dead wanted to play one of his songs for fifteen minutes, it would probably work. If almost any artist wanted to take it and do it their way, there's a good chance it might work. I don't know many writers you can say that about. I don't think the Beatles' music is durable in that same way—it's some of the best music ever made—but I never really liked people covering Beatles' songs very much. I can count the cover versions I really liked on one hand. Not so with Dylan's material. That's part of why his music is so interesting when you put it in a rock context, because it comes from that folk tradition. You start to realize as you listen to him that he's part of a tradition that leads back to what Howlin' Wolf was doing or Muddy Waters.

OPPOSITE:

Tom with Bob Dylan on the True Confessions tour, 1986.

we've rehearsed ever since. Things weren't really spelled out. He would play a song, give us a sense for the feel of it, and we'd follow him. We knew the changes, or he'd show us the changes on the spot. The next day we might try it with a different feel. Or maybe he would call out "Tears Of A Clown" or "Come Together." There wasn't any labored discussion about it, and sometimes you would be like, "That was a great song. What was that?" And he would fill us in. I may never have heard it, but we were playing it. We didn't dwell on a song for a long time, risking fatigue or boredom. Some groups will approach a song and take it apart, spend two hours on it, beat it to death. We just don't do that, and I think that's something we got right around that period, when we learned you don't have to do that.

A lot of Bob's approach comes from his folk background. In the folk world there is less emphasis on playing a song with the same feel every time you do it. More than that, it's typically you and a guitar—you can easily change the feel, play an extra bar, modify the tempo. I think that approach is still very much with Bob, even when a band is behind him. It's a great way to keep the life in music. We got really confident that we could be there, whatever he wanted we could be there, and the moments when the audience is really getting off are earned. There's nothing automatic about it. He really earns it, has the courage to just go for it.

WATCHING THE FRONTMAN

Roger McGuinn: [Dylan] is capable of changing the time signature and the melody and just about everything in the song except the title . . . and you're supposed to stay with him.

Mike Campbell: The Dylan period was incredible for the Heartbreakers because it happened at a time when the band was very bored with each other. That gave us something to do that wasn't just being Tom Petty and the Heartbreakers. I wouldn't take that back for anything. It was backing up this guy that we loved. It kind of restarted the band's juices flowing. Just playing with him was probably some of the most crazy and enjoyable times I've ever had playing live. Because it was so much anarchy, you know? Compared to when our band plays. In fact, we learned some of that from him. We brought a little anarchy back to our trip.

Tom Petty: I don't think he threw us curveballs that much. Sometimes we might play something in a different key but that didn't really baffle us. I mean, it was going to be in a D instead of an E? Or he might say tonight this song's going to be a shuffle instead of a straight beat. Good enough. It made us bold, and we weren't scared to try it and we did it. I enjoyed it. I thought the whole thing was great.

Elliot Roberts: You had to watch him like a hawk.

Steve Ferrone: I've worked with a lot of people, and you've got to keep a close eye on all of them. If you're working with Ray Charles, you better keep a close eye on him. He will yell at a drummer. He loves yelling at a drummer. He yelled at me in front of the whole country, at Clinton's inaugural. That was because I couldn't see him. I couldn't see him. You have to watch his shoulders. All I could see was his legs. And all his legs do, his legs just sort of fly around. They had nothing to do with anything. So I went running over to Ray, and I say, "Ray, Ray, this is Steve. You got to bear with me, man. I can't see you." And Ray said, "I can't see you either, motherfucker."

Tom Petty: At the end of the day, it was an education phase for us. We came out of it bolder. When we went back to play in our own shows, we weren't afraid to try something different. I came out of it better personally because I'd never been behind a singer. For me it was a real eye-opener just seeing what goes on with the guy in front. We also learned how to take a song and make it work. Songs didn't necessarily need to be built on certain parts or rigid structures. We came to see that the songs that were really good always had a number of

ISSUES 478/479 • JULY 17TH/JULY 31ST, 1986 • U.K. £1.90 • $2.95

RollingStone

*THE SUMMER'S
HOTTEST TICKET*
DYLAN & PETTY
TALKING ABOUT
ROCK AND THE ROAD

BASEBALL'S
OUTLAW TEAM
REBELS, HEAD
CASES AND
DRUG CASUALTIES

FLYING WITH
AMERICA'S BEST
FIGHTER PILOTS
IN THE COCKPIT
WITH FRED SCHRUERS

DAVID BYRNE'S
TRUE STORIES

MADONNA'S
NEW ALBUM

FUN, FUN,
FUN FASHION

FICTION BY
FRED EXLEY

THE RITES OF SUMMER
THE BEACH, BACK SEAT,
LIFEGUARD, SUNGLASSES,
SHORTS, BUGS AND MORE

RANDOM NOTES
HANGS OUT WITH
DAVID BOWIE
DON HENLEY
ARETHA FRANKLIN
HEART
EURYTHMICS
MARIA McKEE
R.E.M.

ast EC oast ROCKER

THE ONLY WEEKLY MUSIC NEWSPAPER IN THE U.S.

ISSUE NO. 43 ON SALE UNTIL MAY 20, 1987 $1.00

Featuring Complete Weekly Coverage of Folk Music

THE RETURN OF

TOM PETTY

SEE PAGE 15

PAUL SIMON'S 'GRACELAND' TOUR
PAGE 21

ALL THE LATEST CONCERT AND RECORD INFORMATION

TINY LIGHTS
REVIEWED

FREE CLASSIFIED

BOB DYLAN
TRUE CONFESSIONS TOUR
WITH
TOM PETTY
HEARTBREAKERS
ALONE + TOGETHER

David Zard presents

...MPLES IN FLAMES

...WITH TOM PETTY HEARTBREAKERS

+ ROGER McGUINN

...ERONA
+ DIR. PREV.

...CAVIVA

VIDEOMUSIC in Concert

GIOVEDI
1
OTTOBRE
ore 21.00

ON SALE NOW

TOM PETTY BOB DYLAN
HEARTBREAKERS   AND HIS BAND

THE CONCERT EVENT OF THE SUMMER

PNC BANK ARTS CENTER

AUGUST 9 & 10

HOLMDEL NEW JERSEY

NO OPENING ACT. SHOW STARTS PROMPTLY AT 7:30PM

Tickets available at select ticketmaster outlets, online at ticketmaster.com, or charge by phone at 201-507-8900. Get tickets at CC.com. Ticket limits apply. Produced by Clear Channel Entertainment.

CONCERT LINE: 732-335-8698

www.artscenter.com

ABOVE RIGHT:

George Harrison, Roger McGuinn, Tom, and
Ringo Starr, circa 1986.

SEC 26 DD 9   ADULT EF0803

SECTION/AISLE   ROW/BOX   SEAT   ADMISSION   EVENT CODE

LODGE   WEST

AT THE FABULOUS FORUM

WESTWOOD ONE RADIO NETWORK

PRESENTS

* BOB DYLAN / TOM PETTY *

* AND THE HEARTBREAKERS *

SUN AUG 3 '1986 0:30 PM

SEAT 9

NO REFUND
NO EXCHANGE

136403

ways to interpret them. Bob has a lot of spontaneity in what he does. He likes it to be very fresh. I've heard people say, geez, with Bob you never know what he's going to do. But we rehearsed and pretty much knew what he was going to do at shows. Life couldn't have been better. It was another really good adventure for us. McGuinn was on part of the tour. There was a lot of fun to be had.

Roger McGuinn: The band and Tom would come out, and we all did "So You Want To Be A Rock 'N' Roll Star" and "Eight Miles High," "Turn, Turn, Turn," "Mr. Tambourine Man." The Byrds classics. And it sounded better than the Byrds.

Tony Dimitriades: They learned to be a great band, no doubt about it. They already were a great band, but they learned to be a great band for a whole new generation.

Benmont Tench: Tom had always been the frontman. He was the rhythm guitar player. With Dylan we had the three-guitar attack. It was great. So Tom got to find out what that was like, to be in the band. That must have been fun.

Tom Petty: There's a different camaraderie in the backline, and they sort of welcomed me in, in a way. I think they also enjoyed seeing me struggle with it a little bit. Like if something came up and I didn't know the key or the chords, there would be a few laughs before they would give it to me. "Aw, you didn't do your homework, did you? You don't know the chords. . . . Okay, it's in A." There's a different feeling back there. I got put in the band for a minute, and it was a good feeling.

WELL, IT CAN GET YOU IN THE BACK, BOY, OR YOU CAN LIE AROUND IN ROSES

Benmont Tench: [Playing with Dylan] was alternately amazing and frustrating, and sometimes on the same night. I thought it did wonders for playing with the band. It knit us together. Made us looser. You had to improvise. Boy, I wouldn't trade that. In the course of this we recorded the *Let Me Up (I've Had Enough)* album, at least the rocking part of the album.

Tom Petty: We had the stuff that Mike wrote, which was a little more produced because he worked on it a lot, and the material that I wrote on my own, which was almost improvised in the studio. Very much improvised. Some of them were first takes, and I was still writing the song at the time. I would just make it up as I went along—if it was good, that was it. We were just getting back to something more simple, peeling back a couple of layers. I was probably in that mindset because of the liberation I felt during the time we worked with Dylan. That fired me up.

I was just going right off the top of my head, calling out chords. On the rough mixes you can actually hear me shouting out the changes. This doesn't always work. But it's not always the songs you labor over that come out best. One example of a later song that was ad-libbed top to bottom was "Wildflowers." That was right off the top of my head. Plugged in, set out the mic, took the guitar, and kabang, I sang every word of it and played every chord and then sort of wondered how it happened. Part of my process is that I picture music in my head. I can see something. Getting it to reality is another thing. That's not as easy. Sometimes the really, really great ones come very fast, almost appear there. They were there before I knew it.

Tony Dimitriades: I think that when Tom went into the studio and worked with the band and tried to cut everything virtually live it was an attempt on his part to give the band what they wanted. We are a band. We don't have other people coming in here and helping us write the songs and arrange them. You know, we're a band. Let's go back to the basics—and Tom did that with them. And that was not a good-selling album.

Tom Petty: The songs Mike brought in for *Let Me Up*— "Runaway Trains," "My Life/Your World," and "All Mixed Up"—were tracks Mike delivered pretty complete, minus the vocal. Since his approach was very different from mine, you can hear two different worlds on that record. But I feel like we found a sequence that brought it all together. This was definitely a period in which my relationship with Mike continued to grow. He was already being credited as a producer on certain *Southern Accents* tracks. With *Let Me Up* it was the one time we were listed as the coproducers.

Mike Campbell: Benmont hates "My Life/Your World." He said that sounds like Michael Jackson.

Tom Petty: "Jammin' Me" is a Mike Campbell track. I wrote the lyrics with Bob Dylan at the Sunset Marquis. We wrote a couple of songs at that time, one that went on his record and one that went on ours. Bob and I pored over a newspaper, appropriating the lyrics. Then I took the lyrics I'd written with Bob and put them to a track that Mike had put together. It came out pretty well and was a hit for us.

Mike Campbell: I never even sat with Bob when he was doing it. Later on I saw him. I said thanks for writing those words to my music.

Tom Petty: Mike and I have a lot of the same influences, the same musical tastes. We've grown up together. I'd say 80 percent of all I know about the guitar has been taught to me by him. I've learned everything from him. He's a natural player. He doesn't promote himself in this way, but I'm sure he could shut down most of the guitar heroes. Mutual respect cements our relationship. We've written a lot of songs together that were really good, and I think when I'm not around, he's probably the one that everyone defers

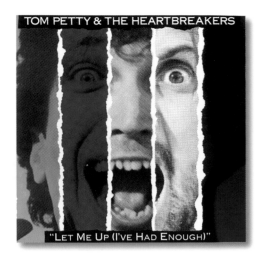

TOM PETTY & THE HEARTBREAKERS

"Let Me Up (I've Had Enough)"

to. He's the cocaptain. We don't see that much of each other these days. He's wrapped up in his life and I'm wrapped up in mine. We've grown up, and we've got families and our own set of responsibilities, but I can always count on him to be there for me and he knows he can count on me to be there for him, musically or otherwise. I don't think my music would have come out nearly as good without him. Without him or Ben, really. I don't think that what I do would have been as good as it has been without them. They played an enormous role in getting it over, getting what was in my head over to other people. But the playing field is level because I don't think they would have been around without me.

THE UNTHINKABLE

Tom Petty: I went through a terrible thing during the Dylan tour when someone burned my house down. We woke up one morning to a house on fire. It was a nightmare. Just a few feet from where one of my daughters was sleeping the fire started. We all survived, but the house didn't. I was told it was arson, and you could have knocked me down with a feather. Arson, are you sure? I just couldn't make any sense of that information. But they'd found that someone had cut a hole through the fence up on the hill and been hanging out for a while watching the house. It was a bad thing for the family.

Benmont Tench: I was asleep and the phone rang. There was supposed to be a party at their house that day. A friend of mine is on the line and says the house is burning. I went over to their hotel that night to see if they were okay, but they were in too much shell shock to even handle any visits. We left on tour within days.

Adria Petty: It was on my mother's birthday that the house burned down. All of these people were arriving for this party as the house burns down, walking up the driveway with gifts, not knowing what was going on. I remember my dad coming over and putting his arm around me. I started to cry, and he went, "Don't do that. This is no time for that. We need to be tough. We'll get through this together. We're all safe and that's all that matters." And I got it. It was true. It was only shit in the house. We're all we've got, and that was cool. I think it was a good moment because the family got very close. We got on that bus together and, you know what, we dealt with each other a little bit more than we did before.

Tom Petty: Then various people started to confess, not just one person but people across the United States. First some guys in New Jersey confessed. Then it becomes this copycat thing that really felt just too strange, too unnerving. It was one of those crazy things that happens to you and makes you aware that there's a lot of unbalanced activity out there, and you don't see it until it has happened. How can you not feel vulnerable? But the choice is to hang in fear, looking over your shoulder, or to start counting your blessings. It's not much of a choice, really.

Stevie Nicks: Everything that he had collected as a little kid, all that was gone. All of us in the business that knew him and knew about it, it scared us all because why in the world would anyone do that, especially to somebody like Tom Petty, who's just cool, you know? He's just a cool guy who makes cool music, and he had no enemies.

Tom Petty: I spent a lot of time trying to figure it out, but I realized I couldn't. That's the hardest thing, realizing that somebody did it. Did somebody really? I kept thinking it must be a mistake—I mean, it must be a mistake. It must be the wiring or something and they're wrong. But they showed me that they were right, that someone did pour gasoline and light it on fire around the house. Damn, I don't know, I don't dwell on it much—I did wonder about who did it, but I will never know. The impulse is to use reason to understand something that lives beyond reason. It's the lunatic fringe. That's why you wind up having security guards and extra weight that you don't have in normal life. You have to keep your eyes open, but you can't live in fear. If I do that, then they've won.

Here's one thing I try to remember: I saw Annie Lennox, Dave Stewart's partner in the Eurythmics. I saw her turn up briefly when they were fighting the fire. I remember seeing her out of the corner of my eye. At the end of the day, when we got to the hotel, Annie was there and had bought everyone a new wardrobe. Kind of broke me up. She had gone out and bought me shoes, bought me a coat, basically everything you would need to get by. When my mind drifts toward the negative, the how-could-this-happen line of thinking, I pull that image up. It's more lasting. It's more crucial.

TEMPORARY HOUSING

Tom Petty: After the fire, somewhere in the middle of the *Let Me Up* tour and the last Dylan run, my family moved to the other side of the hill. Frankly, because of the fire we moved to the other side of the hill. In hindsight it feels like one of those life lessons, that good things come of even the worst you can imagine. It was a strange time, to say the least. The fire. The Heartbreakers tour, with family in tow. An overseas adventure supporting Dylan that took us to Israel, Scandinavia, most of Europe. I'm guessing that all of the activity helped to distract me from the cold, hard fact of arson. Distraction or not, though, it was obvious that eventually I'd need to stop, to create a new place to call home. That's just what I did. After the Dylan tour ended with a string of shows in England, it was back to the States again, with no sense for what was to come next. No master plan. As it happened, I was thrown into one of the most artistically fulfilling, one of the lightest in spirit, and certainly one of the most unexpected periods in my life. Moving to the other side of the hill put me right into George Harrison and Jeff Lynne's neighborhood, right where I needed to be. Here I'd lost everything I owned some months before. I remember the fire—we were supposed to be having a party that day. I can still see the people arriving and the hoses blasting water. And I didn't even have shoes to wear. A moment like that isn't the one when you're thinking, "Soon I'll enter into one of the most magical times in my life." And then, wonderfully, that's just what happens. It's worth remembering that it can work that way.

Chapter Seven/
On the Other
Side of the Hill

I was the youngest one, the kid in the group. And that was kind of fun because I had admired all those guys when I was very young. They were gods to me.

STRANGE WEATHER

Tom Petty: We were in England on the Dylan tour and played Birmingham, after which we were in London for almost a week. George Harrison and Jeff Lynne came to all the shows and hung out, and we all got to be friendly. We made plans to hook up later. Jeff had just finished a record with George at the time so they gave me a copy. On one of the last nights in London, I think, my life changed. We were there with Bob, of course, and there was a long party afterward, and George, Derek Taylor, Ringo, Jeff Lynne, all these people got in this room backstage and just had the best time. We were laughing and drinking and never had such fun.

Then I went home to my room that night and a hurricane hit London, with no warning. There was no warning at all. Meteorologists hadn't predicted anything like this. I didn't know hurricanes hit England. Well one damn sure hit London that night. I remember getting up in the night, hearing the rain hitting the window and thinking, "Man, it really rains here in England." And then I walked out in the morning and huge oaks were toppled. The hurricane came through, wreaked havoc, and moved on. But after the fact I thought, "You know, ever since that hurricane things have been different." Fate is a funny thing. You don't always get a signal. But I sure felt a signal around that time, just a positive buzz running underneath a lot of what was going on.

The Dylan tour ended and we all went back home. When I was home I played the tape that George and Jeff had given me and really liked the production of the record. I thought it was great. That was, of course, *Cloud Nine*, which went on to be a big record for George. But I wasn't home for a week when I ran into Jeff Lynne at a stoplight in Beverly Hills. We'd just been in London together days before, so we were kind of shocked to see each other. He said he was in town doing a track with Brian Wilson and was going into the studio but that he lived just up the road. Of course, now I was on that side of the hill as well. I was renting a house in Beverly Hills. Jeff suggested that we get together because he would be there for the holidays and didn't know anybody. I told him he had to come over. And that was that.

A few days later I was out with my daughter Adria, and we were passing a French restaurant that she and I used to go to on special occasions. She said something like, "Gosh, wouldn't it be great if you could have lunch there?" I said, "You can have lunch there, watch." I pulled in and enjoyed exciting Adria with a bit of spontaneity. We ordered lunch, and while we were eating, the maitre d' came over and explained that a friend of mine was in the next room and wondered if I would come in and say hello. I walked in the next room and there were George Harrison and Jeff Lynne. George holds up his little pad of paper and said, "Look at this, I was just getting your number from Jeff when someone told me you were sitting in the next room." George asked what we were doing right at the moment, and I said we were going back home. "Well, can I come with you?" Sure.

So George came home with me and stayed the rest of the day, just playing guitar at the house. I thought this is wild, but we got along really good. We got along in an unusual way. So he would come back. In fact, he came back the next day and also came back for Christmas when we had a party.

Randall Marsh: We were such fans of the Beatles. And for Tom to hook up with George Harrison? I visited him sometimes in L.A. and would ask him to tell me about George. I would just go, "Tell me more. Tell me more."

Tom Petty: Then I think George went to Hawaii. When he came back we hung out some more. We had an immediate connection. We were really good friends and our families were friends. He brought the kids, and the kids formed lifetime friendships. It was a nice thing. Adria used to stay with George and his family at Friar Park. He told her something that he had never mentioned to me, which is that he had a cousin from Florida who reminded him of me. Before George was really settled at Friar Park, he and this Florida cousin would sleep in every room in this, well, this castle, trying to figure out which one had the best vibe and ought to be the bedroom.

Dave Stewart: The reason why I built a house and a studio in America, in Los Angeles, was because I became very good friends with Tom. I didn't really know anybody else. But he seemed so real. About four streets away I bought some property. George Harrison and his wife would stay there. I was also spending some time with Dylan. I seemed to have a link with Dylan and then Tom Petty. Then George Harrison. You could kind of see the Wilburys coming together. It was quite strange for me to suddenly realize that, one by one, they are in my house all of a sudden. And I saw these pictures of them sitting under the tree in my back garden. It was very surreal.

Tom Petty: It was an idea that George had for a long time. He talked about the Traveling Wilburys. It was just a conceptual band he envisioned, I guess because he was never really interested in being a solo act. You know, rather than being the guy up front he was a team player. He wanted to have a band. It was as simple as that. And if you're George, you get the best guys to be in your band. So, he had an extra track he needed to do for a B-side. He wrote a song, or most of a song, one night. And Jeff was having dinner with Roy Orbison around the same time. George and Jeff were going to record it at Bob's house, where Bob had a studio. It was all very last minute.

George used to store his guitar at my house so he didn't have to fly back and forth with it. He had a couple of guitars in my closet. He drove up one night to get his guitars and told me he had a session going down the next night with Roy Orbison and Jeff Lynne and would I like to come? I was wondering what I was going to do that night, and this certainly filled the bill for an evening's entertainment, you know?

True as his word, he picked me up and we drove up to Bob's house. Jeff and George had finished the music to this tune. Then Bob appeared and was interested in what was going on. So all of us sat down at dinner and over a meal worked out the lyrics of this song "Handle With Care." The title "Handle With Care" was taken off

The first time George Harrison came over to my house, when it was just the two of us there, the first thing he did was pick up the guitar and start to play "Norwegian Wood." I thought, "Well, this is unusual." George said something like, "You know this one, don't you?" It was a funny approach—I was obviously a huge Beatles fan—but he really had an uncanny ability to transcend the fact that he was a Beatle and get you to a place where you weren't thinking about that any more. We just started playing guitars after that.

OPPOSITE:

The Traveling Wilburys in 1988. From left: Bob Dylan, Tom, George Harrison, Jeff Lynne, Roy Orbison.

George, Tom, Jeff, and Bob in the Wilbury Mountain kitchen, 1990.

a road case that was sitting in the garage. I remember Bob saying, "Well, what's it called, George?" George kind of looked around and said, "It's called 'Handle With Care.'" So that was the start.

Bruce Petty: I remember talking to Tom about the Wilburys and the fact that he was in a band with one of the Beatles. I just remember us laughing, like who would have thought that? Not us when we bought tickets at a Gainesville movie theater and stood in line to see *A Hard Day's Night*.

JOINING THE BAND

Tom Petty: The next thing I know, George came over one day and said, "I played the track to Warner Bros., and they said they think it's too good to be a B-side." He got the idea that maybe we could do nine more and we'd have an album—and we'd have a band.

Jeff Lynne: [George said], "We could have anybody." I'm going, "Really?" He said, "Yeah. I would have Bob Dylan. Let's get Bob Dylan in it." And I said, "Can we have Roy Orbison in it?" And that's what happened. And Tom, well, I was working with Tom at that time. We both loved Tom. So we add Tom in as well. And that was the Wilburys.

Tom Petty: We were off immediately to ask Roy Orbison if he would be in our band. We drove to Anaheim where he was performing. We went down and said, "Roy, we're going to start a band. Do you want to be in it?"

Roy says okay. George phoned Bob and the same thing, "Do you want to be in the band?" I think it was George who said, "We need a really good songwriter."

So Bob was in. I'd just been working with Bob, so that wasn't too unusual. But this period was just . . . it was the best time of my life. Just the best time. Some long-lasting friendships were born there. I was learning. In terms of creative work, I was having a ball. We were hanging out around the clock. But it was a good healthy party as opposed to a bad kind of thing. It was all healthy. It was a very special time in my life.

Denny Cordell: The Wilburys, I think, reenergized him. . . . He was reborn after that . . . right back on the horse.

Tom Leadon: I said, "God, Tom, you're playing with Bob Dylan and George Harrison."

Tom Petty: In the period before I discovered the Beatles, probably from the age eleven to thirteen or fourteen, I listened to '50s rock and roll. All that early Elvis, the first-generation rock-and-rollers. That music is really what connected me to the Wilburys. That's where we connected as friends, through my knowledge of this music. Bob, George, Roy, Jeff, they all came

When the Wilburys formed, we were all thrilled to be in a band with Roy Orbison. He was a really sweet person. I know that we never thought of putting anyone else in the band after his passing. We were a circle of friends, and had been for a while, and it would have been really awkward to bring somebody else in. There was no replacement for Roy.

Musically, the Wilburys really counted on Roy's voice as far as the vocal blend and the harmonies went. We knew that if we were to carry on we were going to have to get past that absence. I guess we kind of reconfigured what we did. Bob stepped up and sang a lot more lead than he had been. And I think that the second record is a little more rough and ready, a bit more raucous than the first one. But it's hard to really analyze Roy's absence and know exactly what it meant.

After Roy's passing and, later, after the release of the second Wilbury album, George never looked at it like we were going to break up, like it was over. The next phase was always a matter of trying to find a stretch of time when none of us were working. I think once we even had a rough schedule in place to go back and do more recording. I can't remember what got in the way. But George always talked about it and always considered us Wilburys.

The Wilbury's filming "She's My Baby" in 1990.

up through that music. Especially George, I'd say. It really meant a lot to him. I remember him being really, really amazed that I had a particular Gene Vincent album, one that had meant the world to him. He said, "Man, we learned every song on that album." And, you know, a lot of them aren't classic songs. But he knew every word. We actually learned that whole album. That was the jumping-off point of our friendship.

DAYCARE CENTERS AND NIGHT SCHOOLS

Tom Petty: I was the youngest one, the kid in the group. And that was kind of fun because I had admired all those guys when I was very young. They were gods to me. To be in the group was just a huge, very flattering thing, to be involved with that, to be there when it went down. I had to constantly tell myself, "You know you can't be a fan if you want to be any use to the band. You're going to have to get over that." And I did. I somehow got around that, and we all became friends. We all became pretty good friends. That wasn't so hard to get to eventually, but at first it was kind of staggering.

One comfort was the fact that it was the same with everybody there. I mean, everyone felt a bit the same way. They would be in awe of working with Bob Dylan. George was so in awe of Bob that I remember him saying to Bob on one of the very first days of work, he said, "We're going to treat you like everyone else, is that okay?" Bob says, "Yeah, it's fine." There was a lot of admiration that circulated, which made it all the more remarkable, you know? The plan we came up with was that we would all treat each other like equals, get right past any of that. We really wanted it to be a group in the way it worked. This wasn't a marketing plan. There were no record companies involved, no managers involved until that record was done. Nobody put us together. It wasn't something that somebody dreamed up, with all of us taking Wilbury names because we didn't want it to sound like Crosby, Stills & Nash. We simply didn't want it to sound like a law firm

by putting all of our names up there. We didn't want it to be about that anyway, though of course that was unavoidable. What I'm saying is that it wasn't some manager's dream or some record company's dream. It was our dream.

Jeff Lynne: The Wilburys were five people from the first album, all on acoustic guitars, which is quite a sight, without even writing a song. Then to come up with a song . . . say Bob comes up with a few chords. Then George comes up with a few chords. I would come up with a couple of chords. Tom would. And it would be very much a creative thing and very loosely structured, until we lay down the track—with just a track of five acoustics. Sometimes we would doubletrack that, making it ten acoustics. It's very silly but so much fun. You know, anything would go in the Wilburys. At night we would sit down over dinner and write the lyrics. It was a very sweet way of doing it. We'd sing the lyrics after dinner. And that would be the record, roughly done and sung and played in one day. We did a song a day . . . twelve. A couple of weeks, basically.

Bill Flanagan: Tom Petty is a really, really good lyricist. I remember George Harrison saying that it was fantastic to be in the Traveling Wilburys because you had Tom Petty and Bob Dylan there. If you got stuck for a line, you had a very good chance of getting a great line to fill in the hole.

Tom Petty: Years later, much later on, when the record was a big success, Bob and I were talking about it and I said, "Do you believe how this thing went over?" He goes, "Well, George is really smart. He was in the Beatles, you know."

The Wilburys experience was definitely a rebirth. I felt like I landed in a new pond and things were really good. And they were for a long time after that. I arrived somewhere else. The Wilburys stayed together. Roy Orbison died right as the record was released. It was a terrible loss for all of us. But the band stayed together, and we went on to make another album, and always promised that we would do yet another one after that but we never got around to it.

A PLACE IN THE SUN

Tom Petty: I've said that this was a remarkable period for me. The feeling was light. The creative energy around me was as good as it gets. More than once people have said that they thought I was singing differently. Part of this, I think, had to do with Jeff Lynne's recordings. My voice is more out front than ever before. It's higher in the mix. Jeff likes a pretty dry vocal, which gives him more of a chance to make the vocal big. But I also think that I was in a particularly good place in my life . . . and you can hear it. Now I was never the singer's singer. I didn't have the voice that was going to knock 'em dead at the school recital. I got good at using what I have. I

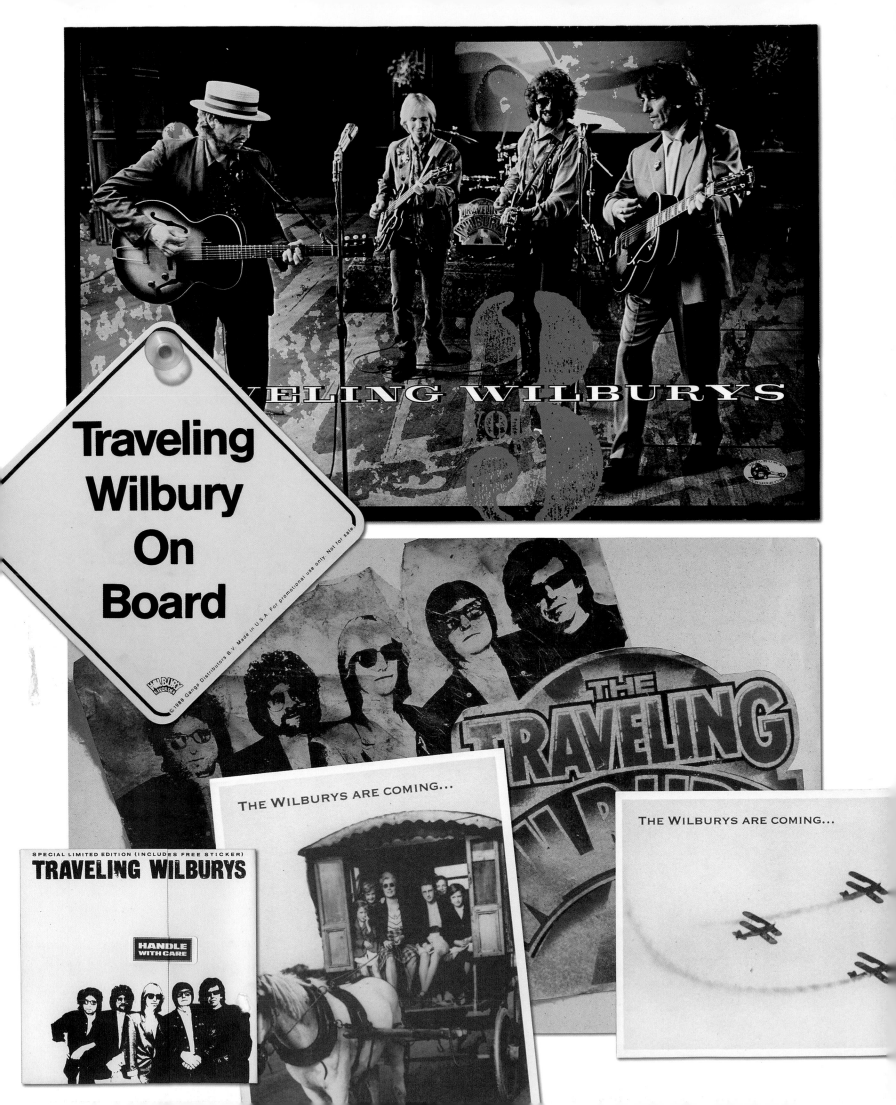

became a better singer, sure. But I also worked hard to know the possibilities of my voice. You've got to create a sound. It's hard to know what you're going to do with a song until you're in the studio. You need to go up to the microphone, start singing it, and then, slowly, you'll find where it feels right. I don't really know what's going to work that well until I'm up at the mic. My question to myself is, "Can I sing this and make someone believe it? Can I get this over with some credibility?" Now if I'm straining or if it's too much effort to sing it, that's going to show and it won't work. But if I'm straining and it sounds, songwise, like I should be straining, then it will work. It's finding that connection between the voice and the song.

Working with the Wilburys and working with Jeff, I was in such a good place. The songs reflected it. And the way those songs needed me to sing them also reflected the positive place I was in. When you think of who was in the Wilburys, we had an amazing group of distinctive singers, all of whom were masters at delivering the material. For a singer, this was a remarkable group to study. And, I think, in the end, I was more comfortable than I had ever been with my voice.

I remember one moment when I had a Heartbreakers session during the same period when we were doing the Wilburys and I was making *Full Moon Fever*. I was trying to fit the Heartbreakers into all of that to prove to them that I could. Which of course I couldn't. So the session is booked. I'm driving to the session. And I have no material. The band is already there. I kind of go, "What am I going to do?" I start beating out a rhythm on the steering wheel and sing, "Well, we're gonna be travelin', travelin', baby." I went through the door, got over to the piano, figured out the changes . . . "Yeah, I got one." And that was that. I wouldn't try to do that every day. Sometimes it's not work at all. Sometimes it's a lot of work. But I love that song. It's on the *Playback* box set. This was the kind of stuff that was more possible in that period, just by virtue of the fact that I was so stimulated by what was around me.

Your artistic peer group can lift you right up sometimes. The Wilburys was that peer group in its best possible version. I've had nice moments throughout my career when an artist I admire weighs in on my material. I remember Bruce Springsteen saying something about the song "Straight Into Darkness," and at a time when I felt like that album, *Long After Dark*, was kind of lost on people. That meant a lot. Bob mentioned that he really liked the song "Something Big" on *Hard Promises*. It just makes me feel great, means so much more than any critic could mean to you because these guys actually do it and know what it's like. The approval of Prince just meant the world to me. I never would have dreamed he would know my music. We hear each other's records. If you got a good one, usually you get a phone call or a note, or when they see you they'll tell you. I remember once when John Mellencamp wrote "Pink Houses," I was so moved by that that I called him and I said, "Now you've really got one, buddy." I think he appreciated that, you know? The approval of your peers means plenty. They're out there doing the same job and struggling with it the same way you do.

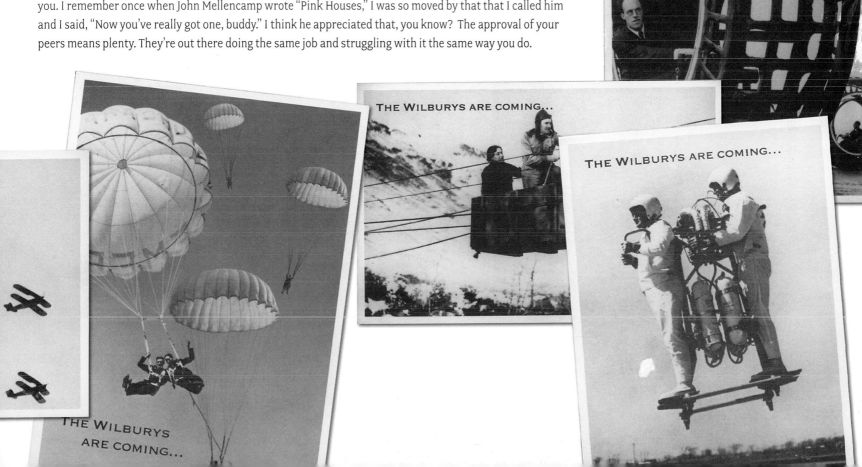

"Your artistic peer group can lift you right up sometimes. . . . I've had nice moments throughout my career when an artist I admire weighs in on my material. . . . We hear each other's records. If you got a good one, usually you get a phone call or a note, or when they see you they'll tell you."

COUNTERCLOCKWISE FROM TOP LEFT:

The Heartbreakers with Eddie Vedder, Denver, 2006.

Alan Weidel, Benmont, Mike, Jerry Lee Lewis, Tom, J.W. Whitten (Jerry Lee's road manager) at the Palomino Club, North Hollywood, 1984.

Tom with John Lee Hooker at the Fillmore, San Francisco, 1997.

Tom and Beck gave an interview together for Musician magazine in 1997.

Tom with Lou Reed, Bob Dylan, Randy Newman at Farm Aid, 1985.

Performing "Free Fallin'" with Axl Rose at the 1989 MTV Video Music Awards.

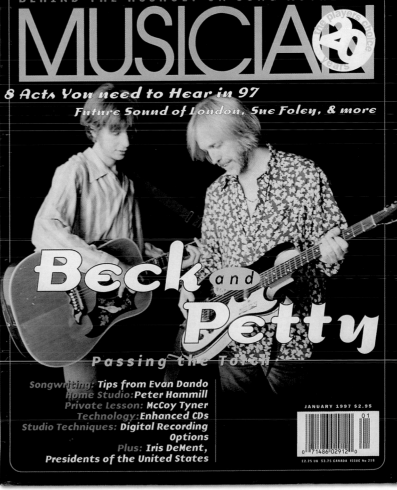

BEHIND THE ASSAULT ON SONG ROYALTIES

MUSICIAN

8 Acts You need to Hear in 97
Future Sound of London, Sue Foley, & more

Beck and Petty

Passing the Torch

Songwriting: **Tips from Evan Dando**
Home Studio: **Peter Hammill**
Private Lesson: **McCoy Tyner**
Technology: **Enhanced CDs**
Studio Techniques: **Digital Recording Options**
Plus: **Iris DeMent, Presidents of the United States**

JANUARY 1997 $2.95

£2.25 UK $3.75 CANADA ISSUE No 219

Chapter Eight/
Free (Fallin')
At Last

It's not going to be a Heartbreakers' project. Jeff's approach was not based on cutting live with a band. He built the track. That isn't how we were used to working. Change is imperative—but it doesn't always go down so easy. That's where the bandleader has to learn to live through the push back, whether it's from the band, the fans, the label, or what have you. At a certain point you're out there and intuition is going to be your only guide.

GOING WHEREVER IT LEADS

Tom Petty: Jeff Lynne became a big part of my musical life.

Jeff Lynne: It was quite a low key for him on that song. I suggested that he just go up a whole octave at a certain point. And it just clicked. The whole song just locked into place.

Tom Petty: I ad-libbed the song for the most part, but Jeff played a key role in the writing. For one thing, the title was his, "Free Fallin.'" He volunteered that to me when I was stuck for a title. I don't remember it that well, but I think Jeff had at least some of the tune. I know for certain that he suggested I take it an octave up at the chorus. This made it happen. Suddenly that title was given incredible musical support. So I gave him credit for it, for sure.

Adria Petty: I remember I had a nanny, like this crazy nanny when I was in high school. We were driving around in my mother's car, and I found a cassette that said "Free Fallin'" on it. I put it in the tape player and it just had that one track, "Free Fallin.'" They hadn't really cut it. It was a demo. Me and a friend were in the car. We were like, "Fuck, that's a good song. Play it

again." We just played it all week, over time, in carpool when we were going home. I would come in the house and say, "God, that's a good song."

Mike Campbell: Working with Jeff was a real eye-opener because he's a musician as well as a producer. He knows so much about record craft that we'd never done before. For me it was like going to musical college. I soaked up so many ideas and little tricks that Jeff knew about for making records. It was really amazing.

Benmont Tench: It sucked. They put on "Free Fallin'" and Tom started singing. I was like, "Oh, God, how lovely." I tried to get my hands on it, but they wouldn't let me. They wouldn't let me near it. They wouldn't let me near it.

Tom Petty: I'd written a couple songs with Jeff, and now he was going to help me record them. I called Mike Campbell. He had a studio at his house that we've done a lot of work in. In a makeshift fashion, he had crammed this gear into a bedroom. M.C. Studios. The guest bedroom. We wanted to cut right away because Jeff was going to go back to England.
  We went over to Mike's. The rest of the Heartbreakers weren't even in town. I rounded up a drummer friend, Phil Jones, someone we've known for

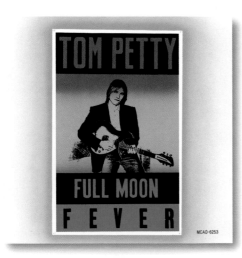

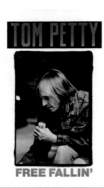

a long time. He played the drums and Mike, Jeff, and I played the rest of the instruments. This was "Yer So Bad." The next day we recorded the second song, which was "Free Fallin.'" Two good days of work, I'd say.

Mike Campbell: Jeff had a system of recording one or two instruments at a time and building the track up quickly. Start the record in the afternoon. By that evening it's done.

Tom Petty: The Heartbreakers didn't like the idea of working with Jeff. They didn't want to work that way, maybe that was it. I remember calling Howie, and he came over to Mike's. When I arrived at the session there's Howie sitting outside looking really irritated. I said, "Well, we'll probably be getting to the bass pretty quick." Then he tells me that he didn't really like this song. I said, "Okay, if you don't like the song, you don't need to play on the song." He said, "Right. Bye." It was "Free Fallin,'" and I already knew that it was one of the best songs I've come up with. No one was going to shake my sense for what I was hearing in that one. Benmont was still wild as an Indian at that point. Stan was in Florida or something. I don't know what the problem was, but I took it right there that this was going to be a solo album. It's not going to be a Heartbreakers' project. Jeff's approach was not based on cutting live with a band. He built the track. That isn't how we were used to working. Change is imperative—but it doesn't always go down so easy. That's where the bandleader has to learn to live through the push back, whether it's from the band, the fans, the label, or what have you. At a certain point you're out there and intuition is going to be your only guide. A track like "Free Fallin'" made it a hell of a lot easier for me to hold my ground.

We would write one day and record the next, then every few days mix down what we had recorded. Didn't take very long initially. I think we probably did about nine songs in a few weeks, and then Jeff went over to England and Mike and I did a few more tracks. We did "Love Is A Long Road" and "All Right For Now" while Jeff was gone. The record company thought the record was too short. So we cut the Byrds' song "Feel A Whole Lot Better," and then we were done.

The whole time I was working on the record I heard it bad-mouthed by the Heartbreakers all over the place. I would run into somebody and they would say, "Oh, I was talking to one of the guys and they said you're doing the wrong thing. You're making a crappy record." I'd just say, "Well, I think I'm doing all right." I don't know what it was. Maybe it was plain old jealousy. They could explain it better than I could. But I think it was just jealousy, like they weren't involved and they were mad about it. I told them up front, I'm not leaving the group.

If you take the Heartbreakers' perspective, I've joined the Wilburys and my next release is going to be a solo effort. But I'm telling them I'm coming back. Well, let's be real, I don't blame them for being skeptical about me coming back. To me it was a great time because I was free at last. I was in a whole new era, with people that were gregarious. They were happy, up people, and the Heartbreakers had been in this closed, dark, old-blood environment. We had come a long way together.

I never thought I was going to leave. I don't think I could have done that and been happy about it. I guess I could have if I had to. I could have just been a Traveling Wilbury. But that was never the idea. All the Wilburys had other projects. Bob Dylan was certainly going to go back to his regular job. And so was I. I never had any thought of leaving the Heartbreakers. I knew they were maybe the best rock-and-roll band there was. You don't walk out on that. They were my friends, and friends were my whole life. So I didn't leave them. Glad I didn't.

Benmont Tench: The Jeff Lynne records sometimes feel to me like a slap in the face. That's not how they're meant, but that's how it can feel.

Tom Petty: There I was, publicly enjoying being free of the Heartbreakers for a while. Publicly enjoying being free of that diplomatic process, just enjoying working with Jeff. Roy Orbison came over and sang. Fate was

BEN | KIT VOX | HOWIE | T.P. | HIKE | KIT | S.R. | S.L

THERE WAS A girl I knew
A long time Ago,
I Remember the Skay (skies?)
(WERE) WAS cloudy & cold

And we were Desperate then
to have eachother to hold
but love is a long long Road

THERE WERE So many Times

doing its thing and bringing the Wilburys together. We were becoming friendly with all those people. Pure fun. Then, on the heels of dealing with some Heartbreaker resistance, I bring *Full Moon Fever* to the record company—and they reject it outright. "Nope, we don't hear a single here." There were five hit singles on that record, but they didn't hear anything. "Start over, we're not going to accept this." It broke my heart. I'd never had a record rejected. I would go home and listen to the record, and there was nothing wrong with it.

George, Jeff, and I were at Mo Ostin's one night in our dating phase. We were doing a lot of playing guitars and singing, just casually. And Lenny Waronker was there, also a key man at Warner Brothers. Mo's wife, Evelyn— God bless her, you know—she heard us playing and said something like, "You guys sing so well together, you should have a group." No one knew that we were thinking along the same lines. Then George called out "Free Fallin'," and we played that there in the living room. Lenny looks at me and says, "Listen, that was rejected?" I tell him, yeah. He says, "I'll sign you right now to Warner Bros. I'll be glad to put that out anytime you want."

Denny Cordell: Tom asked if I would listen to something, and I said sure. He put on the album with "Free Fallin'." I jumped up and shouted and laughed. It was just great. And he said, "I'm glad you like it because the record company doesn't want to release it." He told me that they felt it was inconsistent with his image. I fired off a letter to the president saying he should fire his ass.

Tom Petty: In the end I took an old record-business strategy. I decided to bide my time, hope for a regime change at the record company. That happens all the time. Sure enough, one came. I took it to the new guys and they loved it.

The Wilburys came out and had a big hit record. Then we brought out *Full Moon Fever*, and it became the biggest record I had ever made. It was a huge success with five singles all doing well. Suddenly we're into another world. I've found a new area of music—I sort of reinvented what I did at that point. I look back on that period with a lot of fond memories.

IF IT AIN'T BROKE

Tom Petty: As a producer, Jeff has a great way of clearing space for the song, revealing its characters.

Mike Campbell: *Into The Great Wide Open* was a matter of trying to get those two to fit together, the band and Jeff Lynne.

Benmont Tench: Jeff has always been very, very nice to me. But I don't really know him because he is a guy who can play anything and has an idea of what to play. I think that's what he does as a producer. And there's nothing for me to do there. During *Into The Great Wide Open* I got a phone call occasionally.

Jeff Lynne: I know Tom and Mike better than the rest of the group.

Tom Petty: *Into The Great Wide Open*—that was the return of the Heartbreakers. I tried to make a record with Jeff Lynne producing the Heartbreakers. A successful experiment, but a tough one. Jeff isn't really known to produce groups. He doesn't really like working with a group, so it requires some patience on his part and some patience on their part. I don't think their idea of how they would like to make a record is necessarily the way Jeff goes about it. But I couldn't help but try it. I was so impressed with Jeff, and we'd had so much fun and made such good music, that I wanted to see what happened if we brought them together for a record. It did work out pretty well to an extent. But I don't think I would try it again. The Heartbreakers' way of doing things is to track everything live, all at once, and live or die by that. Jeff likes to make a rhythm track and then—sort of like a sketch becoming a painting—add colors to it. They're Polaroid. They want everything right there.

One issue the band had with Jeff was that he wasn't interested in hearing them play as a unit or hearing them jam. He knew what he wanted the drums to do. He went in and got that. You know, "Here's what I need you to do." And that's what they did, and then they were done. I think they felt like they weren't being appreciated, but they were. It was just a different way of making records than say Jimmy Iovine or Rick Rubin. Jeff is an arranger. He arranges the record in his head—and he's already thinking like, "Well, what are we going to have the drums do to make this song work?"

Me? I like whatever approach results in a great record. I don't care. I'll swim the English Channel if I have to. Whatever you want me to do. I just want to make the record in the way that I think is best in the moment. As I said, my job has often been to navigate through other people's resistance to change. Dave Stewart comes on the scene. Uh, oh. Jeff Lynne. Uh, oh. In cases like this, the evolution of the band is forced. If we don't evolve, everyone suffers, particularly the ones—ironically enough—who are most opposed to those changes taking place. We've been together thirty years, right? Well, we wouldn't have if I had buckled and kept doing it the way we'd always done it. You have to take some gambles, walk out a little closer to the edge at times, in order to keep the thing fresh, to keep it interesting for everyone.

Into The Great Wide Open was very successful. We had two hit singles. I think it's pretty good. I actually heard it not long ago. I checked into a hotel room and—you know how they leave CDs in the room for you to play— there's Bach, then *Latin Favorites* and *Into The Great Wide Open*. So I put it on and listened to it. I thought it was pretty good.

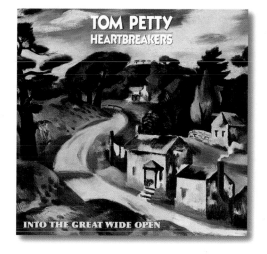

Howie Epstein: Each guy has his own way of doing things. I would hate to compare one to the other. Iovine had his way, where he wasn't really a musician per se but an overseer. Jeff is definitely a musician.

Dave Stewart: Jeff Lynne has done an incredible job of, you know, when he worked with Tom, of keeping the Tom, the Tomness about it. But there is also this pop sensibility.

Jimmy Iovine: Tom needs a partner in the studio. I feel that. That is not an insult. So did the Beatles, and so did the Stones. Jeff was a brilliant choice. A really brilliant choice. The better Tom's relationship with the producer, the better the record. That's what I think.

RECORD PRODUCTION

Tom Petty: Different producers, just like songwriters, have different ways of working. Jimmy Iovine's approach involved us playing it live, over and over and over until we get it right. Very painful way to go. Very painful way to go and expensive. Probably took us two years to pay for *Damn The Torpedoes*. We spent a lot of money in recording costs. Jeff Lynne's way is much cheaper, and I think just as effective. The point is simply that they are different, that's all. I'm not looking to say one's wrong and one's right, one's superior and the other must be avoided at all costs. The moment I start to think in terms of an orthodoxy to the process, I've failed as a bandleader and, actually, as a producer myself.

I always feel that if we don't shake ourselves up we'll stagnate. It's also the nature of the people in this band that if you challenge them, challenge them by bringing in Jimmy Iovine or Dave Stewart or one of the other producers, they are a little bit suspicious of the neccessary change to our way of working. Once an outsider proves himself to them, once there's a playback that's really great, then the band generally gets on board. Not that they'll all jump on at the same time. It usually takes me and Mike to convince them to go along.

It took them a long time to warm up to Dave Stewart. They're really insecure in some ways, the Heartbreakers are. Very insecure. I don't know why, but they can get really fussy about things. I believe that it's good to put them through new things because it feeds the vitality of the band when we do it. When they pull it off, then everyone understands. It's my job as the record producer—and I am a record producer, not just tagging my name on there but taking the job really seriously—to try to take us all places we haven't gone before, to do something we haven't done. It isn't always easy. Rick Rubin was another one where I don't think all of them completely trusted Rick Rubin when he came in.

It's funny, I'm the guy who talked Mike, Ben, Jim Lenehan, these great friends of mine, out of going to college. Completely convinced them that they were making a mistake, persuaded them to avoid campus at all costs. But you won't find another person who is more of an advocate of education. One of my strengths has been to keep the collective learning process going. This means that different producers come in and out of the band's life. I keep taking my education up a notch. It isn't a matter of diplomas and degrees. It is a way of living, a way of staying open to the lessons that might be out there. You will never be told when the next bit of education is coming or where it's coming from or who the teacher will be. That information will only reveal itself after the fact. All that you can do is leave a little room there for the next lesson to come through. Someone will be carrying it. You just leave the door open a crack. Right?

SCOTT TAKES THE EMPTY SEAT

Tom Petty: The Heartbreakers could get really jumpy on commercial airplanes for some reason. It's always been an ordeal. We had real problems in the old days because there were five of us. Somebody was

SPIN

CHINA
Inside the Square with the Student Leaders

TOM PETTY
Won't Back Down

RAP SUMMIT
State of the Hip Hop Nation

INDIGO GIRLS
LOVE AND ROCKETS
SIMPLE MINDS
DINOSAUR JR.
BIKER METAL

AUGUST $2.50
CANADA $3.50

08

0   71098 34394   8

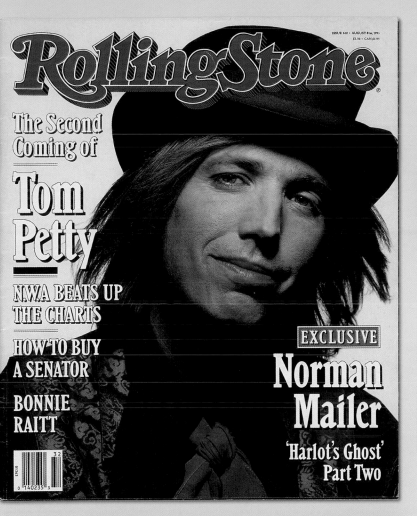

Rolling Stone

ISSUE 610 · AUGUST 8th, 1991
$2.50 CAN $2.95

The Second
Coming of

Tom
Petty

N.W.A BEATS UP
THE CHARTS

HOW TO BUY
A SENATOR

BONNIE
RAITT

EXCLUSIVE

Norman
Mailer

'Harlot's Ghost'
Part Two

Ticketmaster

CALL-FOR-T
(305)356-5
(305)523-3
(813)287-88
(407)839-39
(904)353-3

NO REFUND
NO EXCHANGE
SERVICE CHARGE NOT REFU
EVENT DATE AND TIM
SUBJECT TO CHANGE

ISSUE CODE
EOC1026

FL 3

COMP

SEC.   ROW   SEAT
FL 3   X   19

SECTION/BOX
FL 3

ER STAR PRESENTS
Tom Petty
The Heartbreakers
L CTR-GAINESVILLE
R/RECORDER/VIDEO
OCT 26 1991 8:00PM

EVENT CODE
OC1026

TOM ★ PETTY   HEARTBREAKERS

ALL AREAS

TOURING THE GREAT WIDE OPEN

1991
1992

TOURING THE GREAT WIDE OPEN

Tom Petty & the Heartbreakers

91·92

AFTER
SHOW ONLY

TOM PETTY HEARTBREAKERS

I'M GOIN'
BACKSTAGE

STRANGE BEHAVIOR TOUR '89

Bowie's Big Plans · Rush Gets Respect · Rock's Greatest Fist Fights

MUSICIAN

APRIL 1990

One Wild Year with Tom Petty & the Heartbreakers

I CO-WRITE THE SONGS, I CO-PRODUCE THE ALBUMS, I GET MY OWN BUS.

I CAN OUT-SING ANY OF THESE JOKERS.

THEY'RE A HAPPY BAND.

IF THEY ASK ME TO PLAY SYNTH, I'M GONE.

THIS GIG IS JUST A STEPPING STONE TO SAMMY DAVIS.

ALSO

Lenny Kravitz
···
The Silos

Sibling
Rivalry, Family
Loyalty and
Full Moon
Fever

With prayer and pop music

Song's lyrics help bring Dayton girl, 17, back from coma

"She's a good girl. Loves her mama. Loves Jesus and America, too . . . I want to write her name in the sky. I wanna free fall out into nothing. Gonna leave this world for a while."
— Pop singer Tom Petty

By CINDY HORSWELL
Houston Chronicle

Laura Hight missed her 17th birthday because she had left this world for a while.

But she battled back from a deep coma, and 4½ months after a car wreck that doctors didn't expect her to survive, the Dayton teen-

ager spoke again.

Her father, C.T. "Rusty" Hight, 47, a lawyer and member of the small Liberty County town's school board, and her mother, Leah, a 39-year-old homemaker, never doubted that she would come back to them.

"When I first saw her at the hospital," Mrs. Hight said, "I told her that I knew she hurt bad, but that she would be fine, that we would be with her. Everybody was praying for her, and God was going to heal her. I never really gave her the choice to die."

A single tear rolled down Laura's swollen, red face as her mother

spoke that night.

For weeks afterward, a few tears appeared daily. Each renewed the mother's hope that somewhere inside that battered body was her child, struggling to communicate.

Finally, on June 17, while a tape of the teen's favorite pop tunes played, Laura began to speak the words to one song from memory. The song was *Free Falling*. Perhaps the lyrics held particular meaning for her after all that had happened.

Feb. 1 was memorable because of a steady snow that fell. Because of the snow, Laura, a junior honor

student at Dayton High School, got to skip tennis practice and go home early. She didn't take her normal route because 16-year-old John Gunter asked for a ride to his house.

Her parents had given her the champagne-colored Mazda only five months earlier after she'd earned her driver's license, and — they said — she didn't mind giving her friends a lift, but always insisted that they wear seat belts.

A few miles from the high school, the car's tires began sliding on a snowy curve on FM 1409. It skidded onto the shoulder and she fought to

See COMA on Page 18A.

Betty Tichich / Chronicle

Progress has come steadily for Laura Hight, shown here with her mother, Leah, since she heard a Tom Petty song and surprised her therapist by singing along. The lyrics were the first words to come from her mouth since a head injury sent her into a deep coma in February.

going to have an empty seat next to him. And you never knew who was going to end up sitting in that empty seat, right? We had this thing called the snake bite routine. If it looked like someone was going to take that seat, you would start going, "Snake bite, snake bite, snake bite, snake bite." And they would never sit there. It would be the last place anyone would want to sit. Scott came in somewhere around *Full Moon Fever* as part of the touring band. And we wouldn't let him go.

Scott Thurston: I could have been a roadie, and I would have been happy.

Jackson Browne: I always thought Scott was another unfolding mystery, a guy who's played with the Stooges and Ike and Tina Turner. I mean, those are the poles of rock and roll. In the Heartbreakers, they call him Duckhead. When he's playing with my band he's called Tourette's, because when something is going wrong he starts . . . he just sort of comes apart and starts yelling. Or another nickname for him is Fuck! Fuck!— "FuckFuckFuckFuckFuck."

Tom Petty: Stan suggested Scott. Scott's a good all-around musician. He came down and was just going to do a couple of weeks. He's now been around . . . what is it? Fifteen, twenty years? He can do that high harmony singing. There are also a lot of other parts, particularly around the time of *Full Moon Fever*, that I wanted to reproduce live and couldn't. Guitarwise, we were always frustrated because there was one more part we heard. Scott does a lot of things. He can play acoustic. Or he might play a little extra keyboard part. He's the utility man and more.

Scott Thurston: I come from the same era as Tom and the band. We grew up with rock-and-roll radio and the '60s. I've been playing in bands since I was thirteen.

Tom Petty: Scott was with Iggy and the Stooges, the Ike and Tina band for a while. Impressive stuff. This isn't to mention a few additional assets Scott brings to the band. First, Scott's a good traveler. We've been through some plane rides that really turn everybody a pale white. And there's Scott, waving a drink around, laughing through this incredible turbulence. The band often remarks on Scott's good nature as jets are going through terrible weather. Second, as far as the politics of the band were concerned, when Scott started playing with us, he was neutral. He was new on the scene. He hadn't joined any camp politically. So he had everybody going to him with their troubles, you know? He handled that pretty well, I thought.

Knowing of his neutral politics, one day I even talked Scott into riding on my bus. The rest of the guys were too proud to get off the band bus and come on mine. They weren't going to ride on the, the, uh, star's bus. Because anyone who did that would have been politically persecuted by . . . by Stan probably. But Scott didn't know better. He rode with me for nine or ten months. It was just us on this bus for hours and hours and hours. We never went to sleep, not once. Never touched a bunk. We would pull in after a seven-hour ride and just sit on the bus in the parking lot. We were so in our environment there. Our bus was the Idea bus. Their bus was the No Idea bus. They didn't really have an idea on that bus.

Scott Thurston: It was a good bus.

Tom on his bus, Wildflowers tour, 1995.

Chapter Nine/
Growing Wild

We all put our heart and soul into Wildflowers. *Rick Rubin was great, very dedicated, and almost dogmatic about "We're gonna make a great record" and "We're not gonna accept anything less than great." And damned if he didn't do it. He pushed me like I hadn't been pushed in a long time.*

EVERYTHING CHANGED, THEN CHANGED AGAIN

Rick Rubin: I'd been aware of Tom's music my whole life growing up. It has always been there. I must have listened to *Full Moon Fever* a thousand times, just over and over again and didn't stop for a year or two years. That was sort of my album of choice.

Tom Petty: At first we were just aimlessly playing in Mike's studio, we weren't really . . . no one said we were making a record. I think a few of the *Wildflowers* songs had already appeared. Then Rick came to us through Mike Campbell. Mike had met Rick Rubin when Rick was working with Mick Jagger. They came over to Mike's—I think they were trying to get a song for Mick—and Mike really liked Rick, suggested I meet him. Mike thought Rick had a lot on the ball. A meeting was arranged, and we got along very well. We agreed to make a record together, and it turned into a big adventure. I think maybe it's my favorite of my recordings.

Rick Rubin: Having heard *Full Moon Fever* I remember I called the president of MCA at the time and said, "You know if it ever works out that Tom wants to work with somebody else . . ." Then Mo Ostin at Warner Bros. told me he signed Tom Petty. I said, "Oh, great, any chance I could . . . ?" So Mo set up the meeting.

Tom Petty: It was another time of change for us. It was clear that Stan was unhappy. He was unhappy, and I think what finally tore it apart for me was that Stan told Mike something about not liking the material I was writing. He didn't think it was what he wanted to be doing. I figured there's no point in making someone play something they're not into in the first place, and we'd been having our differences—twenty years with somebody, it's tough. We also weren't nuts about what we were hearing back, like it was clear that Stan isn't really there for us. And word drifted back that he was auditioning with other groups. I'd hear about that, and when he was finally confronted on it, he was very vocal about not being happy with what we are doing. So, setting Stan issues to the side, I figured I'd just make a solo record. That's how it began, but, gradually, it really became a Heartbreakers' record. But without Stan.

Enter Steve Ferrone. Now Steve was a whole different style drummer. He had played blues stuff with Eric Clapton, but came from a jazz background. Despite that, he was really keen on the idea of playing some rock and roll, and we beat it into him. A ridiculously talented musician. Mike met Steve when George Harrison had a show in London and they were both on the show, with Mike replacing Eric Clapton. Steve had been in Eric's band for a few years. I auditioned Steve right there in the studio. He walked in and played a song with us, and in one take cut the track. And I said, "Now this is the kind of guy I'm looking for." He's been with us ever since.

Benmont Tench: I think the difference is that Ferrone drives the band and Stan drove along with the band.

Tom Petty: We all put our heart and soul into *Wildflowers*. Rick Rubin was great, very dedicated, and almost dogmatic about "We're gonna make a great record" and "We're not gonna accept anything less than great." And damned if he didn't do it. He pushed me like I hadn't been pushed in a long time.

He would come over and go through what I was writing and say, "Well, this is good, but could you rewrite the chorus?" It was always, could you do this or that—assignments, long and short. Sometimes I did what he asked and sometimes I didn't. Sometimes he was right and sometimes he was wrong. But he stayed on it, really kept his eye on the ball. There was a lot of that "Let's just do one more take," you know? It got us into a real work mode. We normally leave the studio at 10 P.M., but we'd stay until 12 and 1 in the morning, just because Rick was pushing us and pushing us to do more and more and to keep writing.

Every producer works differently. He just stayed on my back about writing. "Write another one, write another one, come on, you can write another one." Maybe not the most pleasant experience. It was a lot of work, but I'm really glad we did it because it's the album that I'm probably most proud of. I mean, there's a few of them that I'm really close to, that I'm really proud of, but I think that *Wildflowers* is a special one. It's certainly the one that hangs over my head. It's the one that I still feel like I'm competing with, to this day.

Rick Rubin: He was on a real roll. For that album I think we ended up recording about thirty songs. And certain songs just raised their hand up.

Tom Petty: "You Don't Know How It Feels." That particular song is a good example of me arranging the whole thing, which doesn't happen all the time. But I did that quite a bit with *Wildflowers*. I had a drum box and put that on first, arranging all of the instruments on top of it. I think I put down a guitar after the drum track was there. I wrote the guitar solo note for note as you hear it on the recording and played the guitar through a Leslie in a way that we copied on the final recording. Rick really liked the spare character of the demo. It really worked for the song. Lots of restraint. Benmont added a key part on the electric piano, but once the track was there it seemed wrong if anybody started playing a lot. The space was crucial. I remember I had to go back and play the bass myself on the track because nobody could really get a hold of what to play, because if you played too much, it really got in the way.

I liked working with Rick because he's a song producer, like Denny Cordell was a song producer. I absorbed that spirit and focus on the material, making sure not to lose myself in the quest for the perfect sounds. Duck Dunn, the Memphis bass player, told me once, "Did you ever hear four guys playing really great and it sounded bad?" That spoke volumes to me because I hadn't. If you're playing a good song well and there's enough space, it's usually going to sound pretty great. Duck's recordings with Booker T. and the MGs are a case study in just that.

Steve Ferrone: The hardest thing with the Heartbreakers is not playing too much. Typically, it's a great song and all you do is find that pocket.

Tom Petty: The recording of *Wildflowers* went on for two years. It's one of those recordings that was really written just as a collection of tunes. I wasn't making songs along a thematic line. It's not all bright and happy, that much is true. A song like "To Find A Friend" probably reflects troubles I was having at home at the time. "Don't Fade On Me," which is very dark, comes from the same realm of experience. All of the changes going down in my life were probably working in the back of my mind somewhere.

STANLEY

Benmont Tench: I've lived in the same house for twenty-five years. I like continuity. I like seeing my friends. I like going to the same restaurants. I damn sure like playing with the same people I like playing with. And I don't, um, know what the dictionary definition of "band" is, but it has got something to do with that. Stanley being gone was hard to adjust to.

OPPOSITE AND BELOW:

The Heartbreakers in the studio recording Wildflowers, *1994.*

Tom Petty: Stan had said somewhere that he liked the band before we became record makers, when we were just a band. By that he meant that when Mike and I got interested in production and crafting a record, rather than simply using microphones to capture what we did on stage, he lost his interest in the Heartbreakers. I know he had a really tough time with Jimmy Iovine and others. The studio's tough on a drummer, and we were pretty young when we were making those first records. It was a lot of pressure on him.

I also think it's important to recognize that for all of the criticism he took, I can't picture anybody else playing on those records. It took a lot of work to make the recordings, but when we got it done, they were pretty incredible. Jim Keltner could play "Refugee," but he wouldn't play it that way. When I hear those records now, I hear a really great drummer.

When it was time to release *Greatest Hits*, which I was really opposed to doing, I got the Heartbreakers together, including Stan and Howie, and we recorded "Mary Jane's Last Dance." It was the last thing that we all played on. And the song became a huge hit, much to my surprise. One of the biggest we ever had. It was a nice result to having us all together in the studio one last time.

But, really, Stan had done everything he could do to be fired. Just everything he could do to push us as far as we could be pushed, and I didn't want to play with him after that. That was at the beginning of *Wildflowers*, just before that record started. I loved him, and he made a huge contribution to what we did, to our history and everything—but then I'd hear that he was auditioning with another group, looking for another job or something along those lines. And then I heard him, at a gig, talking to another guy in another band, and he described us as not his main gig. And I thought, "Okay, well, you're being paid like it's your main gig." Then I realized he's hanging out to get the dough, because it's a well-paid job being a Heartbreaker. I had the feeling that was the only reason he hadn't walked off yet. So push came to shove and that was the end of it. We didn't speak again for ten years, until the Hall of Fame induction. We got together and played at that and talked and were friendly, but I haven't seen him again since then.

Tony Dimitriades: The vibe was so bad by the end. Stan's last show at the Bridge Concert was sign enough. I remember, Tom said, "Look, I can't, I can't do this. Just call Stan up. He knows it's coming. Call him up and tell him he's out of the band. We got to get someone else." I called Stan, and the first thing that came out of his mouth was, "Greek"—because he always called me Greek—"Am I fired?" I said, "You are, Stan."

I really prefer recording in homes or places that aren't formal studios. Being in a home lends something to the process. I don't know exactly what it is, but when you're in a house you can record in every room. We'll drag wires out to the garage or wherever we need to if we think we've got a particularly good sound in a certain room. People don't listen to music in perfectly tuned control rooms—they listen in living rooms and cars and, you know, in houses.

We have always been like that, where we'll just set up anywhere to make records. Michael was the first one that started the home recording thing in the band. He was always recording at home, and in any nook or cranny he could get something going. I wouldn't be surprised if he's doing it right now. He does it every day. He's gotten more sophisticated with what he can do in a home studio. But over the years we've all made our houses comfortable to record in. It's kind of a prerequisite for the houses we live in.

SHOPPING THE KIT

Dave Grohl: It was October of 1994 and Nirvana had ended. I wasn't really sure what I was going to do with my life. The whole Nirvana thing had become such a big deal, and then Kurt [Cobain] died and everything just stopped. For the longest time it was difficult to listen to music because it would remind me of Kurt or Nirvana. Finally I started getting back into playing a little bit, just by myself. I couldn't imagine joining another band as a drummer. I had all of these songs that I had written over the course of six or seven years. I thought, "I want to go to a real studio and record this stuff by myself." I didn't have a label deal or anything. I was doing it for myself.

By the second day I recorded six or seven songs. I thought, "This is kind of cool. Maybe I will try to start a band and play guitar and sing. Maybe that's what I will do because I've never done that before." It was like a clean slate. The second day I was in the studio, someone from my management calls and tells me Tom Petty just called and wants to know if I will play drums with him on *Saturday Night Live*. I'm like, "What the fuck is he calling me for?! He couldn't find a better drummer?" It was so out of left field. I was a huge Tom Petty fan my whole life. I said, "Tell me when, where I got to be, what do I got to do." It was the first time that I really looked forward to playing the drums since Nirvana had ended.

Tom Petty: After *SNL*, I discussed the possibility of Dave staying on, but he decided to start the Foo Fighters. Our search, not a very long one, really, continued.

Steve Ferrone: I am talking to my girlfriend at the time and she said, "Well, what are you going to do next?" I was like, "I don't know. Something will show up." She said, "Well, what would you like to do?" I said, "I would like to go on the road with Tom Petty and the Heartbreakers." Because I had such a great time doing *Wildflowers* with them. It was totally about the music. But I said, "You know, that's Stan's gig. I don't see how that's going to happen." I should have played the lottery that day. Later the phone rings. My girlfriend tells me, "Tom just called here, and he wants you to call him." So I called Tom. He said, "What are you doing next year?"

Tom Petty: The *Wildflowers* tour was a great one. It was hell on me, because my home life was falling apart and this meant suffering through that long distance as I traveled around. But that tour went for nine months, almost ten. We had a few breaks here and there, but it was almost ten months of just work, work, work. The shows were fantastic. It was great and I remember it really fondly. Having Ferrone along, Scott Thurston still with us. It felt like a great group supporting a great record.

Steve Ferrone: I found the Heartbreakers a little bit strange because they don't really hang out like normal bands. Most bands go out to clubs and hang out. The Heartbreakers go shopping for old instruments. That's their excitement.

I remember we were in upstate New York somewhere. We all walked into this music store and the salesman came over and tried to interest Mike in these brand-new guitars. Mike was trying his best to be polite. Then he started to show Ben synthesizers. So I went up to this guy and I said, "Have you got a room where you keep the stuff you think you won't be able to sell to anybody?" The guy looks at me and says, "We have a room like that." He took us up in the back of the store, opened this door, and all this dust came out. A lot of stuff was bought that day. That's their thing. More of a thrill than going to a bar and picking up chicks.

CONTRACTUAL OBLIGATIONS

Tom Petty: I was so against the *Greatest Hits*. It wasn't my kind of thing. It was a contractual obligation. I hated the idea of it. The songs were meant to be part of the albums they were on. Albums have a particular

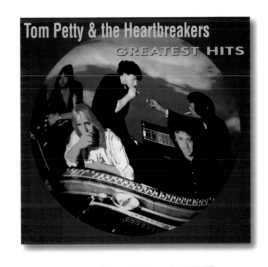

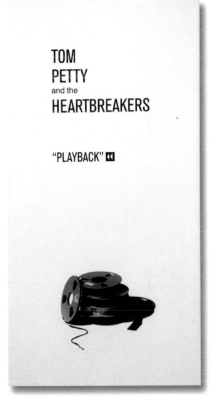

Then I became like a floating musician.

I could play lead guitar. I could play organ.

I could play mellotron, whatever was needed.

Musically, it was a wonderful time for me. . . .

There were some wonderful things happening.

But a crash was coming."

identity, based on the fact that a group of songs, recorded around the same time, is put together in a very specific order. I also didn't see us writing another song for it. I was so offended. I was like, help me to understand this—it's not a hit, how can it be on the *Greatest Hits*? It was just a marketing tool that they use now to sell the record. It's another way of selling product for a second time. You put something new on it. But I was obligated under contract to do it. I was making *Wildflowers* at the time, but the contract called for the Heartbreakers to do this. That was how we happened to get everyone together one more time. We stopped working on *Wildflowers*, worked up another song, actually a song that I started during *Full Moon Fever* and hadn't finished, and it became "Mary Jane's Last Dance."

The album went on to sell over 10 million records. Went on to be the biggest album we'd ever had and one of the very few—I was told this the other day—one of the very few live or greatest hits collections that has sold those kind of numbers. So, go figure. It's a damn good record by virtue of the fact that it has those really good singles, ones that we really worked on. It's not necessarily our best work, just the most popular work.

Playback was another contractual obligation that grew into a really happy project. I brought George Drakoulias in to go through these rooms full of tapes that had been accumulating over the years. George came up with all kinds of recordings that we hadn't released for one reason or another. That turned out to be a full two CDs in the *Playback* box set. That came out and was actually very successful. We got a platinum record for a box set, which is pretty unusual. George did an amazing job. I mean, I wouldn't have sat there all the time it took to go through all that. I just kept checking in with him, and he'd say, "Look, look what I found this morning." He'd play me something that was always fun to hear. He did all the work.

It impressed on me how much time we had spent in the studio. We really stayed in the studio almost every hour we weren't on the road. We recorded a lot of music and wrote a lot of music, much more than was called for on the regular releases. I'm not talking about tracks that were just jams or anything but fully finished records that are really good. One day I'm gonna put them out.

STANDING BEHIND THE MAN IN BLACK

Tom Petty: By the time I'd been through the fire, I was a downright sober person. I was focused on making the most of life, enjoying myself and really wanted to be happy. That lasted for a while, and then things got tough again. When your personal life gets hard, sometimes you can hang around forever trying to convince yourself that that's not what's happening. But it was, and it was probably as much my fault as anyone else's. There was no escaping it. What do you do? The sun came out and then it went behind a cloud again. That's the story of my life in a way.

I remember *Wildflowers* being something I was very proud of when it was done, really pleased with every aspect of it. When it was received with such warmth, that was an incredible high for all of us. There was some fantastic feedback, which you don't always get. That was affirming. It was a very nice feeling, particularly as my life was becoming so chaotic at the same time. I'd been on a roll for so long—*Full Moon Fever*, joining the Wilburys, *Into The Great Wide Open*, *Wildflowers*, *Greatest Hits*, *Playback*. It was quite a run. But tucked in there also were the *She's The One* soundtrack and some work we did with Johnny Cash. The soundtrack was a good learning experience and a low-key situation. The Cash album was a much bigger deal to me.

I had known Johnny Cash since probably about 1982 or '83. We had met up, through a mutual friend, and kept in touch on and off. John came to a show now and then. Then Rick started talking to me about signing Johnny Cash to his record label, to American Records. He asked me one afternoon, "Well, do you think I should sign Johnny Cash?" Definitely sign Johnny Cash was what I told him. Prior to Rick coming along Johnny hadn't been treated the way he deserved by whatever record company he was with at the time. They weren't using his talent. They were just giving him drivel to record. He was getting the Nashville treatment, which, you know, isn't what Cash was about.

I went out to dinner with Rick and John and discussed the whole idea of signing up with Rick. The first thing they wanted to do, which was a really good idea that Rick had, was to make a solo acoustic record with just John's guitar and voice. That went really well. It brought him a lot of critical raves and got him a lot of attention from a younger audience. His next step was he wanted to make a record with a band. They phoned me one afternoon and asked if I would play bass. I'm sure they knew that I was going through a tough time at home. I was just weeks away from moving out. They said, "Why don't you come and play bass on this record?" I went down to play the bass, and without even knowing it, I went to the session Mike and Benmont were on.

It hadn't even dawned on me to ask who else was playing. I can't remember, but maybe Ferrone was playing the drums. It was great, you know. They had brought Marty Stuart, a really great guitar player from Nashville, who we all knew. We were making a record with Johnny Cash and felt great. Then John said, "Well, if we're doing this, I gotta have Howie here because it just doesn't seem right." So, Howie came down. Then I became like a floating musician. I could play lead guitar. I could play organ. I could play mellotron, whatever was needed. Musically, it was a wonderful time for me. Then on the weekends or whatever time I could grab, I'd run over and do *She's The One*, try to come up with a score for this movie. It was bits of score and bits of outtake songs. Though I did write a really nice song, "Angel Dream," that I wrote for Dana. I just met Dana around that point and that song remains a favorite. There were some wonderful things happening. But a crash was coming.

It was really amazing to hear Johnny Cash do "Southern Accents." It was kind of like the song was written for him. I had the same feeling, maybe even to a greater degree, when I heard him do "I Won't Back Down." I just thought, "Well, nobody will need to hear me do it anymore." He gives it such a credibility. But that happened every time he sang. Whatever he sang, it just resonated.

It's hard to say exactly what accounts for Johnny's power as a singer. There was such an authenticity to his voice that when he sang, even if it was another writer's material, you thought, "This is obviously emanating from some source, some human truth." He had such an authority with the material that we all just watched in awe. And he did it fairly effortlessly, not a lot of takes involved. Immediately, he made songs his own.

You can't learn to do what a guy like Johnny Cash could do. You can't get that connection between the soul and the voice from a teacher. You can have all the lessons in the world, but that's not going to get you near that ability. And Johnny definitely had that connection, like a lot of the best ones do. His vocal performances are prime examples of a man's soul making a connection with his vocal cords. It really puts Johnny in a unique class that includes people like Hank Williams, Jimmie Rodgers, Lefty Frizzell, guys who really delivered their material.

When you hear Johnny Cash sing you hear the man himself. He was a very interesting fellow. He knew hundreds of songs, all these folk songs and country songs. He was very well-read, traveled extensively, had a really colorful life. And somehow it all came out in his voice. He was one of those people who was really a joy to talk to. When we were recording Unchained, I used to look forward to lunch with him everyday. We'd all sit with him and with June [Carter Cash] and hear these great stories. That album, I think, was one of the best times I ever had recording.

You could say he had a paternal style. He was older than us and kind of an elder statesman. But age didn't really matter. He was a traveling musician, which supersedes age and category. You could tell this guy has been on the road a lot—and we'd been on the road a lot—and, cosmically, that's where we met. I have a card he sent me once on my birthday that says "You're a good man to ride the river with." That pretty much says it all. Because of that connection we felt, we wanted do right by him, and it resulted in some of our best playing. There's a song on Unchained called "The One Rose." It's not a Heartbreakers' song, but I hear us just playing it so well. We wanted to please him, show him how much we loved him.

TOP AND LEFT:

Tom with Johnny Cash and Rick Rubin, 1994.

ABOVE:

Johnny Cash, Tom, Carl Perkins, 1994.

ISSUE 707 • MAY 4, 1995 • $2.95 • CAN $3.50 • UK £3.00

Rolling Stone

Tom Petty
KING OF THE ROAD

THE SAMURAI AND THE CYBER-THIEF

The Hunt for the World's Most-Wanted Hacker

Moby
THE GREAT WHITE WAIL

ELASTICA • PJ HARVEY
DYLAN UNPLUGGED

Chapter Ten/
Turning Thirty

My friends tell me now, and some told me then, that they were concerned. They were worried about me, and I don't blame them. I wasn't communicating with anyone. Really, I just fell down. It was the only time I remember in my life when I just fell down. The load was too much. I was always the one, no matter what happened, who would soldier on. But not this time.

MY ECHO AND ME

Bill Flanagan: I always felt like *Echo* was maybe the one time in thirty years where in some way Tom's nerve failed him a little bit. It's the big divorce album. It's the *Blood On The Tracks*. But it wants to hide that. He was going through something painful in his life. But he didn't come right out and say it.

Tom Petty: I wasn't in good shape. I just wasn't. I was in deep shit. I had cut myself off from most of the world and become something of a hermit. I was staying at this kind of chicken farm place—literally had chickens in the yard—and was living in a cabin there. I was remote from most of my friends and didn't really talk to anybody. It's not a time I remember fondly.

What was it? It's hard to put a finger on it. It was this incredible disillusionment. It was just a lot of pain. My personal life had blown up. A hand grenade into the hut. It just exploded. But I still had my children to think of. I had to get them situated. I still had one daughter in high school. And it was really left in my hands. I didn't have anybody to help me with it. For a long time I went into what they call clinical depression. I would lie in bed every day, wouldn't get up. And I mean for months. I'd just lie there.

Here I was, I got everything I wanted and it fell apart. My career was always fine, but it was quite a blow to realize that my personal life has gone to hell. I sometimes think that if I had been around more, paying attention to it, I would have understood and been able to respond. But I was running away from it. I'd go on the road for nine months on a regular basis. When I had to face it, and when it did explode, I think it overtook me without me really understanding what was happening. I just got so depressed, like really, really depressed. Not depressed in the sense of unhappy. It's a different thing altogether.

I came out of it at the other end okay, but I think a lot of people were worried. My friends tell me now, and some told me then, that they were concerned. They were worried about me, and I don't blame them. I wasn't communicating with anyone. Really, I just fell down. It was the only time I remember in my life when I just fell down. The load was too much. I was always the one, no matter what happened, who would soldier on. But not this time.

Jim Lenehan: Everything, every big thing that happened to the band was coming for a long time.

Adria Petty: I think he was always a great leader, in all areas of his life. But I think having love fall apart for him was horrible. That was the thing he didn't want to happen. He really wanted the marriage with my mother to work. It was really hard for him. He felt, I think, like he let us down. But he had to go.

Tom Petty: When we made *Echo*, I knew I wasn't doing my job in the studio to the fullest. It's amazing the record came out as good as it did, because it wasn't a situation where I was able to stand at the helm. I wasn't writing a lot in that period. I wrote the songs for the album. But I feel that it wasn't the best stuff I ever did. It's okay. But, then again, it's very hard to judge any project created in a time of turbulence. When I listen back to something, I'm not just hearing the tracks—I'm feeling the moment in which the recording was made. And this was the lowest point in my life. I can't approach listening to *Echo* with anything close to objectivity.

Having said that, however, I heard it recently, and even with all of the associations going off in my mind and heart, it sounded a lot better than I was expecting. But I had great people beside me. I was throwing a lot of work off on Mike Campbell and Rick Rubin. Campbell stepped in, thank God. He stepped in and brought the album home pretty much on his own. I was there, but I don't think I was much help. It was all I could have done to have written the songs. I wasn't much help in recording them. It's a period that really shocks me—like anytime someone mentions that album, I just go, "Oh dear." It was tough. It was a hard, hard time.

In the midst of all this Howie was disintegrating in front of my eyes. We all watched Howie spiraling down, down, down. He couldn't get out of his addiction. He kept saying he was ready to quit drugs. But it really had him.

Benmont Tench: One of the things being lost was right in front of us.

Mike Campbell: *Echo* was very difficult emotionally. There were some dark medical and emotional problems going on with different members of the band. Tom had just been through a divorce and was coming out of that cloud. And Howie was kind of falling into his cloud.

Rick Rubin: I remember it being not that fun of an experience. But that song "Room At The Top," I really like that. I like how it goes from quiet to loud. It's got great dynamics and it's really cool.

Tom Petty: The big mistake we made on that album was starting it with the most depressing song I've ever written, "Room At The Top." Downright depressing. Why it starts the album, I can't for the life of me understand. But I wasn't there that much to make decisions. I was there but not there mentally. I was trying to sort out all my problems. There was just too much going on with me. Overwhelming.

There were some nice things about that period. Dana. I was dating her, and I'd see her every few weeks and it'd be nice. She was helping me. There was that bit of light there that kept the picture from going black.

Stevie Nicks: I totally love Dana.

Adria Petty: Now? I think he's probably the happiest I've ever seen him.

Bruce Petty: Dana, she just seems to brighten up his day. You can tell that she means that much to him.

HOWIE

Tom Petty: In 2002 we were inducted into the Rock and Roll Hall of Fame. Howie and Ron were both inducted. We figured Ron was going to play on one song and then Howie was going to play on another. It was "Mary Jane's Last Dance" with Howie and "American Girl" with Ron. And Stan was going to play on them both. So there were two rehearsals on two different days. One rehearsal, the first rehearsal, was with Ron. And it went really well. We were all really happy and glad to see each other. We wound up jamming for hours. We were only rehearsing one song—but we were there for hours playing. A great time. The next day Howie is going to play. We're waiting on him. Waiting on him for hours. He finally comes in. I remember that Stan, who hadn't seen Howie in a long time, was really shocked. Then we went to play, and the difference between playing with Ron and playing with Howie was stunning. Howie just wasn't completely there and couldn't give it much. That's when my mind was made up. That rehearsal ended in about twenty minutes. Everyone was out the door twenty minutes after we had started playing. And everyone was pretty much thinking the same thing. The dope was killing Howie.

Tony Dimitriades: The very last time I spoke with Howie about cleaning up was at the Rock and Roll Hall of Fame. I grabbed him, found a place, and we sat down and talked about it. By then he was saying, "Yeah, I know. As soon as this is over." Tom had tried everything, from compassion to tough love. When Howie was many hours late for the *Echo* photo session, Tom said, "Let's go. Let's just do the album cover shoot without him." And they did, and they made it the album cover. Have a look.

Tom Petty: I think we all felt that our performance that night was a little off. We hadn't played together much and, frankly, it's not the best audience—a bunch of old musicians staring at you. We did okay. I was just glad that we got through it. You know, I wasn't really thinking about the performance too much.

We were up in a suite at the Waldorf after the induction. Stevie Nicks was with us. She had come to cheer us on. And Stevie said, "Where is Howie? I want to see Howie." Howie didn't usually come around after gigs. You know, he vanished. But she insisted that we call him. So Dana, my wife, got on the phone and told Howie we really wanted him to come up. And he did, and he was in a really good mood. He sat with us for a while but didn't say much. But then, when he got up to go, he stood in the door and waved good-bye. And I knew, somehow, that I was never going to see him again.

Steve Ferrone: I never went to Howie's room until the very last tour. He called me up and asked me to go to his room. I went up there and he had the silver foil. He talked to me about it. I was saying, "Man, you got to do something about this. You've got to stop." He said, "Yeah, after the tour I will do something about it."

Benmont Tench: Boy, could he sing—the loss is staggering to me just on an artistic level. There's no way to come to terms with it. He was a brother.

Tom Petty: I can't describe the loss. We were really good friends for twenty years. What do you say? He's gone.

DREAMVILLE

Jackson Browne: "Dreamville." Amazing song. I mean, you see this little, blue-lipped Tom as a kid with his mom at the public pool, you know? You see these images that are so universal and so human.

Echo was a dark album. It needed a dark cover. And it got one. I think it's a good cover, certainly lines up with what's inside. *Echo* isn't a Heartbreakers record that I reach for, maybe because recordings tend to bring you back to where you were when you made them.

Howie didn't even make it for this cover shoot. He had moved out to Santa Fe, New Mexico, and just kept missing plane after plane to come in for the photo session. All morning long we kept hearing he was on the next plane. He just missed one after another. We were there with the photographer and the whole scene was ready. After a long wait I just got fed up and said, 'Well, why don't we just shoot it without him? Maybe that will send some kind of message." And we did. We just went and shot it without him. I think he showed up at about eight o'clock that night, and it was too late.

Jim Ladd: I love "Dreamville" because it's a wonderful look at a simpler, more loving time—where he's going to go down to a guitar store and buy a black diamond string. Wow. That's a great song.

Adria Petty: "Dreamville" so perfectly captures the feeling of the '50s in Gainesville for those guys—when they grew up and when the music was so great, and they were in this small town in America.

Tom Petty: When I came out of that depression, I felt like I had a whole new lease on life. I don't think I did any music for a while. I just was so happy to be back to normal. Eventually I started doing tours without records. We'd just go out and have a lot of fun. That was another rebirth in a way. I really enjoyed it and felt I was back to my old self. After that I settled in to write *The Last DJ*.

Elliot Roberts: I thought it was a brilliant, brilliant album.

Jim Lenehan: *The Last DJ*. Hard to beat.

Tom Petty: That was my only concept album with a very strict theme. I had become aghast at society, at how everything seemed to revolve around money. Money had become king and it was affecting everything. I used the record business as a symbol for changes that were taking place everywhere. Writers often begin with what they know. I know the record business, and there it was in its last dying breaths. But what I saw there was happening all over the place. I was shocked at how mean things were getting. It seemed like the meaner things got, the more they were applauded.

Once I started working, it came very quickly. There was no difficulty in finding things to write about. It was a weird time. I mean, kids were killing each other in school and rock stars were being invented on game shows. Everything that I'd believed in was being made into a joke. There was not a lot of integrity in what was going down in the music business. Here I was, kind of coming back to it, and it struck me as being just so sad. That's what inspired me to write the record. Now I realize that it was almost a bigger subject than you can tackle. But I couldn't watch the world changing to that degree and not comment on it, you know? It's my job to comment on this stuff and to take note of what's going on. I'm surprised that not many people say much about it. I thought it was worth writing about.

Jim Ladd: The first thing people do in war is take over the media. First thing. When big business came in and Ronald Reagan came in and took over, they deregulated the industry. That allowed Clear Channel and Infinity to buy up all of these radio stations. We used to have a rule called the "seven and seven" rule. You could only own seven radio and seven TV stations max. That ensured mom-and-pop competition. Deregulation changed that. At last count Clear Channel had twelve hundred stations. That's a lot of control over information. For example, Clear Channel put out a list after 9/11 of songs that you couldn't play, including "Imagine" by John Lennon. Put out a list. Don't play these songs.

Tom Petty: I tried to say something about corporate America and what it has done to the small businessmen or the independent businessmen, but also how we all kind of wind up serving these corporations that have become even bigger than the political process. The corporations are driving the political process. It just seemed like something that was old and beautiful was gone in the morning. I thought it was worth writing about. I thought it was worth talking about. My position wasn't that everyone was ignorant about this but that artists could start looking into the effects of it.

It was not received well by many friends. People thought I was arrogant or taking a cheap shot. I saw a lot of curious things written about *The Last DJ*, but in the end, I think the music really does hold up and that the

album is something to be proud of. Radio had given me this great wonderful life and rich tapestry of music over the years, and now it had become this other thing, programmed in relation to market research. I was seeing advertisements for stations that said, "No talk." No radio personality whatsoever, no one there to introduce you to something that might possibly mean the world to you, like music meant the world to me. I thought that was sad that it had to go that way. The first single from the record, "The Last DJ," was banned by a number of stations immediately when it was released. It was banned from airplay for being anti-radio.

I knew I wasn't making the most popular move. But I had to get it out of my system. It was not a good-time record. It wasn't what anyone wanted from me. But that can't be your barometer all the time. That's a dangerous way of thinking. Rick Rubin thought I was doing the wrong thing. When I played it to the record company, you could have heard a pin drop. It finished and no one said anything. Then they said, "Well, that's not about us, is it?" And I said, "Well, I don't know." I can really understand why Warner Bros. didn't get behind it in the way they should have, though saying it wasn't a good album was bullshit. It's good music.

Bill Flanagan: If you put out a record, a theme record, which basically says the record industry stinks, radio has sold out, this whole business is so corrupt it's stinking like a dead dog on a hot day—you know you're probably not going to get a lot of support from radio. But I think it's one of the most interesting records anybody has made in the last ten years.

Tom Petty: The critics were pretty rough. You never like it when critics are rough on you. It's your baby they're beating, right? Of course I would have preferred they all loved it. Some did. But here's the thing that meant the most to me: there was not a single critic who ever suggested that what I described was inaccurate, no one wrote, "Look, this isn't the way it is." I never saw that.

THE OBVIOUS CHOICES ARE OFTEN THE BEST

Jim Lenehan: When Ron came back I sure was happy because he's one of the nicest guys that ever lived.

Tom Petty: If life has its phases, this period had a calm to it, a peace. I went on tour quite a bit, two or three times in those four years. Just for the fun of it, and we had fantastic tours. Was almost like we'd been reborn. We were full of energy. Ron Blair had come back to the band, right at the end of recording *The Last DJ*. I couldn't have faced a stranger coming in and taking over that role, you know? The band is about much more than just being good musicians. It's your family. It came down to me saying, "Hey, pack your case. You're back in." He's been a joy to play with. It was like having new blood in the band. Huge crowds, and I didn't really notice the time going by, to be honest. Life was so good. After seven years of dating, Dana and I had gotten married. I was just very happy. I built a studio at home, would fool around in there and write songs occasionally.

Around that time Olivia Harrison asked me and Jeff Lynne if we'd go to New York with her and induct George into the Hall of Fame, which of course we did. Part of that deal was we would perform a few of his songs. I rounded up Scott Thurston to play the bass, Steve Ferrone to play drums, and then we had Steve Winwood on the organ and Jim Capaldi on percussion. Dhani Harrison played guitar with Jeff and me, and Prince took the lead on "While My Guitar Gently Weeps." Quite an outfit. It was a great trip.

On the plane coming back, Jeff and I—we hadn't seen a lot of each other for some years—started to talk about why we never recorded together anymore. I had written nine or ten songs and felt like recording, so I went over to Jeff's studio and we did a track that night, just Jeff and Mike and me. I played the drums. It went so well, I liked it so much, that I stayed there for another couple of months, going five days a week over to Jeff's and working very casually on an album.

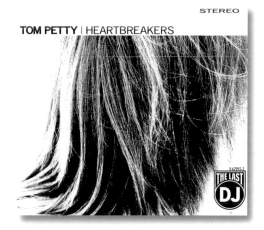

My daughter Adria art-directed The Last DJ. *Being my kid wouldn't be enough to get me to work with you, but Adria is just a really amazing talent. I respect the work she does. We were both kind of hesitant to work together because we're so hard on one another and can really push each other. But at the same time we both kind of have the same goal—and we're going to pull it off when we get together.*

The photographer she hired for the cover, Blossom, was one of Adria's friends in high school. The kids we were driving around in the backseat are suddenly doing the art direction, telling me to turn a little to the left and stuff.

When it was time to come up with a Highway Companion *cover I kept thinking that everyone would expect the dusty desert road with an old pair of steer horns or someone hitchhiking. I wanted to take the meaning of the title to another level. Then the idea of the astronaut and the monkey came to me.*

Dana had found a painter on the Web, a fellow named Robert Deyber. I was sitting around thinking about my cover idea, looking at some of his work, and I thought, "Maybe we could just take a shot in the dark and call him up and see if he'd be interested in letting us commission a painting." So we did. We wrote to him, and he wrote back. I was really nervous to ask him to do one of my ideas, but he was very receptive and really got it on the first shot. It came back to me and I just went, "Perfect."

LIFE BETWEEN THE BRANCHES BELOW

Tom Petty: It's so hard to explain the process of writing songs. When you bump into something as big as a song, all you can do is kind of get out of its way and let it happen. When I wrote the songs for *Highway Companion*, I didn't sit down and say, "Well, I'm gonna write about this or that." I just started to play, and the door swung open. In came the songs. I just tried to get it down, to capture it as quick as possible. From there it was just a matter of thanking divine grace or whoever threw the songs in my path. That album clears my mind when I hear it.

Jeff Lynne: They're great songs. I thought they were brilliant as they were and didn't need any interfering with. We just went straight into the studio and recorded them.

Eddie Vedder: "Square One" off *Highway Companion* is really getting to me. It's just beautiful.

Tom Petty: Based on how I describe songwriting—bumping into something that's bigger than me—you could say, "Well, then anyone could write a song. I bump into things all the time." But this isn't true, because if everyone could do it, they would. I've come to recognize that, for some reason, I have something in me that attracts that kind of inspiration. I believe that it's a little bit like being singled out for something, like there's some greater force that says, "Okay, well, this guy's going to have a powerful enough antennae to bring this stuff in." It's the same, I think, with artists in general, not just songwriters. Anyone can paint a picture, but not everyone can paint the kind of picture that stops viewers in their tracks, that seems to possess that immediacy and contains the kind of truth that arrests viewers. Pure technical skill won't get you there. Same holds for songwriting. There's something more to it. I have a respect for the process and try not to force the results, just as much as I try to be ready when the inspiration comes. Being ready is key, because some songs appear almost as entire entities, you know?

Adria Petty: I remember my dad was always working and always making music. Spending a lot of time with legal pads.

Tom Petty: Many of what I consider the best ones seem to appear almost finished. You're sitting there with your guitar or your piano and something comes, just like that. There it is. Did I do that? I guess I did. Then you can take it and finesse it, if it needs it, and maybe change a chord here, find a better line in a spot. I hesitate to try to understand all of this, but only because it seems like applying reason to this kind of process may just make it go away—it's so spiritual. It's a cosmic endeavor. I'm always a little skeptical of songwriters that tell me that they sat down to write this song about so and so and here's how it goes. I've done that, but I didn't feel that great magic.

Rick Rubin: He can channel material in a pretty strong way. I've seen him do it, and it's incredible. I think he's aware of it all the time and is always open to it.

Tom Petty: I'm old enough now to understand that this wasn't an accident. For some reason, I'm able to catch these ideas and make sure they become songs. I'm able to do it and touch millions of people with it. I'm respectful of that. I think it's what I'm here to do, and I'm supposed to do it. It's a job sometimes, but more often than not, it's not a job, it's something I'd do regardless. It's my place of peace as much as it's something to bring to others.

Johnny Cash said this to me one day: "This is noble work." I wasn't sure what he meant. "Noble work?" He goes, "Yeah, it makes a lot of people happy." That hit me like a bolt to the brain. Why didn't I ever have that thought before? I was probably thinking about me being happy. This basic idea Johnny shared seemed revolutionary in some odd way. It makes millions happy. Then I went and played some shows and looked out and as far as you can see people are jumping up and down. They're happy. It helped me to see the value of it and what it meant in these people's lives, because, really, what it means to them is exactly what it meant to me. Music has always been my passport to a better place.

NIGHTWATCHMAN

Tom Petty: I've done this songwriting thing for so long now that I can, sometimes, feel a little overwhelmed by it. If a song comes at one o'clock in the morning, I know I'm not going to get any sleep. There's been times when it comes and you're tired and you go, "Oh, God, not now." Even if it takes me thirty minutes to write it, I'm going to be so geared up by doing it that I won't possibly be able to shut my eyes for hours. I'll pace and think about the song, and the melody will be in my head and completely overtake me. If I do sleep, it will be restless, like a bad production meeting. When I get up in the morning, it'll be the first thing in my brain. But when it all comes together, there's nothing like it. You do it and then wait for it to happen again.

THIRTY YEARS: FRIENDS WEIGH IN

Jeff Lynne: The picture I have of him is the band setting off in this old van from Florida, aiming to travel across the whole United States to L.A. It must have been like *The Beverly Hillbillies*. The top of the van packed with all their worldly goods. And off he went, rumbling into the night. That picture to me is such a great one. It's enduring, you know? And then they arrived. And then they struggled for a bit. And then, they made it big. Then they still made it bigger and bigger and bigger. It's a really sweet story.

Mike Campbell: How did we survive through all that stuff without breaking up or hating each other? I think it's because whatever might have happened, like the death of a friend or egos in collision or wives that don't like each

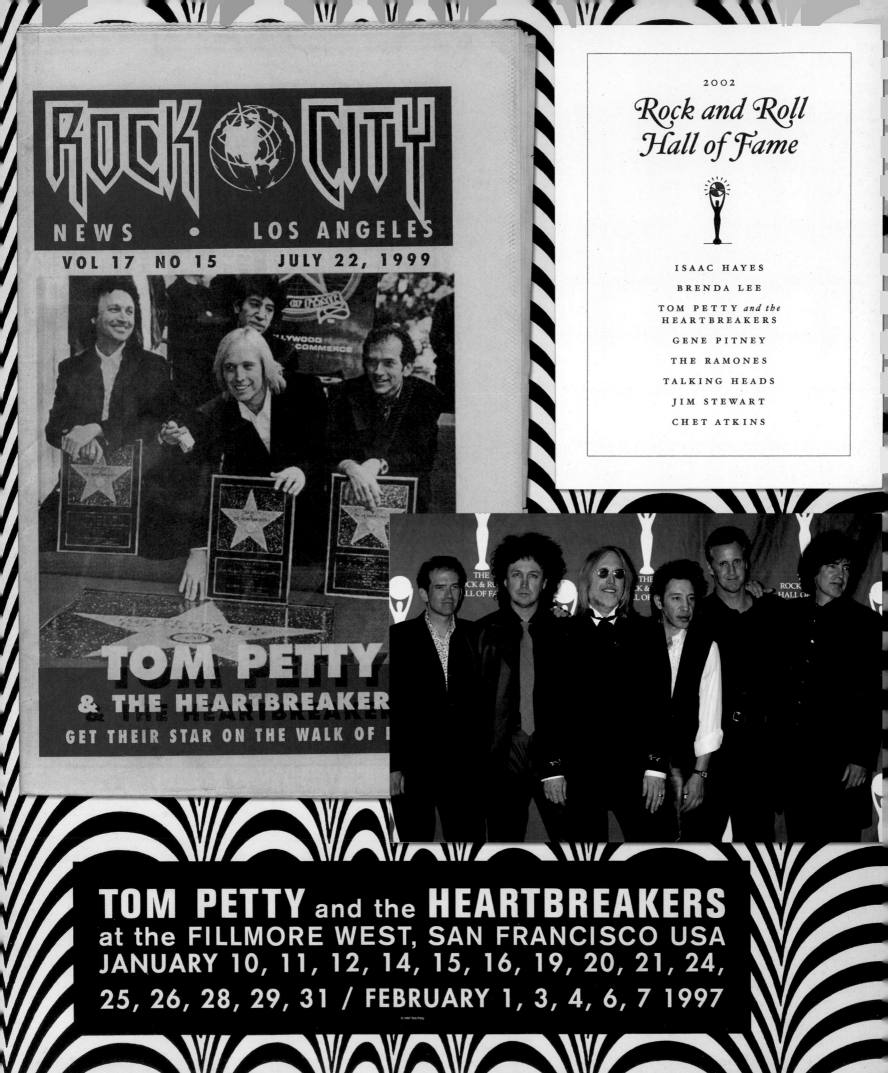

ROCK CITY

NEWS • LOS ANGELES

VOL 17 NO 15   JULY 22, 1999

TOM PETTY
& THE HEARTBREAKERS
GET THEIR STAR ON THE WALK OF FAME

TOM PETTY and the **HEARTBREAKERS**
at the FILLMORE WEST, SAN FRANCISCO USA
JANUARY 10, 11, 12, 14, 15, 16, 19, 20, 21, 24,
25, 26, 28, 29, 31 / FEBRUARY 1, 3, 4, 6, 7 1997

TOM PETTY
AND THE
HEARTBREAKERS

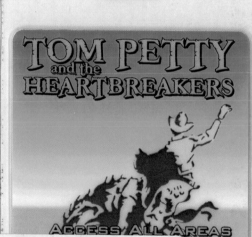

WITH BO DIDDLEY
SATURDAY
AUGUST 16, 2003
AMSOUTH AMPHITHEATRE

PARALLEL 28 EQUIPE
TOM PETTY | HEARTBREAKERS

THE LAST **DJ** **LIVE**
OCT. 12-16
THE GRAND OLYMPIC
AUDITORIUM

PRODUCTION

TOM PETTY
AND THE
HEARTBREAKERS

ACCESS ALL AREAS

WEST
2001

BABY, EVEN THE LOSERS GET LUCKY SOMETIMES
Tom Petty &
the heartbreakers
live at the
Hard
Rock
Hotel
june 1-2, 2001
HARD ROCK HOTEL & CASINO · LAS VEGAS, NEVADA
$5

Dave Grohl: There's that universal element where when you see Tom play and he is singing a song, there's twelve thousand people singing along with him, and they might be singing for twelve thousand reasons. That's the coolest thing in the world when you can get a song that everyone can connect with for their own reasons. You have your reasons for writing—and they have their reasons for singing along. I don't know what the world would be like without Tom Petty and the Heartbreakers. But if I'm still hanging out with the guys in my band in thirty years, fucking shoot me, please.

Rick Rubin: It's incredible that they've managed to exist through so many changes in the world. The world is in such a different place from when they started. But all the young acts seem to look up to Tom Petty. He's one of the people that moves kids in rock bands. They feel the truth of what he's doing. It's sort of a lost art what they do. Great players, great band interaction, and great song writing.

Johnny Depp: There's no real way to categorize it. Yeah, it's rock and roll. You might even say in some instances it's kind of pop. But it's smarter than that. It's, it's sort of intellectual pop or rock and roll. It defies any kind of category really. It's just Tom Petty.

Elliot Roberts: They call it a light in your eye. And whether you're twenty or forty or sixty, if you ever had it, you still have that little light. Tom's got that light.

Jim Lenehan: Somebody asked me how do you get in this business, and I said go to high school with a member of the Rock and Roll Hall of Fame. That helps. But who would have ever known that they would be in the Rock and Roll Hall of Fame? When we were little redneck kids coming out of Gainesville, everybody told us that we were crazy, and we said no, we're right. And we were.

Dave Stewart: They are one of those iconic bands that will be around forever. I am sure that Tom will carry on writing songs and lyrics that will move me, hopefully, until I'm getting older and in a wheelchair. I'm sorry I came along and caused so much turmoil at one point. Now that that's all calmed down, maybe we should get together and have a drink.

Stevie Nicks: The heart of Tom Petty never changes, but he's always evolving as an artist.

Adria Petty: I think it was them against the world in a way. When I imagine them moving to L.A. from Florida—they're like the ultimate American dreamers. There was no doubt in their mind that they were going to make it work. Even the losers get lucky sometimes.

other—all of that stuff that breaks bands up, anytime that stuff happened with this band it always seemed like the joy of playing together outweighed everything else. It never made sense to break up. I don't know why that is with us, but we just love to play together more than anything else.

Benmont Tench: As long as Tom and Mike want to have a band, you know, it would be awfully hard not to play with them. But I didn't think that the band would last thirty minutes, you know?

Denny Cordell: As long as he keeps discovering the inspiration, he will go on forever.

Jimmy Iovine: I think that he captures a side of America that is as relevant today as it was in 1978. There's nothing he can't do. He's that gifted. The minute I met him and he played me those two songs, I knew he would be playing those songs when he was one hundred.

Tony Dimitriades: There are times when I pause and find it almost hard to believe. For thirty years Tom has managed to sustain a vision, without ever compromising, and the band, particularly Mike and Ben, has been right there with him and for him. All the elements were there—great band, great songwriting ability, and a capacity to lead—and Tom respected every one of them. It takes something more than fortitude to do what he has done. It takes inspiration, in the deepest sense of that word.

There's something you get from the crowd, and I really don't know where else you get it. It's an incredible jolt of adrenaline and energy and communication. There's an instant approval and affirmation of what you're doing. You are never going to find that in life except for right there. Which is why it's so intoxicating and performers tend to keep doing it. What exactly it is that keeps me going back for more of that, I'm not really sure. But I need to keep doing it.

I do get a little anxious before I go onstage. But once the band is out there and it's working, everything is okay. I feel pretty at ease, probably more comfortable there than I am anywhere else in life. There's just something about it. For that couple of hours onstage time just stops, and there isn't any other world but that one.

RIGHT:
Bonnaroo Music Festival, Manchester, TN, June 16, 2006.
FOLLOWING PAGES:
The Heartbreakers in 2006.
From left: Mike Campbell, Benmont Tench, Tom Petty,
Steve Ferrone, Ron Blair, Scott Thurston.

yeah and its over before you know it
it all goes by so fast
and the bad nights take forever
and the good nights never seem to last

Acknowledgments

This book could not have found its way into the world were it not for the talent, creativity, and sustained hard work of the following individuals:

Adria Petty, Creative Consultant and Photo Editor; **Reyna Mastrosimone**, Executive-in-Charge of Production; **Tony Dimitriades**, Manager, Tom Petty and the Heartbreakers; **Jeri Heiden**, Art Director; **Warren Zanes**, Text Editor; **Amy Finnerty**, Archivist; **Jason Ware**, Photographer; **Mark Nolan**, Production Assistant.

At East End Management: Mary Klauzer, Management/Lead Archivist; **Robert Richards**, Management; **Brynne Milranny**, Product Coordinator; **Tiffany Goble**, Executive Assistant to Tony Dimitriades; **Stephanie Merrill**, Assistant.

At Chronicle Books: Christine Carswell, Jay Schaefer, Brianna Smith, Jake Gardner, Jane Chinn, and Doug Ogan.

Photo Credits

Martyn Atkins 169 bottom left, 193 top, 196 all photos, 202–203, 207 bottom, 216, 218, 228, 239 second row right

Awest 130–131

Eric Basset 157

Joel Bernstein 69, 71, 72–73, 89 top and bottom, 93

Adrian Boot 64–65

Dennis Callahan Front cover, 13, 57 bottom left and bottom right, 63, 75, 76 top left, 76 bottom left, 76 bottom right, 76 middle right, 80–81, 82, 87 middle, 98, 100, 103 bottom and top right, 104 bottom left and bottom right, 106, 108–109, 120–121 all photos, 122–123 all photos, 124–125, 126–127, 128–129 all photos

Danny Clinch 138–139 all photos, 224, 229, 234–235

© Kevin Estrada 206, 207 top

© 2006 Owen Fegan 231

Deborah Feingold/CORBIS 169 middle right

Piper Fergusen 232–233

Lynn Goldsmith 70 top, 74, 76 top right, 87 top and bottom, 90–91, 94–95, 104 top right, 114–115

Caroline Greyshock 159, 164–165 all photos, 180–181

Frank Harben 27

Jim Herrington 134, 135, 173 bottom left and middle right, 176

Robert John Photography 169 top right

© 2007 Dennis Keeley 99, 110 lower left Heartbreakers' portraits, 112, 151, 153

Annie Leibovitz 22, 23, 78 all photos, 215

Courtesy of Buster Lipham 29

Robert Matheu 92, 143

© Jim McCrary All Rights Reserved 1970 51 bottom

Camilla McGuinn 147 bottom right

Tony Mott 144–145

© Andee Nathanson 2007 47 top, 50, 57 top

Michael Ochs Archives/Getty Images 168 bottom

Adria Petty 10 all photos

Courtesy of Tom Petty 28

© Ron Pownall/RockRollPhoto Spine

Neal Preston 2, 20–21, 104 top left, 105, 148, 156, 160, 161, 162–163

Aaron Rapoport 103 top left, 173 top

Paul Rider/Shoot Group 136 all photos

James Schnepf 178, 219

Robert Sebree 137, 191, 192 all photos, 193 bottom, 194–195 all photos, 197, 198, 200, 204, 210–211, 220

Mark Seliger/Contour Photos 9, 174, 179, 185, 186–187 all photos

Red Slater 33 bottom left and top right, 34 right, 36–37, 38, 41 all photos, 42

Courtesy of Sound Stage 223

Jim Spellman/Wireimage 226 middle right

Blossom Spring 222 all photos

Courtesy of Benmont Tench 34 left

Tom Tomkinson 168 top

Unknown Endsheets, 14, 31, 55, 58, 60, 132, 133, 209 middle left

Tracy Wilcox/The Gainesville Sun 227 top right

Steve Wilson Back cover, 46 top and bottom, 47 bottom, 49, 56 collage artist, 57 bottom middle collage artist

© Zox 16, 18–19, 59 top and bottom, 118–119

The publisher gratefully acknowledges the photographers who have provided for the reproduction of their work in this book.

Every effort has been made to trace the ownership of all copyrighted material. Please contact the publisher about any inaccuracy or oversight and it will be corrected in subsequent printings.

Whisky

SOLD
OUT

TOM
AND
HEARTB